The
KENT
Village Book

THE VILLAGES OF BRITAIN SERIES

Other counties in the series include:

Bedfordshire	Leicestershire & Rutland
Berkshire	Lincolnshire
Buckinghamshire	Norfolk
Cambridgeshire	Northumberland
Cheshire	Northamptonshire
Cleveland	Nottinghamshire
Cornwall	Oxfordshire
Cumbria	Powys Montgomeryshire
Derbyshire	Shropshire
Devon	Somerset
Dorset	Staffordshire
Durham	Suffolk
Essex	Surrey
Glamorgan	East Sussex
Gloucestershire	Warwickshire
Gwent	West Midlands
Hampshire	Wiltshire
Herefordshire	Worcestershire
Hertfordshire	East Yorkshire
Kent	North Yorkshire
Lancashire	South & West Yorkshire

A list of the volumes currently available can be obtained
by writing to the publisher

The
KENT
Village Book

ALAN BIGNELL

with illustrations by Arthur Prosser

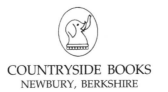

COUNTRYSIDE BOOKS
NEWBURY, BERKSHIRE

First published 1986
New expanded edition 1999
© Alan Bignell 1986, 1999

COUNTRYSIDE BOOKS
3 Catherine Road
Newbury, Berkshire

ISBN 1 85306 571 4

Designed by Graham Whiteman

Front cover photo of Upnor, near Rochester
and back cover photo of Eynsford
supplied by Robert Hallman

Produced through MRM Associates Ltd., Reading

Typeset by Techniset Typesetters, Newton-le-Willows

Printed by
J. W. Arrowsmith Ltd., Bristol

 Introduction

While touring the villages in order to be able to rewrite and expand this book, I have been struck by how much has changed in some of them, but also by how little many of them have changed at all in the last thirteen years.

Few have escaped the pressure for new houses and that is both inevitable and, in some cases, desirable if they are not to become decaying museum exhibits in the countryside. My constant concern is that too little modern building will delight the future as that of the past delights us today.

Where there has been change, it has tended to be considerable: absorption by neighbouring towns; total extinction (as with some of the villages neighbouring the Channel Tunnel terminal); change of character as a result of industrial development or, indeed, abandonment by formerly thriving rural industry.

It remains difficult to know quite where to draw the line between small town and large village and even local advice is not always decisive. However, I have omitted both Paddock Wood and Snodland this time, and given the benefit of the doubt to some other entries.

Every village has its own legends and local lore and during a 30 year career as a *Kent Messenger* journalist I 'collected' these stories, much as I might have collected stamps or anything else. With the benefit of unstinted access to the paper's files, for which I am very grateful, I have used the stories to characterise the villages in a way that 'eye of the beholder' descriptions cannot.

As with the original book, I have again been fortunate enough to have the collaboration of my former colleague, artist Arthur Prosser, and the benefit of his own unrivalled knowledge of the county and the talent to illustrate it so delightfully.

I have taken the opportunity not only to up-date the book and to add more than 50 villages that were omitted originally, but also to make some alterations in the light of knowledge or information I did not have then.

As before, some readers may feel their village has been unfairly treated. But there has to be an element of selection, even when a book is enlarged as this has been and my major concern has been, as it was originally, to feature all that is best among Kent's unique treasury of more than 350 villages. I hope I have achieved that.

Alan Bignell
Maidstone

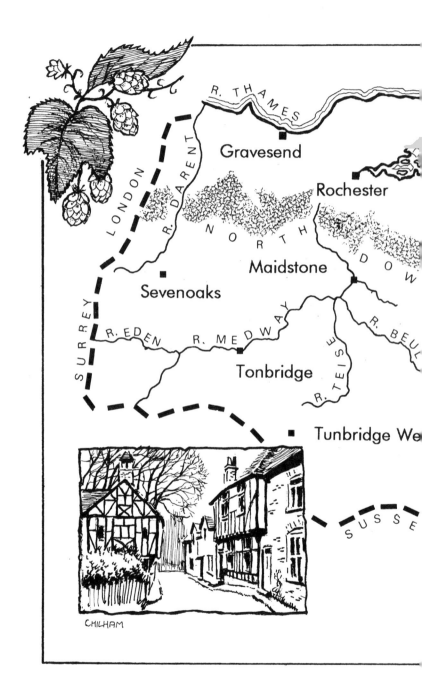

R. THAMES

Gravesend

Rochester

R. DARENT

LONDON

N O R T H

D O W

Maidstone

Sevenoaks

SURREY

R. EDEN

R. MEDWAY

R. TEISE

R. BEUL

Tonbridge

Tunbridge We

SUSSE

CHILHAM

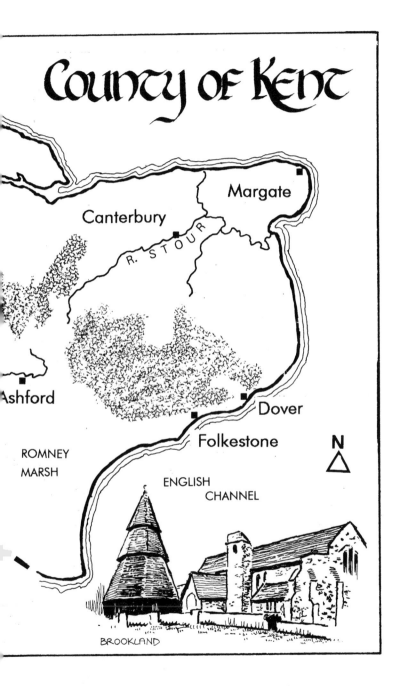

County of Kent

Margate

Canterbury

R. STOUR

Ashford

Dover

Folkestone

ROMNEY
MARSH

N

ENGLISH
CHANNEL

BROOKLAND

Typical Kentish oast houses.

❦ ACOL

This is a splendid place to start a tour of Kent villages. It is slap in the middle of the Isle of Thanet, where nearly all of Kent's history began, although the surrounding terrain has been described, a little uncharitably, perhaps, as a cabbage prairie.

That is because Thanet is characteristically flat and relatively tree-less and much of the land is given over to growing market garden crops. But Acol has tried hard to be – well – inconspicuous, and as far as I know only that irrepressible cleric and author of the *Ingoldsby Legends*, Richard Barham, ever learned anything worth recording about it.

Barham's story begins with his prose introduction to *The Smuggler's Leap – A Legend of Thanet*, in which he wrote: 'Near this hamlet is a long-disused chalk-pit of formidable depth known by the name of The Smuggler's Leap'. He went on to versify the tradition of the parish that the name derived from an incident in which a Riding Officer called Anthony Gill from Sandwich, lost his life in the early 18th century while in pursuit of a smuggler, when both rode their horses over the pit's edge.

According to the *Legend*:

> Below were found next day on the ground
> By an elderly gentleman walking his round
> (I wouldn't have seen such a sight for a pound),
> All smash'd and dash'd, three mangled corses,
> Two of them human – the third was a horse's.

The story went that Exciseman Gill, in his eagerness to catch the smuggler, bargained with the Devil for a horse that could match his quarry's. He got it, but of course it was no mortal animal and so, when they all tumbled into the pit, the Devil-lent steed survived, leaving the locality to be haunted by the ghosts of Smuggler Bill and Old Gill, but only one of their horses, the smuggler's grey. The cliff-faced pit is still there.

❦ ACRISE

Even local people may well question the inclusion of Acrise among a collection of villages. There is no discernible village centre in the usual sense, and the only impression of any kind of community is to be found among the scattering of houses around the 16th century red brick mansion that is Acrise Place.

Actually, Acrise Place is two houses, one Tudor and the other Carolean, joined by a Georgian portico. It came into the ownership of the Papillon family in 1666 after David Papillon came to England in 1588 from France. He became a prosperous civil engineer and it was his son, Thomas, who bought the house, which he enlarged. It was the family's home for almost 200 years until, in 1861, it was sold and changed hands several times before it was bought by the War Department in 1938. Then, in 1950, it was bought back by Arthur Papillon who began the work of restoring it from its semi-derelict condition but died in 1955 before the work was completed.

The little church of St Martin hides itself away in the grounds of Acrise Place although it is much older than the house, with some surviving Norman stonework and lots of memorials to various members of the Papillon family.

🍁 ADDINGTON

The parish of Addington contains some of Kent's most ancient antiquities although many of the houses could encourage the casual visitor to think the village is relatively modern.

In fact, it regards itself as one of the oldest continuously inhabited places in England. Stone Age people lived hereabouts 4,000 years ago. At least, they certainly died and were buried here, as evidenced by the Neolithic burial chambers in Park Road, between the village green and the village hall. They date from about 2,500 BC and the descendants of their occupants were probably still farming the area when the Romans arrived and also lived and died in the vicinity, as did their Saxon successors.

Addington was part of one of those Kentish manors that were given to Bishop Odo after he was made Earl of Kent as a reward for his part in the Norman Conquest. After his fall from grace and banishment from England, successive owners included a long line of the Watton family, who held it until 1750.

The old Manor House was demolished after the Second World War, but some of the present properties are built on the site, including The Bungalow in Addington Park and The Lodge in Park Road. Addington Park Lodge identifies one of the entrances to the park and the stables have been converted to chapels by the Seekers Trust, who bought the estate in the 1930s.

There are four fairly distinct areas of the parish. The Green is the most obviously old part, with the 14th century one-time coaching inn, the Angel, and several other rather fine old buildings.

The house now called St Vincent's was formerly 15th century Hedgehogs Farm. It was enlarged in the 1770s by Admiral Parry, who was the father-in-law of Captain Locker who taught Midshipman Nelson his seamanship and it has been said that it was Nelson who suggested the name for the new house.

On a mound behind a screen of trees, the later tower of the Norman church of St Margaret of Antioch is something of a local landmark. The four bells in the tower have been described as some of the most interesting in Kent, having sounded over the parish for more than 500 years, although recast in the 17th and 18th centuries.

Across the road from the church is the prehistoric burial chamber known as The Chestnuts, a group of leaning sarsen stones, all that remains of a once earth covered barrow first recorded by John Harris in the 18th century and by Josiah Colebrook, who thought it was an Ancient British temple, in 1745. Flinders Petrie recorded 24 standing stones in 1880. A local parson who dug into the site in 1845 found some pottery pieces and more pottery was found at the beginning of the 20th century. The barrow was in ruins by the time the site was excavated properly by Dr John Alexander in 1957, when some of the fallen stones were restored to their former upright positions. Today, the site is most easily identified by a group of modern houses, called The Chestnuts, near the Angel inn.

Addington has the A20 on one side and the parallel M20 on another side. At the foot of the Downs, its near neighbours include commercial sand pits, West Malling golf and country club and the 37 acres of Addington Park which for more than 50 years has been owned by the Seekers Trust as a centre for prayer and spiritual healing, attracting without any sort of ostentation visitors from all over the world.

ADISHAM

This is one of the Nailbourne valley villages, watered by that stream that, legend has it, resulted from a spring that welled up where St Augustine knelt to pray for the end of a 6th century drought. The miracle so incensed the Saxon pagan gods that they conjured up a great storm that dammed the offending stream but the greater deity prevailed by insisting that, nevertheless, the stream would flow once every seven years.

The village groups round its long, narrow main street which ends at a triangular open green where the Early English Holy Innocents' church stands on the site of a much earlier, perhaps 7th century, one. The present church is an unusual (in Kent, at any rate) cruciform building with a pyramid-capped 13th century flint tower.

One of its rectors, the Rev John Bland, was among the first of the Kentish martyrs of the Marian persecutions when he was burned at the stake at Canterbury in 1555. He was accused of heresy, imprisoned, bailed and then re-arrested two months later, spending ten months in prison before he was led to the stake which he shared with a colleague from Rolvenden.

 ALDINGTON

While not one of Kent's most picturesque villages, Aldington has managed to achieve distinction on several counts.

During the 19th century, it lent its name, however reluctantly, to the infamous Aldington Gang of smugglers, also known as The Blues and led by members of the Ransley family. The Walnut Tree inn, once frequented by the gang, is said to be haunted by the ghost of a man who was killed there during a quarrel and thrown down a well in the yard.

But long before that, the village was even more famous as the 16th century home of Elizabeth Barton, the so-called Holy Maid of Kent. She was a servant girl in the household of Thomas Cobb, Archbishop Warham's bailiff at Aldington. She achieved a reputation for visions she claimed to have during what became known as her 'ecstacies', which later historians have suggested were probably some kind of epileptic fits. But at the time they impressed the local parish priest, a man called Richard Masters, through whom she became known to the archbishop. She began making predictions during her 'turns', which was relatively harmless until she began to speak about the king's (Henry VIII) plan to divorce his queen, Catherine, and marry Anne Boleyn.

It is now generally accepted that the poor girl's 'ecstacies' were manipulated by her politically motivated betters but word got out that she had predicted, under divine instruction, that if the king married Anne, God's vengeance would plague him and he would lose his kingdom.

The king was not amused. He had Archbishop Warham arrested and ordered his successor, Archbishop Cranmer, to look into this Holy Maid's predictions. Cranmer succeeded in getting her to confess that she had never had visions at all. Confessions were also procured from Warham and his associates that they had, indeed, used her for their own political motives and in April 1543, as Richard Barham put it so eloquently in his Ingoldsby Legend of *The Leech of Folkestone*, her series of supernatural pranks procured for her head an unenvied elevation upon London Bridge.

That particular Legend featured Aldington Frith, a wide tract of unenclosed country stretching down to the very borders of Romney Marsh, as a favourite rendezvous of 'warlocks and other unholy subjects of Satan'.

But Holy Maids and smuggler gangs apart, Aldington takes some pride in having been the chosen home of none other than Noel Coward, who had his home from 1929 until 1956 in 17th century Goldenhurst farmhouse. Here he composed many of his most famous melodies and lyrics, including *Room with a View*, which was said to have been inspired by the view from one of the rooms.

Another writer, Ford Madox Ford, also lived in Aldington where he wrote a poem called *Aldington Knoll*, which tells how the owner of the land once wanted to level it, but could find no labourers to do the work because of a local belief that anyone who disturbed it was sure of a bad end. Eventually, however, a man from outside the village was employed and he dug up a skeleton and a sword before he died.

During the Second World War, the Knoll was used as an observation post from which, it was said, could be seen the towers of 36 churches and, presumably, many more enemy aircraft.

Aldington's St Martin's church stands on the northern slopes of hills bordering Romney Marsh and the tower is a landmark for seamen. The earliest parts of the church date from the 12th century but the tower was begun in about 1530 and never properly finished until the early 20th century. One of the finest Perpendicular style church towers in the country, it was built free-standing from the church, which was then extended to it. The 14th century choir stalls are among the finest in Kent.

There used to be an archbishops' palace near the church but, at the Reformation, it was taken by Henry VIII for himself and all that remains today is to be found in the wall of Court Lodge farm.

In the 1980s, Central Electricity Generating Board plans to build a converter station on a 34 acre site in Church Lane to transform British AC to Continental DC current, enabling exchanges of current by sub-Channel cable, aroused a great public outcry. But, as is so often the way with public outcries, it failed to influence Authority which went ahead and built the converter station anyway.

 ## ALKHAM

> Here lieth Herbert, offspring of
> Simon. A man open-hearted, assured
> by hope of good things, fluent in
> words of faith.

That epitaph was inscribed on the lid of the stone coffin of Herbert de

Averenches, monk of St Radigund's Abbey at Alkham and first recorded rector. He held the living from 1199 to 1203. The coffin lid is now in the church of St Anthony the Martyr and the inscription is claimed to be the earliest to be found in any Kent church.

Alkham is a pleasant little village, snuggled into the woods and the Downs west of Dover and well worth a visit just for the pleasure of finding such a delightful spot.

The flint church was built in the early 13th century by monks of nearby St Radigund's Abbey. There was almost certainly a church here during Saxon times but the present one dates from the 13th century and was once larger than it is today.

When the Abbey was closed by Henry VIII, most of the stone of which it was built was carted away to help build Henry's coastal defence castle at Sandgate during the invasion scare after 1538. The remains brood demurely over better days at the end of a narrow country lane leading out of the village.

🍁 ALLHALLOWS

Several of the villages on the Hoo Peninsular, where the Thames and the Medway would meet if this fist of land were not between them, are known by the name of their church with the addition of 'Hoo'. Thus, there is St Mary Hoo, Hoo St Werburgh and this one, which is Hoo Allhallows, its church being All Saints.

For most of its life Allhallows has been an agricultural outpost, but in the 1930s the river frontage a mile from the village was advertised as a popular resort, served with a railway line from Gravesend and its own railway station. It never quite caught on and today there is neither line nor station, but there is a holiday camp and a chalet park and the village is a fair-sized one, with its own school, pubs and a scattering of shops of different kinds.

Properly enough in any village, the church has a pub, the Rose and Crown, opposite and the riverside holidaymakers have the British Pilot to cater for their needs.

There is said to be treasure buried in the grounds of Allhallows Place but unfortunately no one knows quite where that was. The Kent historian Edward Hasted wrote in about 1760 that the house, once the home of the memorably named Sir Harbottle Grimstone, Bart, survived 'though much decayed'. Sir Harbottle, 17th century Speaker of the House of Commons and holder of a number of other high offices too, died in 1683, aged 82, and now there is no sign of the house.

The little 11th century church that gives the village its name stands on a slight eminence, a reminder that this part of Kent has been inhabited for a very long time. There is some evidence that there was a church on the site before the present one was built and the area was certainly inhabited by early Britons before the Romans came and by Saxons after the Romans left. Indeed, the village was once much more important than it is now and during the 8th century it was a royal residence of Mercian kings who held sway over Kent at that time. Later, its remoteness made it a convenient place for smuggling gangs to land their contraband.

Yet, but for its resuscitation by the railway during the 19th century, it might have continued its 18th century decline and disappeared as completely as Allhallows Place.

Allhallows boasts an unusually high level of annual sunshine. What it does not boast about, however, is the bitingly cold north winds for which it is equally noted. In his book *The River and the Downs – Kent's Unsung Corner*, Michael Baldwin referred to it as the Boneless Wind and suggested the description may have been a local corruption of the name by which Roman navigators knew the north wind, the boreas. He may have been right. What is certain is that however it got the name, it is somehow peculiarly appropriate for a wind that, in the countryman's telling phrase, 'fair goes right through you'.

Still, it must be said, on one of those fabled summer days that England cherishes for their rarity, this part of Kent can be enviably delightful.

🍁 ALLINGTON

Today, Allington is almost wholly new, its antiquity vested almost exclusively in Allington Castle, down by the River Medway. The castle was originally built by Sir Stephen de Penchester, 13th century Constable of Dover Castle, on the site of an earlier manor house. Later, it was owned by the Cobham family and in 1492 it was bought by Sir Henry Wyatt who carried out some restoration work but is far better remembered for the legend that, while imprisoned in the Tower of London by Richard III because of his Lancastrian sympathies, he was saved from starving to death by a cat which brought a pigeon to his cell every day.

It was afterwards that he was knighted and came to Kent where his son, later Sir Thomas, was born at Allington in 1503. Thomas became a renowned soldier, scholar, statesman, poet and self-confessed lover of Anne Boleyn. His son, another Sir Thomas, benefited substantially from Henry

VIII's Reformation by the acquisition of property of the dissolved friary at Aylesford, and when Queen Mary declared her intention to turn back the clock and marry the Catholic King Philip of Spain, Wyatt led an insurrection against the marriage. But he misjudged the support he could expect in London. He was arrested and, a few months later, executed and the castle was forfeited to the Crown while Maidstone lost its Charter for five years for supporting him.

When Elizabeth came to the throne she restored Maidstone's Charter and leased Allington Castle to one of her courtiers, John Astley, but after his successors moved into Maidstone, the castle was left to deteriorate. By the mid-19th century the whole place was derelict and remained in that state until, in 1905, it was bought by Sir Martin Conway, who spent £70,000 on restoration.

The castle again changed hands in 1951 when it was bought by the same group of Carmelite Friars who rebuilt Aylesford Priory. They carried out further restoration work and used Allington Castle as a retreat and study centre until they, in their turn, sold it and it became an international conference and residential training centre.

The last service was held in the old riverside church of St Lawrence, just outside the castle gates, in 1969, after which it was converted into a private residence. During conversion, efforts were made to open an old safe in the vestry, the keys to which had been long lost. In the end, oxyacetylene cutting equipment was used and the old safe yielded up its secret at last – a single sheet of lining paper charred by the heat of the cutting. Ah well!

The new development of Allington, on either side of the A20, brought demands for a new church and during the 1930s, St Nicholas' church was built in Poplar Grove. Then, in 1973, the present church, still St Nicholas', was built next to the previous one, in Poplar Grove, continuity being achieved by furnishing it with the font, a bell and three stained glass windows from old St Lawrence's.

🍁 APPLEDORE

Today, Appledore is more than eight miles from the sea, on the banks of the Royal Military Canal, which was built between 1804 and 1807 as part of the country's defences against the threatened invasion by Napoleon's army. Once, though, before the River Rother changed its course during a series of 12th century storms, it was an important trading and ship building riverside port.

The canal was never put to the anti-invasion test but it served Appledore well, nevertheless. It gave the village back its access to the sea, and it also gave Appledore an overland route along the military road to Hythe in one direction and Rye in the other.

Most of all, though, it drained the swampy land that had made the area notoriously unhealthy for centuries and it changed Appledore from a damp, fever-ridden place into the delightful little waterside resort it is today.

Long before Napoleon, Frenchmen attacked Appledore in 1380 and burned the church and most of the rest of the village. The church was rebuilt and has

Pillbox on the Royal Military Canal.

since been restored and its treasures include some very fine stained glass windows.

The exceptionally wide main street leading up from the canal is a reminder of the former importance of the village. The Street is lined with attractive houses dating from Tudor times and the little square sets off very prettily the ivy-clad Red Lion Hotel, 18th century Swan Hotel, the church and the old forge, all of which are worth a visit for their different reasons.

In 1991, Appledore's primary school achieved the distinction of being the smallest in Kent, with only 16 children on its roll. Despite parental protests, the school was closed and the children admitted to nearby Wittersham school instead.

For centuries the most prominent local family were the Hornes of Hornes Place. They arrived in 1366 and the restored oratory which they built has been a national monument since 1951 in the care of English Heritage.

A little mystery of Appledore surrounds the old chair which was found in the attic at the Swan in 1967. It was made of wood, with an engraved silver plate ascribing it to Sheikh Mbaruk Bin Raschid Mwele and dated August 1895.

The general belief is that the Sheikh displeased the British Government of his day so much that Admiral Rawson was sent to East Africa with a naval squadron and an Army punitive expedition under General Sir Lloyd William Mathews. The soldiers, it seems, attacked the Sheikh's stronghold but failed to find him and the assumption is that the chair was brought back in lieu of its owner, although no one seems to know how it came to be at the Swan in Appledore. Perhaps a former landlord, whose name was Mathews, was related to the general. Oddly enough, in 1973 another wooden chair was discovered in the hotel's attic. This one was larger and much older, probably about 14th century, with a carved Latin inscription.

It is probably not true that local journalists are still hoping for the discovery of yet another chair, so that they can proclaim the news under the headline: 'Three chairs for Appledore!'

🍁 ASH-NEXT-SANDWICH

Locally, it is enough simply to call it Ash, of course, but on a county scale it is necessary to distinguish this one from several other villages in Kent also called Ash. They are all smaller, this being one of the largest parishes in the county.

Strangers to East Kent have no excuse for not finding it. The distinctive green copper spire that tops the 15th century tower of St Nicholas' church is a landmark for miles around, both on land and at sea. The church is noted for having the best collection of medieval effigies in Kent.

A long, straight village, Ash is known for its market gardens and the nearby hamlet of Marshborough claims to include land that has probably been cultivated for as long as or longer than any other in the country. It is an attractive place, with timbered houses, old cottages and welcoming inns, although they are a mere remnant of the number the village had in the days when it had its own brewery. Opposite the Lion public house, No 75 at the top of Moat Lane is a plaque-bearing Historic Building of Kent, now a dental surgery, and the lane is fronted by a number of Tudor cottages.

The area boasts two vineyards, one at Moat Farm and the other at nearby Church Farm, Staple, both of which welcome visitors.

According to persistent legend, somewhere within the parish bounds lies hidden a fabulous solid gold image of the Saxon god Woden, three or four feet high. Stranger legends have been proved true. Certainly, when Bryan Faussett excavated in the area in 1759 he uncovered a series of Saxon graves. Perhaps the burial place of the golden treasure remains to be found somewhere near them.

Nearby Richborough Castle was once a stronghold of the Roman legions and for about 350 years Richborough was the foremost trading and military Channel port in England. Today, the castle is an imposing ruin but the old port was pressed into service again during the First World War as a supply base for the British Expeditionary Force in France and in the Second World War part of the D-Day Mulberry Harbour was assembled there.

Since then, though, the great cooling towers of Richborough power station have been the dominant landmark on the rather flat landscape thereabouts.

🍁 AYLESFORD

The most casual visitor to Aylesford can see at once that it is old. It is, in fact, said to be one of the oldest continually occupied sites in England.

The Royal manor of Aylesford was first owned by William the Conqueror and the church of St Peter and St Paul is of Norman origin, with a list of vicars dating from 1145. But this River Medway crossing point (the name is said to derive from an Anglo-Saxon description meaning the ford by the church) was old long before the Normans arrived.

There was certainly a Bronze Age settlement hereabouts and in the mid-5th century local tribesmen lost a vital battle against Jutish settlers led by the warlords Hengist and Horsa. In AD 893 Alfred the Great defeated the Danes

in a battle here, or near here, and in 1016 the village was the scene of another defeat of the Danes, this time by Edmund Ironside.

The 14th century ragstone bridge, for centuries the only road across the Medway between Rochester and Maidstone, no longer disgorges modern day traffic directly into Aylesford High Street. The new bridge also offers a good view of the old stone bridge, which is probably one of the most photographed and painted landscape features in Kent, and of the very pleasant riverside grounds of the Hengist Hotel, behind the free car park.

There is no mistaking the antiquity of the houses that overlook the river on both sides of the old bridge. They include the Chequers Inn and the George House, formerly a coaching inn and still bearing the evidence on the windows which make it necessary for the owners to display a notice advising strangers that it is now a private dwelling. A little further along, the Little Gem claims to be the smallest pub in Kent and certainly one of the oldest, if the date above the door, 1106, is to be taken quite literally.

The village is built around a square from which Rochester Road passes by the Tudor group of Trinity Court almshouses, founded by John Sedley in 1605 and restored in 1841, with a new wing added by the Brassey family in 1892.

The actress Dame Sybil Thorndike's father was vicar of Aylesford and she was married there in December 1908 by the Bishop of Rochester and her uncle the Bishop of Thetford. Her mother played the organ during the ceremony. Dame Sybil's last visit to the village was in 1972 when, at the age of 90, she opened the new village community centre.

Only just outside the village is The Friars, England's first Carmelite priory in 1242, but closed like many others by Henry VIII in 1538 after which it became a country mansion. It was visited by Samuel Pepys in 1669, when it was owned by Sir John Banks. Then, one night in June 1930, the building was virtually destroyed by fire and although there was no loss of life a rare collection of Venetian glass and other valuables were lost.

The building remained more or less derelict until after the Second World War when Carmelite monks from Europe pooled their resources and bought and restored what had once been theirs anyway. Today, The Friars is open to visitors and welcomes thousands of pilgrims every year.

A little further from the village in the opposite direction is Kent's 'little Stonehenge', the 5,000 year old Kits Coty. It stands, surrounded by iron railings, on a steep hillside, to one side of, though not visible from, the Blue Bell Hill road between Maidstone and Chatham. The three great upright stones capped by an equally massive table stone are all that remain of a 200 foot long burial chamber that was still recognisable 200 years ago, before soil erosion bared it to today's visitors.

Lower down the same hillside are the remains of another chamber, Little Kits Coty. Legend has it that its reputation as the Countless Stones was challenged once by a baker who thought he would invalidate the name by placing a loaf of his bread on each stone as he counted it so that he would know which he had counted and which he had not. But he found that the loaves were disappearing in his wake and, convinced that the Devil was guarding the secret of the stones, the baker abandoned his task, leaving the stones still un-numbered, their reputation intact.

Unfortunately, that particular legend is told, pretty much the same in every detail, of other heaps of old stones all over Britain and none can say where it began.

Just east of the village itself, in Station and Forstal Roads, the traditional local industries of brick and tile making have been replaced by a large area of warehousing and distribution centres. Beyond that again is Cobtree Manor Park, a very pleasant area of woodland and open space that was once part of the old Cobtree Manor estate where the showman and several times Mayor of Maidstone, Sir Garrard Tyrwhitt-Drake had his zoo. When he died, he left the property to the town and as well as the public park there is now a golf course and the Museum of Kent Life.

Part of what was once the site of the giant Aylesford paper mills is now home to the Meridian television studios and also to Kent Newsprint, a leading newsprint recycling plant.

 BAPCHILD

The old Roman Watling Street (A2) runs almost arrow-straight between Sittingbourne and Faversham through just two villages, Teynham and Bapchild.

Bapchild is much the smaller of the two but although it is a village of relatively little importance to the county generally now, during the 7th and 8th centuries it was important enough for Kings of Kent to hold Councils here. A spring on the outskirts of the village is still known as Becket's well, although it almost certainly has less to do with the 12th century archbishop than with some much earlier inhabitant who left his name (Bacca, perhaps, or Becca) to the spot that later became the site of a pilgrims' oratory.

The village was on the route of the real Pilgrims' Way, as distinct from the long distance footpath that has been given that name and which follows, roughly, the meanderings of the much earlier west-east trade route for tin, wool and other exports bound for the short sea crossings to the Continent from the Kent coast. As recently as the late 18th century, this would have been one of the more lonely stretches of the Watling Street route between London and Dover and travellers on it were always at risk from footpads and highwaymen. Newspapers regularly reported the activities of these robbers who, according to some accounts, at any rate, could behave with commendable gallantry.

One such report in January 1789 told how a Whitstable man was held up near Bapchild by two men, one armed with a cutlass, the other with a pistol, and robbed of three shillings and sixpence. The robbers were said to have behaved very civilly and to have given their victim fourpence-ha'penny back 'to bear the expenses'.

There was a Saxon church at Bapchild before the present Norman St Lawrence's church was built of rough flints, to which the Tudor brick porch was added. The church is unusual in having its tower, topped by a slender broached spire, at the end of the nave.

Inside, the church gives the impression of being over-endowed with fairly massive chalk-block pillars, each carved with a different design, and one of the curiosities of the church is a mammoth's tooth, said to have been found when the church was built and now displayed in a glass case.

Today, the village is little more than a few shops and houses on both sides of the road, dwindling to a few scattered cottages and farm buildings on the outskirts.

🍁 BARFRESTON

High on its hill, some eight or nine miles inland from Dover, this little village, which the locals call 'Barson', by the way, is remarkable only for its church, which boasts one of the finest examples of Norman architecture and stone sculpture to be found anywhere in England.

The exterior walls and doorways of St Nicholas' church are decorated with a profusion of figures of all kinds, ranging from the commonplace to the frankly bizarre. One, over the south door, is said to be a representation of Archbishop Thomas Becket. The carvings are all of 800 years old but they are still capable of capturing the imagination of visitors as they must have done when they were new, about a century after the church was founded by Hugo de Port, a sub-Constable of Dover Castle and, later, a monk at Winchester.

Most famous and most-often pictured is the south doorway, with its carvings of Christ in glory giving his blessing, surrounded by a heavenly host and a variety of beasts of all kinds, most of them mythical. All around are small scenes depicting the activities of the manor house community: a minstrel, cellarer, armourer, labourer, miller, etc.

But the artist (artists?) had a lively sense of humour, for also depicted are a dog (or is it a bear?) playing a harp, a monkey riding on the back of a goat with a rabbit over its shoulder, a hare drinking a toast to a partridge, a horse and rider, even a couple kissing and, at the nave north door, two dancing girls, each holding one ear of a severed head.

It really is an extraordinary gallery, especially for such a small church where, in the absence of a tower, the single bell hangs in a yew tree in the yard. It has been suggested that the decorative stonework may have been brought here from a monastery at Hackington, now part of Canterbury. It was begun by Archbishop Baldwin in the 12th century but bitterly opposed by the monks of Christ Church so that after he died during a Crusade in 1190 the unfinished monastery was demolished.

There is certainly nothing in Kent or Sussex and little anywhere else to compare with the exuberance of the carvings that make this pretty little village unique.

🍁 BARHAM

More than most villages in Kent, Barham has had a ringside seat for the pageant of history.

It lies among the Downs to which it has given its name and it was on those Downs that Romans camped on their way inland from their Thanet landing. William the Conqueror here met the Men of Kent, heard them swear fealty and took delivery of the hostages they surrendered against their fulfilment of that oath.

It was here that William, son of King Stephen, fell from his horse and broke his thigh on his way to Dover to meet the Earl of Flanders, and it was here that King John camped with 50,000 men in preparation for war with France.

Simon de Montfort assembled a huge army on Barham Downs in 1265, during the Barons' War; and in 1422 Henry VI came from his crowning in Paris to be met here by his Barons and Commons and escorted to Canterbury and on to London.

Margaret, Duchess of Burgundy met her brother, Edward IV, in a tent on these Downs; Charles I picnicked on them during his return to London with his bride-to-be. During the Civil War, Royalist troops massed here for their attack on Dover Castle; and Charles II was welcomed home here after his long years of exile by the Kentish Regiment of Foot, in 1660.

In 1799, the village witnessed 38 baptisms of infants born in the camp of 18,000 troops waiting to go to Holland and, during the Napoleonic Wars, Barham Downs was again covered with the tents of an Army awaiting embarkation.

There are those who will tell you that it is on Barham Downs – perhaps in one of the hundred or so prehistoric burial mounds there – that the legendary golden statue of Woden that crops up in the lore of towns and villages throughout East Kent lies buried. Henry VIII took the legend sufficiently seriously to order one of the mounds to be excavated and the diggers did, in fact, find gold-embellished armour.

Broome Park at Barham is a 17th century mansion designed by Inigo Jones. It is probably the original of Richard Barham's Tappington Hall in his *Ingoldsby Legends*. During the 18th century it was the home of Henry Oxenden who, while still at Cambridge, invented an ice-yacht that had four skates, a tablecloth sail and a dragoon sword for a rudder. He tested it satisfactorily and later adapted the idea to a land yacht which he 'sailed' on Barham Downs at speeds – so 'they' say! – of up to 30 mph.

In 1911 Sir Charles Oxenden sold Broome Park to Lord Kitchener of Khartoum. His alterations to the house were said to include a cupboard built into the panelling of his study in which he could hide whenever he spotted a lady approaching the house, in case she turned out to be another of those suffragettes who besieged him from time to time.

Barham is an attractive village, with a long street over which towers the green copper spire of the 13th century church of St John the Baptist. Nearby Barham Court was once the home of that FitzUrse who was one of the knights who murdered Thomas Becket in Canterbury Cathedral in 1170, and the three bears on the village sign that stands on the green are a reference to the FitzUrse family.

Incidentally, an unusual feature of that same village sign is the little mouse carved into the woodwork, the signature of the craftsman who made it and who was known locally as Mousey.

For many years the most distinctive local landmark, after the church, was Barham windmill but that was destroyed by fire during restoration in 1970.

🍁 BARMING

The old village of Barming is almost lost now among the houses and bungalows of 20th century estate development. If it is still to be glimpsed at all, it is on the River Medway side of the Maidstone-Tonbridge road, where the road falls steeply down to the river and the bridge that crosses it.

Until very recently, the 18th century wooden St Helen's Bridge carried all classes of traffic across the river but time took its toll and it became unsafe for vehicles. It was closed in 1997 to traffic, which must now use the next nearest crossing points at East Farleigh or Teston.

The bridge has been replaced with a new footbridge as part of Maidstone Council's millennium River Medway Countryside Park scheme, much of which is being financed by a national lottery windfall. Local people were not happy about it. They wanted the unique (on the Medway) wooden bridge to be repaired and preserved, but their pleas were not heard.

There used to be another wooden bridge across the Medway, connecting Court Lodge at West Farleigh with Barnjet Manor at Barming. The 18th century Kent historian Edward Hasted recorded that St Helen's Bridge was carried away by river ice in 1740 but, in fact, it seems it was Barnjet Bridge, not St Helen's Bridge, that suffered that particular fate.

The 17th century Bull Inn and the war memorial just opposite used to be the turning point for the old trolley bus shuttle service from Maidstone and it is still the destination for one of the local bus services. It was inevitable that homes would be built along such a route and that the land behind them would succumb to the mounting pressures for development. Those pressures are continuing and more new homes are planned for the parish.

St Margaret's church looks as if it heartily disapproves of all the new building and stands well apart from it, surrounded by fields on the hillside above the river. It is a pretty little church with some interesting features but its very isolation has made it a target for thieves and vandals from time to time.

Pre-Christian Roman remains were found near the church during the 19th century, including some apparently elaborate stone coffins. But after the excavators had gloated over them they rather lost interest and went off to dig elsewhere. The coffins were lost and now no one knows what became of them.

The village also has a much more modern and rather less eye-catching little church, St Andrew's, alongside Tonbridge Road, just short of the junction with Queen's Road.

In 1086 the Domesday survey distinguished East Barming, around the church, from West Barming, also known as Little Barming. The two remained separate until the end of the 15th century, by which time the West Barming church was in ruins and the parish could not afford to support its own minister. Having no West Barming to compete with, East Barming dropped its qualifying compass point and muddled through another 300 years until the turnpike road put the village into commuting distance from Maidstone and made it a favourite spot for some of the county town's more moneyed classes to build in.

Barming Heath was chosen as the site for the new county asylum in 1828. It became the Oakwood psychiatric hospital but that is now closed and the old (listed) buildings are being redeveloped for housing alongside the new Maidstone General Hospital.

James Syms, in his self-illustrated book, *Kent Country Churches*, notes that from 1780 until 1820 the rector of Barming was a forebear of his. He wrote a history of the village which, Syms said, consisted largely of criticism of some of its more important parishioners. On the whole I'm inclined to be grateful that my own sojourn in the parish has not coincided with that of the critical cleric. Fancy having to make up your mind whether it was better to have come in for his public criticism or to have been left out as not important enough for it!

 BEARSTED

Of all Kent villages, few cling more tenaciously to their independent character in the face of pressure from a bloated neighbour than Bearsted does.

Maidstone, the county town, has been reaching out towards it since the 1930s and in one direction the estates of both have pretty well joined together. But the old village, around the green, is still as picturesquely villagey as anywhere in the county.

The cricket ground on the green is said to be one of the oldest in Kent and it is surrounded by picturesque old houses. At opposite corners of the green are the White Horse inn, which overlooks the village sign, and the Royal Oak, behind which is a seven-kiln oast house.

A road separates the pond from the rest of the the green and another road separates the pond from more houses. A lychgate-style shelter for the site of the former village pump commemorates Queen Victoria's diamond jubilee and at the opposite end of the green a drinking fountain commemorates the silver jubilee of Elizabeth II.

Tucked away at the end of Church Lane, Holy Cross church is unique in Kent for the stone beasts perched on three corners of the top of its tower. Once generally supposed to be bears (appropriate enough for a village called Bearsted), they are now more usually supposed to represent a lion, a panther and a griffin, and are probably the work of local stone masons, who had something of a reputation.

Stone quarrying was an important local industry in the 16th century and one of the leading families of masons was the Berties or Bartys. Robert Barty, who died in about 1501, owned a house in Maidstone and farmed in Bearsted and in 1532 Thomas Barty was Master Mason of Winchester Cathedral. Today, that part of the parish that is known as Barty includes the property still known as Barty House, now a private nursing home.

According to local legend, one night of every year the three creatures come down off the tower and stretch their legs in the churchyard before taking up their posts again, but it is difficult to find reliable eye-witnesses to the event!

In the churchyard is the ground-level stump of a Canadian cypress tree which was known as the Mourning Tree. The stump is carved with the date, 1996, when the tree was felled and in the angle formed by two paths that went round it there is a tablet inscribed: 'This tree marks the grave of John Dyke, who was hanged for rick burning in 1830 at the last public hanging at Penenden Heath. Subsequently it was found that he was not guilty of the crime.'

In fact, years after Dyke was hanged, another man made a deathbed confession to the crime. He was buried on the opposite side of the church, so that the innocent Dyke's unjustly maligned spirit should not be offended by his proximity.

Bearsted cricket club celebrated its 250th anniversary in 1999. A Bearsted team was beaten by a London side, in London, in 1749 and there was certainly a Bearsted cricket club in 1875 because one of its members was the famous Kent cricketer Alfred Mynn, known as Mighty Mynn, the Lion of Kent. He was born in Goudhurst, the son of a gentleman farmer, and trained as an architect. But he devoted most of his life to cricket and became known as the finest all-rounder the game had ever had.

He was an 18-stone man, over six feet tall, yet he claimed he ate only bread and drank only beer. He was renowned as a very kindly, good-natured man and when, having neglected his business for the game, he was bankrupted as a result, friends clubbed together to pay his expenses so that he could carry on playing his beloved cricket. Mynn eventually died in London in 1861 and was buried in nearby Thurnham churchyard, but it is on Bearsted green that he is best commemorated, with the village sign which shows him, top-hatted, at the wicket.

Baroness Orczy, creator of *The Scarlet Pimpernel*, lived with her husband, artist Montague Barstow, at Snowfield in Bearsted. She was something of a character herself. Living like a lady of the manor, she travelled about in a carriage and four and threw tantrums if the local girls did not curtsey and the boys doff their caps when she passed. She lived in Bearsted until her death in 1947.

The poet Edward Thomas lived in Bearsted after he moved there aged 23 with his wife Helen and son Merfyn, in 1901. The first cottage they rented is gone now and the site lost, probably under part of the rash of new homes on the Roseacre estate, but they later moved to Ivy Cottage, now Ivy House, which still overlooks The Green just across the road from the pond. Thomas earned a precarious living and very little recognition as a literary drudge until he turned to poetry in 1914. He was killed in France in 1917 but in those last three years he poured out a great deal of very good poetry that earned him his place in the annals of Kentish literature.

Today, Bearsted has joined the growing number of Kent villages that have their own vineyards. Bearsted's was an orchard in the 1980s but by 1998 was producing 10,000 bottles of wine a year.

🍁 BEKESBOURNE

In 1705, Bekesbourne featured, if somewhat remotely, in a very odd little story told by Daniel Defoe. His journalistic instincts were so aroused by it that he published a pamphlet entitled *A True Relation of the Apparition of one Mrs Veal, the next day after her death, to one Mrs Bargrave, at Canterbury, the 8th*

September, 1705 – which apparition recommends the Perusal of Drelincourt's Book of Consolations against the Fears of Death.

Having relieved himself of the title, Defoe summoned up enough energy to tell the tale, as told to him, of a Mrs Veal of Dover who visited her friend Mrs Bargrave in Canterbury in September 1705.

Mrs Bargrave was the daughter of a Bekesbourne yeoman who had cut her off with the proverbial (and in this case, it seems, literal) shilling for marrying a second time against his wishes. Her husband was a drunken maltster called Richard Bargrave who ill-treated her and no doubt fully justified the lady's Bekesbourne father in everything he had forecast when he opposed the marriage.

However, on the day of Mrs Veal's visit to her friend Mrs Bargrave, they chatted about a long journey that Mrs Veal said she was about to make. She asked Mrs Bargrave to arrange for a tombstone to be made for her mother's grave, large enough for Mrs Veal's own name to be added to the inscription in due course.

That agreed, Mrs Veal left, saying she was going to visit a cousin while she was there in Canterbury. It was only when Mrs Bargrave later learned that Mrs Veal had, in fact, died in Dover the day before her visit that she began to broadcast her experience.

The story soon circulated and even claimed the attention of Queen Anne and her consort, Prince George of Denmark, who asked a local expert to investigate the odd affair. The investigation revealed nothing to invalidate the story which, thanks to Mr Defoe's comprehensively titled pamphlet, survives as one of Kent's many ghost stories.

More recently, Bekesbourne was associated with another celebrated story-teller. The 18th century Old Palace was owned by Ian Fleming until 1968, during which time he wrote some of his James Bond books there. The Old Palace was built in the grounds of a palace built for Archbishop Thomas Cranmer in 1552 and he spent some time there before his imprisonment for treason and martyrdom at the stake in 1556.

Bekesbourne was once a borough and a limb of the Cinque Port of Hastings and during the two 20th century world wars it hosted a military airfield, but today it is just another of that string of villages threaded together by the Nailborne stream. St Peter's church stands a little aloof from the rest of the village; a long, low flint and tiled building, the principal feature of interest of which is the Norman doorway on the north side.

The village provides a postal address for Howlett's, John Aspinall's privately-owned zoo, which is actually just outside the village.

BENENDEN

This is the first, alphabetically, of the Wealden 'dens' that commemorate the Saxon practice of appending forest clearings in the sprawling Andredsweald (the Weald) to their coastal manors. These clearings, dens, were where the manor pigs rooted for the acorns and other 'pannage' on which they were fattened and from which timber and brushwood was collected. The people who attended them built rough shelters and enclosed small plots for their own sustenance and gradually, as bigger areas were cleared, farms were established and the villages grew up. Some of them retained the names of the manor from which they evolved (as in Tenterden: Thanet's den) but more adopted the name of the man or the family who owned the manor and the den – thus Benenden: Bynna's woodland pasture, or den.

Today, the village is one of Kent's more tucked-away beauties, with a large village green overlooked from one end by the exceptionally large church and from the other end by some attractive old weatherboard and tile cottages. They once housed the village school which was founded by a member of the Gibbons family (of *Rise and Fall of the Roman Empire* fame).

When the Normans carried out the first major exercise in English bureaucracy, their Domesday surveyors noted that Benindene was one of only four places in the Weald that had a church, although it was probably not the same church that was ruined by a storm on 30th December 1672, and rebuilt in 1677/78.

Today's village was largely created by Lord Cranbrook in the 1860s. Until then, it was a typical Wealden parish of scattered properties, where the names of such 16th century yeoman farmhouses as Pympne Manor, Mill House, Manor House and The Moat meant more to the locals than the name of Benenden itself did.

One of those old houses was Hemsted, which was owned for 400 years by the Guldeford family. In 1573 Queen Elizabeth I was the guest of Sir Thomas Guldeford and his wife Elizabeth at Hemsted, where she planted a walnut tree which remained standing until 1857.

The last of the Guldeford owners of Hemsted sold the house to Admiral Sir John (Foulweather Jack) Norris in 1718.

In 1766 the most celebrated of all Hemsted's occupants came to live there as the bride of Foulweather Jack's grandson, another John. She was pretty Kitty Fisher – the one who found Lucy Lockett's pocket in the nursery rhyme. Born Catherine Maria, she was a milliner of humble parentage who wiggled her way into high society's drawing rooms by way of several of its bedchambers.

However, after her marriage it seems she settled happily enough into the role of mistress of Hemsted. She was well regarded by local folk, not least for her generosity to the poor. Unhappily, she died of smallpox only four months after her marriage and was buried, according to her own wishes, dressed in her best ball gown, in the local church.

Hemsted was rebuilt in 1860 by Gaythorne Hardy, later Lord Cranbrook, and when Lord Rothermere bought it in 1912 he made more alterations, allegedly using cattle urine and small shot to 'age' some of the new stonework he added.

Now, Hemsted houses Benenden School, one of the top private girls' schools in the country, which numbers Princess Anne, the Princess Royal, among its old girls.

After William Cobbett took one of his Rural Rides hereabouts, he wrote a testimonial to the 'singular humanity' of the people of Benenden. He was particularly impressed with the bench which was provided for the village stocks, 'so that the patient, while he is receiving the benefit of the remedy, is not exposed to the danger of catching cold by sitting on the ground.'

Perhaps it was another manifestation of that 'singular humanity' that enabled Benenden to play host to the chest hospital which was established there by the Post Office in 1905, to give free medicine and treatment to tuberculosis victims among its staff. After 1933 all Civil Servants and their wives and children were admitted too. The hospital was enlarged and as TB became less of a scourge than it had been, it was equipped to care for sufferers from a wide range of chest and respiratory illnesses.

What illness, if any, was suffered by the man on the Castleton's Oak inn sign at Benenden, I really do not know. But there he sits on his coffin, in memory of a local man called Castleton who is said to have made his own oak coffin half a lifetime before he finally needed it.

In 1984, gas and oil prospectors probed the geology of different parts of the Weald, including Benenden, and there were hopes and fears of a new industrial revolution that would bring to the countryside a wholly unfamiliar crop of the notorious 'Nodding Donkey' oil drilling rigs. In fact, what finds there were proved to be not worth exploiting commercially and the prospectors packed up and went elsewhere. It has been suggested that it was the huge sigh of relief that was responsible for the devastating 1987 'hurricane' – but perhaps not!

 BETHERSDEN

This is another of those Wealden 'dens' derived from a family name, this time (according to Judith Glover's *The Place Names of Kent*, at any rate) Beaduric. The village's major claim to fame results from the so-called Bethersden marble which found its way into the two Kent cathedrals, Canterbury and Rochester, as well as many humbler churches and some large houses throughout the county. Bethersden's own church of St Margaret has none except that which paves the south porch.

But then, Bethersden would have known better than most that the local stone was not real marble at all, even though it could be fashioned and polished to look very like it.

In fact, it is the product of a geological curiosity. At some period, it seems, this area was part of some kind of crustacean Sargasso Sea, to which a particular species of water snail resorted for what no doubt seemed good reasons at the time. The creatures died there in their millions and their shells were compressed into a rock strata during a million years or so, to be quarried as Bethersden marble for a very few short centuries.

The local people had a more practical use for it than mere interior decoration. They laid slabs of their mock marble across the sticky Wealden clay fields to make causeways across which pack horses loaded with raw wool and finished woollen goods could pick their way to the markets that made the local industry one of the richest in England for 400 years.

The stone is no longer quarried and Bethersden has lost its textile industry but it remains an attractive little village, its main street lined with typically Wealden weatherboard houses and several old hall houses. The village inn, the George, is properly adjacent to the church, in this case just opposite.

Once, the village was the home of that Richard Lovelace, the Cavalier courtier and poet, who rejoiced in the reputation of the handsomest man in England and who whiled away a term of imprisonment by philosophising (against all the evidence of his condition at the time) in his poem *To Althea, from Prison* that:

> 'Stone walls do not a prison make
> Nor iron bars a cage;
> Minds, innocent and quiet, take
> That for a hermitage.
> If I have freedom in my love
> And in my soul am free,
> Angels alone, that soar above,
> Enjoy such liberty.'

He earned the opportunity for such ruminations in April 1642 after he was imprisoned in the gatehouse of Westminster Palace for trying to deliver, to both Houses of Parliament, the Kent Petition. The petition had been drawn up by the county's leading gentry in the name of the knights, gentry and commonalty of the county of Kent, urging 'a good understanding' between King and Parliament so that law abiding people should not have to choose to offend either one or the other. Four months later, the Civil War broke out.

Lovelace's loyalty to Charles I cost him dearly and he had to sell all his land in and around Bethersden. St Margaret's church, however, is still custodian of a number of family monuments and the south chapel is known as the Lovelace Chapel.

There has been a church at Bethersden for a thousand years or more, certainly before the Normans came, although no trace of the earliest one remains now and the list of incumbents begins with John atte Broke in 1319. The present church is 14th and 15th century, much restored in the late 19th century. A curiosity in the churchyard are the oven vaults, not unique, but certainly unusual, built for three families, the Jacksons, Wilmotts and Witherdens, in 1796.

After several slumbrous centuries, Bethersden found fleeting fame in 1985 through the local engineering company of W. & D. Cole, which supplied new gates and railings for St Paul's Cathedral in London. Rather more recently, Buss Farm became the location that was used for the Larkins' Home Farm in the TV series, *The Darling Buds of May*.

But apart from occasional impingements upon the public attention such as these, Bethersden keeps itself pretty much to itself and seems content to be numbered among those Kent villages with more eventful pasts than presents.

Nevertheless, it does boast a very distinctive village sign, installed in 1996. It is in the form of a 3-foot diameter iron frame on an oak post set in Bethersden marble. Around the frame are symbols of local significance: an anvil, horse-shoe, oast house, a pig, a sheep, shearing clippers, a rocking horse (signifying a local industry) and a book (in memory of the Cavalier poet, Richard Lovelace). The whole frames a picture of the village and buried beneath the sign is a 20th century time capsule.

❦ BIDBOROUGH

The clock on the tower of the 13th century sandstone church of St Lawrence, Bidborough, looks out over the neighbouring rooftops away into a beguiling distance. It is well worth the effort of climbing up the worn sandstone steps and passing through the lychgate into the churchyard just for the windy, top o' the world peace and quiet to be found there.

The clock itself dates only from 1851, but it is remarkable for its long pendulum which reaches almost to the floor of the tower inside the church. Anyone who can synchronise his eye movements with the steady swing of the big round weight on the end may read on it the inscription:

> When as a child I laughed and wept,
> Time crept.
> When as a youth I dreamed and talked,
> Time walked.
> When I became a full grown man
> Time ran.
> Soon I shall find when travelling on
> Time gone.
> Will Christ have saved my soul by then?
> Amen.

Nearby, on an adjoining tower wall, is a memorial brass to Albert Peter Thurston (1881-1946) who lived in the parish for 42 years. He was a pioneer in flying from 1902 and the first doctor of science in Aeronautics, founder of the first aeronautical laboratory in the country at the East London (Queen Mary) College. He also initiated the metal construction of aircraft. A memorial postscript adds, on a slightly reproachful note, perhaps: 'Buried at Over Wallop, Hants'.

The window in the tower, behind the swinging pendulum, is a memorial to 'those men of Bidborough who gave their lives for the country in the Great War 1914-1918', and the north aisle west window is particularly admired for the beauty lent to it when the setting sun shines through the coloured glass. The windows contain glass by the William Morris Company, some of it designed by Burne-Jones.

The church itself is old, with one remaining Saxon wall. It stands on a spur of the Bidborough ridge overlooking the Medway valley to the north and the land that falls away to the Ashdown Forest to the south. Among the many churchyard memorials is one to a Countess of Darnley who was buried there in 1803.

But the village, which, despite its age, has a prosperous modern look about it, has only about 500 homes. In 1955 one of its residents was Kew Gardens curator William Dallimore, who identified a rare variety of chestnut tree growing in and around the village. Now it is known as the Bidborough chestnut – *Aesculus Dallimorei Sealy* for long.

🍁 BIDDENDEN

If there is such a thing as a 'typical' Kent village, Biddenden is probably what most people would like to think was just that.

It began, inauspiciously enough, as one of the many 'dens' or manorial outbacks where the manors of east and north Kent kept their hogs and cut their timber. In this case, it was the 'den' of Brabourne, a village near Ashford. But it was already affording a degree of personal prosperity to the Chulkhurst family when their daughters, Eliza and Mary, were born in about 1100 and gave the village its abiding fame.

The girls were England's first Siamese twins, joined together at shoulder and hip, and they lived together in the fullest possible sense for more than 30 years. When one of them was taken ill and died, the other refused to allow surgeons to separate her from her dead sister, saying that they had come into the world together and would leave it the same way. She died a few hours later.

That, at least, is the handed-down story. In fact, the Chulkhurst twins are more legendary than historical. There is no hard evidence that they ever lived, although that, of course, is not to say that they never did.

At any rate, they are credited with the bequest of what became known as the Bread and Cheese lands, income from which was to pay for a dole of bread, cheese and ale (later to be paid in tea) to the local poor. The dole is commemorated today with the Easter distribution of special biscuits stamped with a representation of the two Maids, who also feature on the very distinctive village sign.

The ceremony of distributing the dole was not always a very decorous one. In 1682 the Rector, the Rev Giles Hinton, reported to Archbishop Sancroft: '... even to this time (the custom) is with much disorder and indecency observed.' After that, the bread and cheese (but no more ale) was doled out in the church porch until the end of the 17th century, and then from the old workhouse.

Today, the Chulkhurst Estate is built on part of the Bread and Cheese lands and Cheeselands is a housing trust development.

After the Chulkhurst twins had lived and died, Biddenden shared the Wealden woollen wealth. A building boom in the 14th, 15th and 16th centuries bequeathed later centuries such local features as Standen, a fine old timbered house about a mile outside the village; Biddenden Place, home of Sir John de Mayney early in the 13th century; Vane Court, which was once owned by a former King of Siam; and Great Batchelor, the home of Gervase Adlard (or Allard) who was Captain and Admiral of the Navy in 1272.

The core of the village is the High Street, where the pavement is of ancient slabs of Bethersden marble. Like all Wealden villages, Biddenden was practically cut off every winter and sometimes throughout the year when any prolonged rain turned the roads into a morass of mud. As recently as 1807 the Rev Edward Nares recorded that even with four horses harnessed to his carriage he could travel no more than three miles from the rectory. In the 15th century, the local weavers laid causeways of Bethersden marble along which packhorse trains could carry their loads of wool and some remnants of those causeways are still to be found across fields and beside roads.

The village main street has some picturesque weavers' cottages and other old houses between the small triangular village green and the church. The Red Lion inn is said to have been built by an Agincourt veteran in 1415. A hundred yards north of the village green is the Old Cloth Hall.

The street leads up to All Saints' church, itself a sandstone monument to 14th and 15th century prosperity and almost certainly the successor of an earlier Saxon church. The local Bethersden marble has been used in the construction of the tower and there are very fine brasses on some of the memorial tablets that form part of the floor inside the church.

The 20th century made its contribution to village fame with the development of the 22-acre Biddenden vineyard, the oldest vineyard in Kent, about a mile and a half outside the village.

🍁 BILSINGTON

The little East Kent village of Bilsington takes its name from Bilswip's tun – Bilswip being a queen and abbess who owned the manor which, in 1243, belonged to two sisters and was divided into Bilsington Superior and Bilsington Inferior.

St Augustine's Priory (Bilsington Superior) was built by Sir John Mansell, among whose many high offices was that of Henry III's Lord Chief Justice, and it provided shelter for pilgrims travelling to Canterbury. But the board and lodgings fees paid by the 'tourists' were evidently not the only source of the Priory's income because in 1437 the Prior was pardoned for his part in the local wool smuggling industry. He was also 'exonerated from all claim for the recovery of the King's Jewels'. It seems that Henry V left his war chest at the Priory, from which it was never recovered.

Court Lodge, immediately west of the church, from which it was separated by a moat, was the administrative centre of Bilsington Inferior.

Like so many of its kind, after the Dissolution the Priory became a farmhouse and gradually declined into ruin. It was a reputed hideout for the notorious 19th century Aldington Gang of smugglers but in 1906 it was partly restored and the red brick house that adopted its name was added to it.

In former times, the owner of the Manor of Bilsington was required to carry the last dish of the second course to the king's table and to present him with three maple cups at a coronation, a tradition that was discontinued after George IV's reign.

In 1825 the house became the property of William Cosway, a baker's son who became secretary to Vice-Admiral Collingwood and who served aboard the *Royal Sovereign* at the Battle of Trafalgar. Sir William was a supporter of the Reform Bill and in June 1834, when Lady Cosway and their children were at Brighton, he left London on the Criterion Coach to join them. He was travelling on the outside of the coach when the horses bolted on London Bridge. The runaway coach overturned and he was thrown off and killed. He was 50 years old. Other supporters of the Bill met in Canterbury and resolved to commemorate him, as a result of which, in June 1835, work began on building a monument in Mill Field, Bilsington.

Built of Kentish ragstone, the 52 foot high obelisk became a landmark for shipping and during the Second World War it had to be removed for security reasons. After the war, however, it was replaced and was struck by lightning in October 1967. It would have cost £5,000 to repair it and the village decided that Sir William's memory could be adequately preserved by the inscribed base of the monument alone. But Bilsington is not much more than a church, a pub and a village hall and it missed its obelisk and in 1998 it gave a grateful welcome to a national lottery grant of £83,500 towards the cost of restoring the Cosway memorial and providing a footpath as the village millennium project.

 BIRLING

For nearly 600 years the Nevill family has owned land at Birling, ever since the manor came into the family by marriage in 1435. They came to England with the Conqueror and successive Marquesses of Abergavenny have traced their title back to Sir Ralph Nevill, sixth son of the first Earl of Westmorland, who was summoned to the English Parliament of 1450-1472 as the first Baron Bergavenny.

Since then, the family has given England many famous sons, including that Richard Nevill, Earl of Warwick, who became known as Warwick the Kingmaker after his nephew won the War of the Roses and became Edward IV. First to use the new form of the title, Abergavenny instead of Bergavenny, was William, 14th Baron, who died in 1745.

The Hon Rev William Nevill built Birling Manor in the late 1830s, having become vicar of Birling in 1816. He became the fourth Earl of Abergavenny in 1845 and his three daughters, Caroline, Henrietta Augusta and Isobel, are credited with having carved the 10 foot high imitation 15th century font cover in the church.

The manor was destroyed by fire in 1917, but the compact little village centre around the church still includes the old forge and the village inn, which changed its name from the Bull to the Nevill Bull in 1953 in memory of Michael Nevill who was killed in the Second World War. The Nevill family crest features a bull's head and two chained silver bulls for supporters.

Artist Rowland Hilder's mother came from Birling. His father, Roland Hilder, was under-butler at Birling Manor and after their marriage, Mr and Mrs Hilder emigrated to the United States in 1904. It was there, in 1905, that young Rowland was born. The family came back to England and to Birling several times and Rowland studied art at Goldsmith's College in London.

Margaret Collins' book *Birling, A Backward Glance*, in which she gathered together a great many interesting and entertaining details of life in the village in the past, was illustrated for her by Rowland Hilder.

Among the many stories of former villagers, there is one about the Hon Rev E.V. Bligh, vicar of Birling in the mid-19th century, who tried to commercialise the Birling Cure for rabies. The recipe was a close-kept secret, but it apparently included herbs and drugs infused in milk and it was sold in large wine bottles costing a guinea each. This proved to be too expensive for most of the potential customers, so the enterprising cleric re-bottled some of it and sold it for 3s 6d a small bottle. According to Mrs Collins' researches, business was good for a while, but then Louis Pasteur developed his anti-rabies vaccine in 1864 and the Birling Cure went the way of many another patent medicine into oblivion.

Birling is now another of those 'dormitory villages' with no school and, since 1947, no village store or post office. But the church, All Saints, much of which is 14th century, still stands on its little rise. It is reached from street level by a flight of stone steps, from where its later Perpendicular-style tower dominates the village centre and much of the surrounding countryside. Not altogether surprisingly, the names of various members of the Nevill family feature prominently on the memorials inside the church.

Nearby, the wrought iron village sign, unveiled in December 1989, is a relatively rare example, in Kent, of the silhouette style, in which the symbols are unpainted metal cut-outs. The work of village blacksmith, Len Kilner, features the Nevill bull and the White Horse of Kent, above which two medieval pilgrims cavort in merry memory of the many pilgrims who would have passed through Birling on their way to Canterbury.

❦ BISHOPSBOURNE

Bishopsbourne is a bit of a backwater, in the least possible derogatory sense, through which flows, when the fancy takes it, that slightly mysterious stream, the Nailbourne. It is supposed to feed the Little Stour only once every seven years when it flows in obedience to a decree by St Augustine himself, after Saxon pagan gods had tried to frustrate his efforts to relieve a terrible drought.

It is a pretty, peaceful village. Local features include Bourne House, one of the finest Queen Anne houses in Kent, and Charlton Park House, an elegant Georgian mansion, with a grand salon built specially for George IV who often visited the house during his romance with Lady Conyngham. The house, in its open parkland about three-quarters of a mile south-east of the village, had a varied career after it was taken over by the Army during the Second World War. A 16-inch gun was mounted on a railway carriage nearby to bombard France, although it was not actually fired very often because it did almost as much damage to local homes as it could expect to do to its target area, and their owners' complaints were judged to be more valid.

After the war the house was used by the Dr Barnardo organisation as a home for some of their children, who gave the house a reputation for being haunted. In 1970 it was taken over and restored by Lt Col Michael Underwood, who later sold it to George de Chabris, the Canadian financier and Liberal party benefactor. It has since changed hands again and undergone more repairs and renovations.

The village has been the chosen home of a number of celebrities. Theologian Richard Hooker, who died in 1600, once lived here and is commemorated with a bust inside the church. Joseph Conrad lived and wrote in the house known as Oswalds, near the church, where he was a neighbour and some time collaborator with another author, Ford Madox Ford. Later, Alec Waugh and another writer, Jocelyn Brooks, also lived in the village.

At one time, Sir Horace Mann, a great Kent cricketer, had a house here and in 1773 the *Canterbury Journal* published a poem called *The Kentish Cricketers* which told how in July that year Kent and Sussex teams played cricket there. Kent won and, according to the poem:

'The matchless cricketers were seen
In rich white vestments tread the green
Where the smooth grass was laid compleat
Before Sir Horace Mann's retreat.'

There was a church at Bishopsbourne before the Normans came, although the present knapped flint church of St Mary and St Nicholas is 13th century and later, with a massive-looking Perpendicular style tower. Among the more celebrated churchyard residents is Rev Joseph Bancroft Reade, who was rector from 1863 to 1870 and one of the signatories of the scientists' declaration of 1864 which attempted to reconcile Biblical teaching with the theories of Darwin and other scientists.

🍁 BLEAN

The name of this strung-out village lining the road between Canterbury and Whitstable is taken directly from the ancient Forest of Blean which once surrounded it. The parish is more grandly titled St Cosmus and St Damian in the Blean.

Why? — you naturally ask. Neither I nor anyone else can satisfactorily explain that. The nearest we can come to it is to say that Cosmus and Damian were Arabian doctors who became Christians, took no fees for their professional services and were martyred in about AD 303. The likelihood is that their names were brought back to this part of Kent by a returning

Crusader – possibly the same one that was responsible for a similar dedication of the church at Challock, near Ashford.

The 13th century church at Blean is not one of the more distinguished of Kent churches and its shy retirement, well apart from the village it serves, suggests a hint of embarrassment about it. In the churchyard, however, is the unmarked grave of little Agnes Gibbs, who died in 1851, two years old and only 18 inches tall.

The child was born at Luckett's Farm, Blean and her size attracted a lot of attention, including that of the Duchess of Kent, mother of Queen Victoria, who asked to see her. Little Agnes was sent to London, where she was examined by the Queen's own physicians and pronounced perfectly formed in miniature. Nothwithstanding that, the child lived only two years and when she died her father and the local vicar buried her secretly by night in the churchyard, leaving her grave unmarked to foil grave robbers.

The grave of blacksmith Benjamin Linton, however, was not unmarked when he died, aged 80, in October 1842. His memorial is another version of the epitaph to Thomas Clampard, the Wateringbury blacksmith who died in 1748:

> 'My sledge and anvil I've declin'd
> My bellows too have lost their wind
> My fire's extinct, my forge decay'd
> And in the dust my vice is laid.
> My coals are spent, my iron's done,
> My nails are drove, my work is done.'

That epitaph crops up, more or less the same, in a number of churchyards, not only in Kent either, and seems to have originated at Aylesford in 1742.

The Forest of Blean once wooded the whole area between the Great Stour east of Canterbury and the sea, but is now reduced to a few scattered areas including the national nature reserve south of Seasalter.

It was in Blean Woods that the famous pavilion of white woollen cloth was set up so that, lacking a palace in crowded Canterbury, members of the royal house of Lancaster could shelter on summer nights when they came on pilgrimage to Becket's tomb in the cathedral. The first to use it was Queen Margaret, wife of Henry VI, who made the pilgrimage in 1445.

BONNINGTON

On a roadside vestige of village green is a carved wooden sign identifying the site of the Bonnington Oak, once known as the Law Day Oak, where the old Leet Court met once a year.

Bonnington is one of those scattered Romney Marsh villages with a little church, said to be the oldest on the Marsh, remote from all habitation along a lane that leads out of the parish, across the Royal Military Canal.

The church dedication, to St Rumwold (or Romwold) is odd, to say the least. The saint had nothing at all to do with Kent, having been born, during the 7th century, in Northampton, the son of the King of Mercia. He was denied any opportunity to travel from there because, although he distinguished himself by preaching a sermon to his parents on his second day, he died on the third. Modern parents of less precocious children may well feel it was probably all for the best!

However, this was the child-saint whose image was one of the wonders of Boxley Abbey, near Maidstone, and which was unaccountably lost after its 'miraculous' properties were publicly exposed as fraudulent in 1538.

It was, however, another image of the saint that, in 1282 (if that jocular cleric the Rev Richard Barham is to be believed – and he himself would not have expected to be believed all the time), played a part in the downfall of Sir Alured Denne of Bonnington Hall.

The tale is told in *The Lay of St Rumwold (or the Blasphemer's Warning)*, one of the *Ingoldsby Legends*, how Sir Alured earned a rebuke from the saint for swearing on his wedding day. He mended his ways until, at a royal feast, some ice cream made his tooth ache and, forgetting the little saint's warning, he swore fluently. At that point (so the *Legend* asserts), St Romwold appeared in a window and Sir Alured's bride disappeared in a puff of perfume, leaving only her clothes behind to console her tardily repentant husband.

Much more recently than that, Bonnington was the home for two years from 1894 of the author Ford Madox Ford, after his runaway marriage with a London chemist's daughter when he was 21. He wrote of the village then as a scattered, little-populated place on what had once been common land peopled by squatters, so that it grew to be a maze of little hawthorn-hedged closes, each with someone's home upon it.

The Fords lived in Bloomfield Villa, a tall house the name of which was later changed to Fir Trees Villa. He described some of the local characters in his books and recalled the village in *Return to Yesterday*, which was published in 1931.

🍁 BORDEN

The church of St Peter and St Paul at Borden is reckoned to be about 800 years old and was possibly built on the site of a Roman temple by monks of Leeds Abbey. The Norman tower is the oldest part of the present church and its most eye-catching feature is the fairly elaborate carving around the west door.

The parish, though, was founded in 1160 when the first vicar was appointed and today Borden is an undisturbed little village about a mile south-west of Sittingbourne from which it has managed to remain very positively separate. The approach from Sittingbourne takes the visitor past several modern homes but where the road bends past the church, old farm buildings and some picturesque timbered cottages give a glimpse of the old village.

In 1802 the bells of Borden church were carted to Milton for shipment to the Whitechapel foundry to be recast and six months later they were rehung and rung. But before that, bells for the church were cast more or less in situ by the Wilnar brothers, Henry and John, both of whom are buried in the churchyard.

Their bell-founding gave rise to one of those entertaining legends that abound in Kent villages. It was said that the Devil once paid a visit to Borden, where he was so incensed by the ringing of the church bells that he went up into the belfry and hurled one of the bells down. It fell into a nearby field which swallowed it up, leaving a hollow to mark the spot.

Like most of these legends, there was a grain of fact among the fiction. In 1959, a ploughman in Boundary Field, the site of the legendary hollow, was responsible for the discovery of what is now believed to have been the Wilnar brothers' bell-casting pit.

🍁 BOROUGH GREEN

Long before it broke out in the rash of new homes that made this one of the largest of the Mid Kent villages, Borough Green was, in fact, the 'green' to which residents of the neighbouring borough of Wrotham (itself now a village) resorted on high days and holidays.

The village had its beginnings at the crossroads of the Gravesend-Tonbridge and Maidstone-Sevenoaks roads and it was natural that such a spot should attract innkeepers and other businessmen to set up shop to serve the travelling public. The Red Lion inn was established there in 1586; the Black Horse in 1592. The Bull arrived in 1753 and the Fox and Hounds in 1837, although it is now a private house, despite the old inn sign. The Rock was a Friends Meeting House before it was converted into a public house.

It was the arrival of the railway in 1874 that began the big expansion of Borough Green. In 1877 much of the Tomlyn family's Yew Trees Farm was bought by the Beehive Shoe company of Northampton and not long after that the land was being parcelled off into small plots on which homes were built. Thus was modern Borough Green born.

The railway gave the new residents easy access to London and the sprawl continued. After being partly in the old Wrotham borough (later Wrotham urban district) and partly in Ightham, Borough Green became an independent civil parish in 1934, and is now part of Tonbridge and Malling borough, with a compact village centre.

The immediate neighbourhood is almost ringed with about 500 acres of old, working or planned quarries, producing sand, clay, brick earth and ragstone. Once, one of the disused claypits provided a swimming pool for local school children. A prefabricated 'cradle' was submerged in the water to provide a safe rectangular pool that was used for 30 years until 1942, when the claypit was filled in.

The parish is home to Great Comp, an early 17th century house, privately owned, with gardens administered by the Great Comp Charitable Trust. They are well worth the price of public admission, especially early in the year when the rhododendrons and azaleas are at their best. Part of the property was originally owned by Sir Roger de Leybourne, who died in 1270. Then it was known as Caumpe, but the present house was built by Sir John Howell and the estate was owned by descendants of that William Lambarde who wrote the first Kent county guide book, *A Perambulation of Kent.*

🍁 BORSTAL

The village is best-known for the institution to which it gave its name and which was originally the first attempt to separate boys from men in the British prison system, and the first attempt to cure wrongdoers instead of only punishing them. It was opened in 1904 in what had been a military prison since 1876. Borstal House (also known as the Manor House) stood behind St Matthew's church, but it was demolished in the 1960s and now there is a modern estate on the site.

Rather less well-known than the institution but, in their way, more remarkable, are the Borstal Lamps. The story of how they came to be in St Matthew's church was told by Donald Maxwell, author and Royal Academician, who although born in London in 1877, lived for many years in Kent and did much of his writing here before he died at Goddington in 1936.

He told the story of the lamps in his book, *Unknown Kent*, published in 1921. On a visit to Damascus just before the First World War, he visited the Street Called Straight of Biblical renown, where he ordered from a lamp maker seven brass lamps to take back with him to hang in the church at Borstal. As it happened, he had to return to England without the lamps, fully intending to return to collect them. But in the meantime, the war began and he could not make the trip. He resigned himself to never seeing the finished set of lamps.

However, after the war was over, he went back to Damascus hoping he might be able to order another set for the church. He went to the same shop, where he found the same lamp maker who told him there was no need for him to have more lamps made. He could have the ones he had originally ordered. He led the Englishman to a deep cellar of his house where he showed him the lamps he had hidden away for safekeeping throughout the war years, during which the occupying Turks had taken such things for war materials.

So Mr Maxwell brought home his lamps at last and they were duly dedicated and hang now in the church, his memorial to two friends killed in the war, Victor Morgan and Luke Taylor. Each of the lamps is hand-made and unique and they bear testimony to the honesty and faith of the un-named Damascus lamp maker.

Maxwell lived in Borstal at the time he told that story and he described the village then as 'frankly hideous' despite its position on a hillside with a glorious view of the Medway river and valley that many famous towns might envy. 'For that reason,' he thought, 'it is rather a tragedy that it should be so exceptionally ugly.'

Perhaps he was a little harsh on poor Borstal, or possibly more recent planning laws have led to some improvement. It is still not one of Kent's more picturesque villages and probably never will be, but 'exceptionally ugly'? Well, visitors must judge for themselves.

A hundred and fifty years ago, Borstal was nothing more than a few farms, farm workers' cottages and the White Horse Inn. Today, it is virtually a suburb of Rochester and almost indistinguishable from the city itself. Borstal Marshes were renamed Baty's Marshes in memory of the late Robert Baty, the Director of the Royal Academy of Dramatic Arts who retired, after a lifetime in the theatre, to Borstal where he led the campaign that resulted in the Marshes being made a local nature reserve in 1987.

BOUGHTON ALUPH

Alphabetically, at least, the first of four Boughtons in Kent, the others being Boughton under Blean (near Faversham), Boughton Malherbe (between Maidstone and Ashford) and Boughton Monchelsea (near Maidstone). This one is north of Ashford and is pronounced 'Borton Alluf'. At one time it was known as Boughton-next-Wye and it has also been known as Boughton in the Bush.

According to Judith Glover, in her book *The Place Names of Kent*, the word began as Old English 'boc tun', literally meaning a beech farmstead, but because the early books were handcut into beechwood 'pages' it came to mean a book or, more precisely, a charter. Thus Boughton Aluph was a farmstead or manor granted by very early charter to the Aluph family, whose connections with the village, incidentally, lasted less than a century.

The village today surrounds a large green, most of which is occupied by a cricket field and pavilion. The houses are of all ages and styles: weatherboard, brick, stucco and even one of green corrugated iron. The most significant green-side building is the red-brick Flying Horse inn.

Of the church, Pevsner said it was 'to be respected architecturally', although he judged it more quaint than beautiful. Other beholders have been rather more generous; James Antony Syms, in his splendid and very comprehensive self-illustrated series of *Kent Country Churches* books (1984-89), claimed the 13th century church of All Saints at Boughton Aluph as the pride of his collection.

The village is another of those that are linked by the Pilgrims' Way and would have been known to medieval package-tour pilgrims to Canterbury. In their day, small groups of pilgrims foregathered in places like Boughton Aluph in order to be able to embark upon the more hazardous parts of their route (in this case Challock Forest) in sufficient numbers to discourage robbers. The All Saints' porch was equipped with a fireplace in front of which the travellers could get themselves warm and dry before setting off once more.

🍁 BOUGHTON MALHERBE

The local pronunciation is 'Borton Mallerby' and it took the name from the Malherbe family. Today only a church and some scattered farm buildings remain of the village that once supported the great mansion of the Wotton family.

Successive Wottons held various high offices and left a heritage of legends about themselves and their times as well as a wealth of memorials in the church. The family's links with Boughton stemmed from that Nicholas Wotton who settled in Kent during the reign of Elizabeth I after a prosperous City career that included twice being Lord Mayor. He married a Kent heiress whose family owned Boughton Place.

The will of Edward, the first Lord Wotton, expressed his wish to be buried as near as possible to the font in which he was baptised. In fulfilment of that wish, his widow had the font removed completely and his body buried beneath where it had been. For doing so she was fined £500 and ordered to replace the font which, however, it seems was never done.

Other members of the Wotton family have included a Dean of Canterbury and York and that Sir Henry Wotton, diplomat and poet, who was born at Boughton Malherbe Place in 1568 and grew up to become famous for such lines as:

How happy is he born and taught
That serveth not another's will,
Whose armour is his honest thought
And simple truth his utmost skill.

It was a Wotton, too, himself an ambassador for Elizabeth, who defined an ambassador as 'an honest man sent to lie abroad for the good of his country.'

Another, Thomas, was jailed on a charge trumped-up by friends to prevent his joining the ill-fated rebellion led by Thomas Wyatt in 1554 against Queen Mary's plan to marry Philip, heir to the Spanish throne. As a result, Wotton was able to continue in Royal favour and inherit the Boughton estate where in 1573 he entertained Elizabeth I during her Progress through Kent. She marked the occasion by planting a yew tree just north-east of the church.

After the Wottons, the house was inherited by the Earl of Chesterfield and it was the 4th Earl – he who introduced the Gregorian calendar in England in 1742 and was accused of robbing common folk of eleven days of their lives – who plundered Boughton Malherbe Place for his great house near Park Lane in London. Ironically, the London house has quite disappeared while Boughton Malherbe Place became a farmhouse. It has since been owned by the son of Galfredus Mann, once MP for Sandwich and known as the King of Cricket. One of his more memorable oddities was a game of cricket played on horseback which he promoted in 1800.

It was at Boughton Malherbe in 1574 that 17 year old Mildred Norrington, known as the Pythoness of Westwell, was tried before Thomas Wotton and George Darrell. Mildred's 'possession by the Devil' attracted a lot of interest in Kent at the time. She was a servant girl in Westwell, where prayerful efforts were made to cast out the Devil who, however, roared his defiance at the lot of them and became so violent that poor Mildred had to be held down by four strong men. When he calmed enough to speak rationally, the Devil blamed an old woman called Alice, who also lived in Westwell, saying that he had lived at the old woman's house, shut up in a bottle, until she sent him to Mildred with instructions to kill the girl because she did not love his mistress, Alice.

After more prayers, the Devil was finally persuaded to evacuate the girl's body and leave her in peace. Later, though, Mildred confessed that she had faked the whole 'possession' and gave a demonstration to show that she could do so at will.

The Old Rectory at Boughton Malherbe is supposed to be haunted by the ghost of a hunch-backed monk and there is a story that a former rector who lived there used to give lodgings to passing tramps, just to test the reputation of the house's haunted room. According to the story, none ever stayed more than an hour or two in the room.

One of the owners of nearby Chilston Park was created Baron Douglas of Baads and Viscount Chilston of Boughton Malherbe in 1911. He was Secretary of State for Home Affairs in the cabinet of Arthur Balfour, who became Prime Minister in 1902 and remained leader of the Unionist Party in the House of Commons until 1911 when he retired. There is a memorial shield with the coat of arms of the first Lord Chilston on the west wall of the nave of the church.

Chilston Park has a long history stretching back certainly to the 13th century when it was among the possessions of the FitzHamon lords of Leeds Castle. Since then it has been owned by several notable Kent families, including the Husseys and the Hales, and altered and added to by successive generations until today, when it is a very select guest house and a trove of architectural and artistic treasures.

There are a number of memorials to various Viscounts Chilston and members of their families in St Nicholas' church, which stands well away from the main centre of population, between a farm and the old school house, now Bell House, on a hill that gives it a commanding view across the Weald. The church actually has three bells, although two of them are never rung because the tower is not sufficiently structurally sound to stand up to the exercise.

Propped against the wall of the church in the churchyard is an old headstone, the original inscription on which has been weathered away and into which has been chiselled the name of Tom Baker and the unfinished dates '1934 –' . Tom Baker is still alive, the actor who is remembered for his role as the television time-lord Dr Who. He has lived in Boughton Malherbe with his wife, Sue, for many years and he bought the headstone for £100 some years ago.

🍁 BOUGHTON MONCHELSEA

As one resident told Denis Tye, when he was collecting material for his book *A Village Remembered*, which was published in 1980: 'Once I knew almost everyone I passed in the village streets. Today I hardly know a soul.' There are old-timers in many of Kent's villages saying much the same thing, for the pace of change is still accelerating, in the villages as much as anywhere else.

Until the 1930s, Boughton Monchelsea was a small stone-quarrying community a little way out of Maidstone. The great excitements were likely to be the daily departures of teams of great horses bringing the stone up from the quarries or, once a year, wagons bringing hop-pickers in to the neighbourhood hop gardens.

But the last quarry closed in the 1960s and the hop-pickers come no more. The village has expanded to provide whole estates of new homes for the seemingly endless growth of the population of this part of Kent.

The locality, if not the village, was inhabited by Iron Age settlers and by Belgae tribesmen long before the dawn of the Christian era. What the Romans, whose villa remains were excavated in 1841, called the place we don't know, but we do know that they quarried ragstone from the local quarries and used it to build, among other things, the walls of London.

The quarries were part of the possessions of the Saxon Godwin, Earl of Kent and after the Norman Conquest they were given to the Montchensie family. They left it their name, now corrupted, before dying out in 1287 with William de Montchensie, who was prematurely interred in Wales during the under-mining of a rebellious castle.

William de Montchensie's daughter, Dionysia, owned the first known French grammar book written in English, which was made for her by Walter de Bibbesworth of Herefordshire. It is now in the British Museum. An intriguing glimpse into the way the scholarly Walter's medieval mind worked is afforded by one of the exercises he devised for the book:

'Of ladies, one would say "the company". Of geese, also "the company". These two are linked together. What can be the reason? Guess now!'

Boughton ragstone was used in the building of Westminster Abbey and the repair of Rochester Cathedral and in many a more modest church and other buildings in Kent, too. In 1419 Henry V ordered 7,000 stone cannon balls from Boughton for use in his Normandy campaign.

It is said that on that proverbial clear day it is possible to stand at the 15th century lychgate of St Peter's church – a lychgate, incidentally, that claims to be one of the oldest in England – and see right across the Weald to the South Downs beyond. Even on a more typically English day, the church overlooks the deer park that for 300 years surrounded Boughton Place. Although 11th century in origin, with 14th and 15th century additions, much of the church was rebuilt after a fire in 1832 and there was more rebuilding in 1874-5 when the south aisle, north and south porches and the vestry were added. The 15th century tithe barn beside the lychgate is one of the oldest in the country

Boughton Place, one of Kent's most notable Elizabethan houses and built on the site of an even earlier house, is sometimes open to visitors. It has had many different owners during its long history, including Robert Rudston, who forfeited it to the Crown for his part in the Kentish Rebellion of 1554. He was imprisoned in the Tower, but after his release he was permitted to buy back the estate for two-thirds of the price he had originally paid for it just four years before when he bought it from his friend, Thomas Wyatt of Allington. The house and the church are separated from the rest of the village by Heath Road.

Boughton Mount was once owned by John Braddick, a West Indian trader who made a fortune and was suspected of keeping slaves in the cellars of the house before he took them to London to sell them. The house has also been the home of George Foster Clark, founder of the Maidstone factory that became famous for its custard powder and other culinary delicacies.

Among the permanent residents of the village now is William Reiffgens, who is buried in the churchyard. He was a Flemish beggar who was befriended by villagers, became rich and repaid their kindness by leaving a bequest to the poor of the parish.

Boughton embraces the hamlet of Wierton which includes Wierton Grange. This was once the official lodgings for Assize judges when they came to Maidstone and is now the lodgings for senior circuit judges whenever they preside over trials at Maidstone Crown Court.

The village is identified by a distinctive village sign which stands on the little vestigial village green. It was designed by artist Graham Clarke, who lives locally, and mounted by local blacksmith Stuart Potter. It features a hilltop church, a single deer to represent the herd of fallow deer that once roamed the deer park, a white-cowled oast house, and a typical cottage, separated by stylised fruit and other trees. The foreground is held by a smocked shepherd on one side and a pick-carrying quarryman on the other, all in typically Graham Clarke style, which makes it something of a collector's piece for anyone interested in village signs. The artist also designed some stained glass for the church's millennium windows.

🍁 BOUGHTON UNDER BLEAN

This is the only one of the four Kentish Boughtons that is not distinguished by a family name. The 'under Blean' refers to its geographical situation under (or, more accurately, south of) the old Forest of Blean. Unlike the others, it is the only one that is commonly known simply as Boughton, logically enough since the forest has long since dwindled away into a few wisps of scattered woodland.

Until 1976 this was one of a string of traffic-tormented A2 London-Dover road villages. Like the others, it grew up along the great Watling Street highway after travellers forsook the older Pilgrims' Way, beside which Boughton's church of St Peter and St Paul was built, a mile away from the present village at Boughton Street. The village gets a mention in Chaucer's *Canterbury Tales*, where it is called Boughton under Blee.

The church is very picturesque in its rural setting amid a small cluster of houses and farm buildings. Parts, including the chancel, north chapel, nave and the arcade of the north aisle, are 13th century and there are very fine crown post trusses to the nave and north chapel. Much of the rest of the building is 14th and 15th century and there are an unusually large number of distinctive monuments.

The villagers at Boughton, like those at Bridge, on the other side of Canterbury, asked for, pleaded for and finally demanded a bypass. Eventually they got it and when it opened in March 1976 they held a carnival and danced in their main street where, before, 500 of them had sat down and brought one of the busiest routes in the country to a standstill in protest. Boughton could breathe again air as fresh as most of us can hope for in these pollution-plagued days and could entertain serious hopes that its old buildings would not, after all, be shaken into ruins, at least for a few more centuries yet.

Buildings like the big old timbered houses that introduce the village to arrivals from the Faversham end, and the 15th century White Horse inn opposite. The main street is lined with attractive houses of all ages, from medieval to Victorian and modern, some virtually at the roadside; some, like those at the Queen's Head end, nearest Canterbury, looking down haughtily from a-top a grassy bank.

At the Faversham approach to the village is the 17th century red-brick Nash Court, built by Sir Thomas Hawkins. His memorial figure, together with that of his wife and their seven sons and six daughters, carved in stone by the sculptor Epiphanius Evesham, is a feature of Boughton church. There is a brass, too, commemorating his father, also Thomas, who was a servant of Henry VIII and who died in 1587 aged 101. Nash Court is now the home of the Farming World visitors' centre with its rare breeds and sundry pastoral pursuits for all who hanker after the rural life relieved of its realities.

 ## BOXLEY

Today, Boxley lives in retirement along a narrow road, not so much at the foot of the North Downs as ankle-high on them. There are a few houses, a pub – the King's Arms – the church and the abbey remains.

Boxley House continues to survive a number of changes since it was the home of the Maidstone brewery family Styles from 1865 until 1945. It has been a boys' school, a country club and a hotel, and is now the home of the European School of Osteopathy.

Boxley parish is, in fact, the largest in the Canterbury diocese, reaching up and over the Downs, and is on the route of the Roman road from Rochester through the Weald. The cobbled approach to the church of St Mary and All Saints may actually be a remnant of that road and the church itself is quite possibly on the site of a Romano-British chapel.

The first definite date we have for a church at Boxley is about 1100. Certainly, there was a church here during the reign of Henry I (1100-1135), but the present building probably began life as the work of 13th century monks at the Cistercian abbey. On either side of the west door is a carved head, one a king, the other a bishop. The king is generally supposed to be Edward II who stopped at Boxley Abbey on his way to besiege Leeds Castle in 1321.

After the Reformation, Boxley Abbey was given to the Wyatts of Allington as a private residence and inside the church there are memorials to members of the family. They forfeited the property when Sir Thomas Wyatt was beheaded for his opposition to Queen Mary's marriage to Philip of Spain, but it was returned to his widow by Elizabeth I.

Cecilia Lushington, sister of the poet Alfred, Lord Tennyson, lived at Park House in Boxley and there is a commemorative tablet to her and other members of the Lushington family in the south aisle. Also remembered is George Sandys, a 17th century poet and traveller who, in 1610, toured Middle-Eastern Moslem countries and returned to write a best seller about his adventures.

Boxley Abbey, which was founded in 1145, was once famous, and later notorious, for its miraculous Rood of Grace and its wondrous statue of St Rumwold. The two were, for pilgrims trekking to Canterbury, rather like the lions of Longleat or the vintage cars at Beaulieu: tourist attractions not to be missed by anyone passing that way.

The Rood was a figure of Christ on the cross, made of wood, wire, paste and paper, so that it could be made to move and even to weep most realistically in the incensed dimness of the abbey. According to William Lambarde, it was made by an English prisoner of war in France, who brought it back to England when he was released. During a refreshment stop at a Rochester alehouse, the horse carrying the mechanical marvel wandered off and found its way to Boxley Abbey, which it refused to leave, even after its owner caught up with it, until the monks bought the Rood and installed it in the abbey. Denounced as trickery at the time of the Reformation, it has since been said to have deceived no one, but was regarded by those who came to see it as a minor marvel of mechanical ingenuity, worth seeing for that reason alone.

The abbey was also noted for its statue of the child saint, Rumwold. That might have been rather less defensible because the statue was reputed to be movable only by anyone who lived a pure life. The degree of purity was judged by the weight of the donation handed to the monk in charge who could, if suitably motivated, operate a discreet ratchet to assist the pious pilgrim's efforts.

The two marvels of Boxley were big money earners for the abbey, but their secrets were revealed to a gawping public in Maidstone market place before the Rood was taken off to be publicly burned in St Paul's churchyard in London, after the abbey was closed in 1538. The statue of St Rumwold escaped a similar fate by being lost, probably when it fell off the back of a wagon (!) on its way to London. It was, after all, a nice piece of timber if nothing more.

The principal remains of the abbey now include a fine 13th century tithe barn, 200 feet long.

 BRASTED

Brasted Place is one of only two houses in Kent designed by Robert Adam. It was built in 1784 for John Turton, physician to George III, whose retirement present to the doctor was a clock from Horse Guards in London, which now graces a turret at Brasted Place. Later, the house was bought by a minor railway magnate, William Tipping, who made a number of alterations.

It was here that Prince Louis, later Napoleon III, dreamed of reconquering France. He was a nephew of the Napoleon Bonaparte who gave so much trouble to so much of Europe until the Duke of Wellington put the boot in once and for all at Waterloo.

Louis drilled his handful of zealots in the splendid parkland around the house at Brasted and in August 1840 decided the time had come to take his little band of 56 followers and fulfil his destiny. They crossed the Channel to Boulogne, but were immediately rounded up with the minimum of fuss and imprisoned. Louis was tried and sentenced to permanent confinement in a fortress, but he escaped and returned to Britain in 1846. Two years later he was back in France to become at first President of the Second Republic and later Emperor of France in 1852. Twenty years later, after the fall of the Empire, he and his Empress Eugenie were back in England, at Chislehurst, where he died in January 1873.

Brasted Place became the property of the Church of England. They established a theological college there and more work was carried out by a local building company which, however, went into liquidation in the late 1980s. After that, the theological college extension was demolished and the house was converted into apartments.

A former rector of Brasted, a Mr Skinner, who did not live there, wrote in 1788 that the parish appeared to be remarkably healthy, its inhabitants a very quiet, good sort of people, rather less polished and perhaps less corrupted than might be expected so near the capital. Brasted is, in fact, about 25 miles from London.

If the name really does derive from an earlier form meaning 'sprawling village' it is no longer altogether appropriate, although it could perhaps be said to ramble a bit alongside the A25, which was the main route through the Holmesdale Valley before the M25 was built. It is still a very busy road and, in response to public demand, Brasted was made the guinea-pig for a pilot traffic-calming scheme introduced into this country from Denmark. It incorporated a series of traffic islands and chicanes which did, indeed, slow the traffic, but to such an extent that villagers' voices were again raised in protest at the long tailbacks it caused.

Roughly in the middle of the village, alongside the main street, is a pretty little green surrounded by some fine old buildings, including a row of Tudor cottages. On the green itself the village sign depicts a medieval Archbishop of Canterbury blessing the garden of Brasted – a reference to the fact that the village, with neighbouring Sundridge and Chevening, is still known as the Archbishop's Garden and the living is still in his gift.

A side road leads to the church, St Martin's, on the other side of the little River Darent. The foundations of a Saxon church were found in the churchyard in 1966 but the present church began life in the 13th century. Most of it was rebuilt in the 1860s and in 1944 it was badly damaged by a flying bomb (V1 'doodlebug').

A little way outside the village, the valley sides climb up to Brasted Chart and Toys Hill, the highest point in Kent, part of which was one of the earliest acquisitions, in 1898, of the National Trust.

🍁 BREDGAR

Bredgar is one of those hideaway Downland villages, 350 feet up on the north slopes of the North Downs. The M2 has cut away the north end of the village, which is roughly bisected by the B2163 Sittingbourne-Hollingbourne road, with a nucleus formed by the pond and the church.

The typically Downland flint church of St John the Baptist at Bredgar has drawn the village round it for something like 800 years and looks set to do so for many more years yet. There has been a church here certainly since the 11th century although the present one is mainly late 14th century, probably on the site of an earlier wooden one. Its tower doorway is one of those that are distinguished by surviving Norman stone decoration, probably preserved from an older building.

Buildings around the church and pond include several prominent old timbered houses and behind trees near the pond lies the College which was founded by Robert de Bradegar in 1393.

In his *Second Kentish Patchwork* (published 1968), Kent author Robert Goodsall quoted a *Kentish Gazette* story of July 1768 about a Mr Cary, a shoemaker of Leeds, near Hollingbourne, who was returning from a Bredgar feast when he was stopped by footpads and robbed of eight guineas, 15 shillings and sixpence. The story concluded: 'It is thought they dogged him from Bredgar.'

The main claim to fame of the village, currently, is the Bredgar and Wormshill Light Railway, a privately owned light railway with two narrow-gauge steam locomotives and other attractions. The working museum is the result of the passion shared by two brothers for collecting and restoring narrow-gauge steam engines.

 BREDHURST

The North Downs, more than anywhere else in Kent, delight in conducting travellers on rambling tours of their pleasures, punctuating the route with secretive signposts that hide their clues among wayside foliage or take almost audible delight in repeating again and again that your destination is still the same distance from the next junction as it was from the last.

It is a phenomenon the traveller through the Downs will experience often and some of the approaches to Bredhurst will demonstrate it very well. Having found it, there may well be a temptation to wonder if it was really worth the trouble. There is little enough to see apart from the Bull inn, which has been there since Tudor times, and its neighbouring group of old cottages, opposite the school (founded in 1866), and a straggle of mainly relatively new and some very modern houses in and immediately around the village itself.

Bredhurst manor was acquired by the Treasury under orders from Edward III and given to the chapel founded by King Stephen which Edward completed. John of Gaunt bought it in 1379 and Richard II gave it to Sir Simon Burley in 1384. He lost it, however, after he was accused of high treason in 1390 and by 1551 the manor had passed into the ownership of Sir Thomas Cheney. When the local Kemsley family took it over later in the 16th century, Isabel Kemsley stipulated that her son John should hold 'a drinking' in the village on All Saints' Day. That particular tradition was continued until the 19th century, by which time the manor had come into the possession of the Romilly family. Their ownership ended when the widow of the fourth Baron Romilly, William Guy Gospard Romilly (who died in 1983), sold it.

St Peter's church at Bredhurst squats among woodland, just properly aloof from its congregation, with an adequate area for car parking bitten out of the woods and an additional detached churchyard on the opposite side of the lane. It is a typically Downland flint church, apparently unsure whether it is most proud of its 13th century origins or its 19th century additions, including the little bellcote with its two bells.

Despite its size – the population of Bredhurst in 1990 was just 330 – the village is very much alive and thriving. It has had its own parish council since 1975 and in 1998 it welcomed news of the success of its campaign to keep heavy lorries – working on the twin projects of M2 widening and Channel Tunnel rail link building – out of the village centre.

 # BRENCHLEY

Visitors must make up their own minds about whether they agree with Kent's much-quoted 18th century topographer and historian Edward Hasted that Brenchley is 'dreary and gloomy', or with Thomas Dearn who, in 1814, found it 'rather cheerful, with no more timber than is barely sufficient for the purpose of embellishment.' A clear case of beauty being in the eye of the beholder.

Certainly, the main street of the village has been described as one of the finest in England. There are several very attractive old timbered houses, as well as a number of newer ones that have almost completed the amalgamation of Brenchley with neighbouring Matfield.

The village was certainly established by 1170, when the first church was built as a chapel of Yalding church, although the present All Saints' church dates from 1233. The honey-coloured sandstone building is almost hidden behind the ornate lychgate that was erected (as the commemorative plate recalls) 'in grateful memory of Queen Victoria's 60 years' reign', and by the avenue of 400 year old yews. According to records of 18th century Brenchley, these were kept clipped by men who were paid a quart of beer per tree for their labour.

The Kentish rebel leader Wat Tyler is said to have lived in a cottage near Brenchley before he led revolting peasants to air their grievances to young Richard II in London in 1381.

The Old Palace, now a row of much-restored half-timbered cottages near the village centre, was once the home of Nell Gwynn's son by Charles II, George Beauclerk, Duke of St Albans. Other picturesque buildings include the 14th century Old Vicarage and the Old Workhouse which, despite its 19th century name, is as Tudor as it looks. The Bull inn, on the other hand, despite appearances is a late 19th century replacement for the original Old Bull Inn which was destroyed by fire. The Rose and Crown, notwithstanding the sign that lays claims to origins in 1495, is part of a mainly 18th century white weatherboarding block.

Just outside the village is Brattles Grange, a 16th century house where Kent historian William Lambarde lived for a time.

Brenchley was one of the iron-founding centres of the Weald where industrial prosperity was succeeded by the agricultural well-being that depended upon the local orchards and hop gardens. In the 17th century, the village boasted one of the largest of the Wealden iron works, owned by John Browne and employing 200 men. One of the reminders of those great days of Wealden industry is the hammer pond about a mile south of the village, one of the largest of its kind in Kent.

Half a century ago, all the low-lying Wealden countryside around Brenchley foamed in a wonderland of orchard blossom every spring. It was one of the scenic wonders of the county, attracting coachloads of tourists to follow the Blossom Tour routes. Today, many of the orchards, like most of the hop gardens, are gone and the new, smaller fruit trees hide their more modest candy-floss glories behind high hedges.

🍁 BRENZETT

It was in 1970 that I had my first encounter with the Romney Marsh village of Brenzett. I went there to seek out and meet a fairly remarkable man called Capt John Noel, who had been the official photographer with the Everest expedition that tackled the north face of the then unconquered mountain in

1922 and again in 1924.

Capt Noel was, in fact, also one of the last to see George Mallory and Andrew Irvine that day in June 1924 when they left the main party in their bid for the mist-shrouded summit from which they never returned.

That 1924 expedition disproved the belief, commonly held by climbers until then, that men could not live above 24,000 feet without extra oxygen. Members of the team reached a new record height of 27,000 feet and Capt Noel himself won a record by living and working at 23,000 feet for two and a half weeks without supplementary oxygen. Afterwards, he travelled the world lecturing and exhibiting some of the photographs he took on that expedition, and he lived to share the excitement of that June 1953 Coronation Day news that a Commonwealth expedition had conquered the mountain at last.

My visit to Brenzett on that occasion was marked with most cordial hospitality – tea and ginger biscuits, I seem to remember – but poor old William Cobbett, when one of his Rural Rides took him to these parts in 1823, carried away a very different memory. He wrote that he found Brenzett a miserable place where he had difficulty getting a rasher of bacon for breakfast and had to go without an egg altogether. But he did comment that the surrounding farmlands looked to him to be full of sheep and cattle 'fatting', as he called it, and fields loaded with corn.

It hasn't changed all that much in 175 years. Between times, Rudyard Kipling found Brenzett and seemed to enjoy the solitude of its Romney Marsh remoteness which, presumably, inspired him to write:

> 'I've loosed my mind for to cut and run
> On a Marsh that was old when Kings begun;
> Oh, Romney Level and Brenzett reeds,
> I reckon you know what my mind needs.'

Brenzett is a crossroads village on the A259 between Old Romney and Appledore. The only really significant building is St Eanswith's church: an old grey rubble-walled building, the oldest parts of which date from the 12th century. Very few Kent churches, even here on the Marsh where time never seems to have quite the same relevance as it does elsewhere, cling to the names of Saxon saints like St Eanswith. She was a grand-daughter of King Ethelbert who welcomed Augustine's little band of missionaries to Kent in AD 597, and the founder, in AD 630, of the first nunnery in England at Folkestone. The first miracle accredited to her was performed during the building of the nunnery when one of the beams was cut too short by a carpenter and she caused it to be extended to the right length by the power of prayer alone.

The village is also home to an aeronautical museum, just a short distance outside the village centre.

🍁 BRIDGE

Villagers of Bridge made world-wide headlines in the 1960s and 1970s during their 14 year campaign for a bypass that would take the A2 London-Dover traffic out of their village.

It all began in January 1962 when pensioner George Smith walked to the village to buy sweets and cigarettes for friends at the local hospital. As he left the shop he was knocked down and killed. The incident was the last straw for villagers who had been predicting some such tragedy as a result of the ever-increasing and increasingly heavy traffic that was thundering along the A2, right through the middle of Bridge. Authority promised a bypass would be built, but was carefully non-committal about exactly when. Then in 1963, two lorries and a bus collided in the main street and the campaign for a bypass gathered momentum. By 1964 the villagers decided the time had come for action and they blocked the street by walking in it, causing delays for Easter traffic.

There were other demonstrations, too, until in 1969 they held the first of a series of sit-down protests – actually sitting down in the road, en masse, forcing traffic to a complete halt. Of course, they were moved, but when in 1972 a meat truck demolished a shop, trapping a young girl and killing the driver, the villagers repeated their sit-down protest, this time with 300 of them filling the road. Later that year, more than a thousand people joined in yet another similar demonstration and closed the village street to all traffic for an hour. The tail-back was impressive and it showed what could be done – what the villagers vowed would be done, too, as often as it took to get the action they demanded.

Until the completion of the M2, the A2 was, after all, one of Britain's major highways, linking London with Dover and the Continental mainland even though, in those days, it was little more than a country lane in places. Repeated disruptions of this kind had to be avoided if carriers and tourists, both British and Continental, were not to be angered by delays, and trade affected.

This time the Government promised urgent action and work began on the bypass the following year. The village victory over Governmental delays inspired a theatrical performance called *The Road Show* scripted by Peter ('Doc') Watson of Canterbury's Marlowe Theatre Company, which toured the South-East during 1977. By that time, life in the village had returned to something the residents were prepared to accept as normal. It was a very famous victory indeed.

The village takes its name from the bridges that, for centuries, have crossed the Little Stour (also known as the Nailbourne) and were responsible for the settlement that grew up at this crossing point along the old Roman Dover-London road. Apart from the present 18th century bridge, which is not an intrusive feature, the most prominent village building is the church, which retains Norman details among its much restored fabric. Bridge was formerly the manor of Blackmansbury which, until the Reformation, was one of the many possessions of St Augustine's Abbey at Canterbury.

Bridge House was built during the 17th century by Sir Arnold Braems, a Royalist who made his fortune developing Dover seafront – and lost it building Bridge House. At the time, it was one of the largest houses in East Kent, with an avenue of trees lining the path from the house to nearby St Peter's church. His son, Walter, inherited the estate and after he died in 1692 his widow sold it to a John Taylor, who demolished most of the house. What remained was later bought by the Marquis of Conyngham and became part of the Bifrons estate.

A more recent resident was Count Louis Zborowski, the multi-millionaire racing car driver and miniature railway enthusiast. He was partly responsible for the famous Romney, Hythe and Dymchurch Railway and almost wholly responsible for the Chitty-Chitty-Bang-Bang cars made at least as famous by the Disney film of the same name. He drove for the Aston Martin Company in Europe and the USA and was killed in 1924, when he was only 29, while competing in the Italian Grand Prix at Monza.

Other notable local houses include Higham Park in its spectacular 17th century landscape park and gardens, which are open to the public on specified days throughout the summer.

🍁 BROOKLAND

Of all the many interesting features of the Romney Marsh villages, the wooden belfry of St Augustine's church at Brookland is surely the most remarked upon. It is, certainly, a curiosity: a great wooden octagonal pyramid in the churchyard, apart from the church itself, commanding attention on the approach road into the village. It is taller than the church and topped by a winged dragon weathervane that makes it even taller.

All sorts of tales are told about why the belfry should be alongside the church instead of, as more usually, on top of it. The most likely prosaic explanation is that its builders, in the 13th or 14th century, recognised that the reclaimed marshland on which the church stood would not support the extra weight of the bells. So they hung them in the churchyard, where they were later enclosed in the rather odd shingled three-tier structure we see today.

Much more popular, though, is the local story that the belfry did, once, stand on the tower. That story relates how the village lapsed into a state of moral laxity at one period and the villagers no longer bothered with the formality of church weddings. Then, one day, a young virgin presented herself at the church to ask the vicar to marry her to one of the local lads. On hearing this, the old church was so shaken (literally) that the belfry toppled off its tower and fell into the churchyard, where it has remained ever since.

St Augustine's church at Brookland is also famous for its circular lead font, which is generally supposed to have been carried back to Brookland among the spoils of war from one of the many raids on France during the 13th and 14th centuries. Very likely all eleven children of John and Mary Munn, who died early in the 19th century aged 75 and 89 respectively, were christened in that font, but only one of them lived longer than 27 years, according to the memorial inside the church.

Brookland is the largest of the Marsh villages. Like many of the others it used to be noted for its medieval Passion Plays and the Brookland players not only entertained their own villagers but also travelled to give performances in other towns and villages on the Marsh. These plays were based on Bible stories and while some were common to all, several groups of players developed their own specialisations.

Later, Brookland also became a centre for Romney Marsh sports and games meetings, and no doubt the old Kentish games of Bat and Trap and goal-running were played there.

Brookland lies on the Rye road and could hardly have escaped involvement in the Romney Marsh smuggling trade if it had wanted to. In fact, its villagers engaged in the trade as enthusiastically as practically everyone else in this part of Kent. The village featured rather more prominently than it might have wished in one encounter between smugglers and the forces of law in 1821, when the notorious Aldington Gang, known as The Blues, fought a pitched battle with Preventivemen just outside the village.

On that occasion, as on previous ones, Brookland's Dr Ralph Hougham of Pear Tree House was called upon to tend the wounds on both sides. Doctoring wounded smugglers with the necessary discretion – and, no doubt, for the appropriate rewards – was part of the common experience of medical men, especially in the Romney Marsh villages and towns, for centuries. Dr Hougham carried about with him a specially made tooled leather wallet containing medicines and instruments so that he was always prepared for just such emergencies.

🍁 BURHAM

Burham moved inland about a mile during the 19th century, after whatever prosperity it had enjoyed stopped coming from its river frontage and began to be provided by chalk quarrying for the new cement works.

From very small beginnings, Burham grew rapidly to house a population of about 500 in 1851 and almost 2,000 by 1900. It was during this period of growth that the 12th century waterside church of St Mary the Virgin became too small and too distant and a rather grand new one was built, for the 'new' village. It lasted less than a hundred years, however, and was declared unsafe and demolished in 1980. The old one, down by the waterside, is still standing and was restored in 1956 after being disused for many years.

Today, St Mary's church is officially 'redundant' and cared for by the Churches Conservation Trust and both Church of England and Methodist worshippers share the unobtrusive little 19th century church in Church Street. One of the curiosities of the old churchyard used to be a memorial stone, now lost, with a twisted face on it and the words:

Behold Burham's Belle, a delight
With her curls assymetric and tight;
Let us hope that her Biz
Was as straight as her Phiz
And she kept, like her nose, to the right.

Great Culland House lasted from 1592 until 1953 and then it was pulled down. The French Ambassador to Elizabeth I stayed in it to be near his friend Sir Walter Raleigh, who was staying at nearby Aylesford Priory. The old house, though gone, is not forgotten, nor will be while the great donkey-powered wooden treadmill which used to draw water from the nearby well remains preserved outside Maidstone Museum.

A more recent memorial to a more ancient event is the ragstone monument on the bank of the River Medway close to the old church. The inscription reads: 'This stone commemorates the battle of the Medway, AD 43, when a Roman army crossed the river and defeated the British tribes under Caractacus.' It was possibly the most decisive battle of the Roman invasion and opened the way for the Roman conquest of Britain. The idea of marking the spot in this way came from the author Nigel Nicolson of Sissinghurst Castle.

 BURMARSH

Burmarsh is one of the earliest known Romney Marsh settlements. The manor of Burmarsh was given to St Augustine's Priory at Canterbury before 1066 and there is still a farm called Abbott's Court north of the village.

Although much of the present All Saints' church is Norman, the chancel may once have been a Saxon chapel. A memorial tablet inside the church commemorates Edward Coleman, the first veterinary surgeon-general to the British Army cavalry.

Next to the churchyard is that other indispensible feature of any Kentish village, the inn – in this case the Shepherd and Crook. A wholly appropriate designation for a village that, like all Romney Marsh villages, still dwells upon the days when the famous flocks of sheep were the true Lords of the Levels even though, today, much of the former pasture land has surrendered to the plough.

CAPEL LE FERNE

There is a distinctly new look about this little village overlooking the Straits of Dover. St Radigund's church was dedicated by the Bishop of Dover as recently as 1966, its building, like that of the new primary school, made necessary by all the new development that has pretty well overwhelmed the original old village.

One of the few reminders that the place has a history is the old Norman church of St Mary. Now redundant, it seems to have been shouldered aside to dream away its dotage in a rural retirement that has little relevance to the present village that has mushroomed alongside the Folkestone-Dover road. Yet the new church was built with a piece of stone from the ruined St Radigund's Abbey incorporated into it, a nod, at least, in the direction of historical continuity, and there have been claims that the Royal Oak pub could date from 1100.

But, for the rest, the few 20th century years of the Second World War have left more evidence than all the centuries before. This was the site of a gun battery, 400 feet above the Channel, from which 16-inch guns shelled

Occupied France, visible on a clear day from the cliff tops. The site was fortified at a cost of more than £2m, with deep underground installations that included a hospital, ammunition store and barrack rooms and consumed thousands of tons of concrete. The site is marked with the Battle of Britain memorial: the figure of a fighter pilot, which was unveiled by the Queen Mother in 1993. The stone base is carved with the crests of 66 RAF squadrons that fought in the Battle in 1940 and there are various other wartime relics still remaining in the vicinity.

The roadside pub, the Valiant Sailor, was there in 1855, in front of the spot known as Steddy Hole. This was the scene of a notorious murder when a Serbian soldier called Dedea Redanies, who was serving with the British Army and stationed at Shorncliffe, killed an 18 year old Dover girl, Caroline Back, and her 16 year old sister Maria.

Redanies had courted Caroline for some time and her parents agreed to let her go with him to see his sister in Folkestone on condition that Maria went too. But it seems Caroline gave Redanies cause to suspect she was less serious about him than he was about her and when they reached Steddy Hole, according to his subsequent confession, he stabbed first Maria and then Caroline to death, leaving their bodies there while he went on towards Canterbury, where he was arrested.

The crime caused quite a stir at the time, as did his trial at Maidstone Assizes. His execution on New Year's Day 1857 was witnessed by a crowd of up to 5,000 people filling the street in front of the scaffold, on top of the porter's lodge of Maidstone prison.

❧ CHALK

If it had not been for Charles Dickens, the village of Chalk might well have been forgotten by now, absorbed into the sprawl of Gravesend.

But whatever else is forgotten about it, Chalk will be remembered for a long time yet as the place where Dickens spent his honeymoon in 1836. His bride, Catherine (Kate), was the daughter of George Hogarth, editor of the *Evening Chronicle*. Opinions still differ about exactly where the newly-weds stayed, despite the metal plaque with which the Dickens Fellowship advertises its own choice.

When they went there, the couple intended to spend two weeks in the village, but in the event Dickens could only spare one week away from his demanding work on the first instalments of *The Pickwick Papers*, the work that really established him as an important literary figure of his time.

They returned to the honeymoon cottage a year later, however, to help Kate over a difficult period of post-natal depression. Later, of course, Dickens was to use the old forge in Lower Higham Road at Chalk as the model for Joe Gargery's forge in *Great Expectations*. After falling into disrepair after the last village blacksmith left it, the forge and cottage are now Grade II listed buildings, expertly restored and occupied as a charming weatherboarded private home.

Another literary association with Chalk is that which Richard Barham gave it in his *Legend of the Ingoldsby Penance*. This tells how it was that the ghost of a former Sir Ingoldsby Bray, who founded Ingoldsby Abbey alongside the Rochester road at Gravesend, came to haunt the ruined walls of the vanished abbey.

There is, though, no literature to identify for us the merry little fellow carved in stone over the porch of the church of St Mary the Virgin. He has been described as holding a flagon between his thighs. Ireland, in his *History of the County of Kent* in 1830, supposed the undeniably tipsy-looking figure was an embodiment of the old custom among villagers of brewing the Whitsuntide strong ale which was used to lubricate the seasonal merrymaking and was known as Church Ale.

It has also been suggested that this is none other than Puck, the mischievous and sometimes pretty lewd little imp whose ancestry can be traced back to pagan mythology.

🍁 CHALLOCK

If the claim of a Challock nurseryman in 1983 had been upheld, the village might well have become world famous. Instead, it continues to lie almost unnoticed from the A252 between Charing and Chilham, behind The Lees and amid the Forestry Commission's Challock Forest.

The claim was made by the local Kent Country Nurseries that it had developed a blue dahlia. Now, as one horticultural expert explained when the claim was challenged, growing a blue dahlia 'would be like finding the lost Ark'. More aptly, perhaps, it would be like growing the black tulip that caused such a to-do in Alexandre Dumas' novel of that name. So, naturally enough, there was a lot of interest when the nursery catalogue offered its customers blue dahlias.

Unfortunately, a claim was lodged against the company under the Trades Description Act alleging that the 'blue' dahlia was in fact no such thing. The judgment against the nursery decided that the colour was actually purple and not the blue that gardeners had been trying to develop for a century, almost ever since the dahlia first came to Britain from Mexico in 1804. The nursery is no longer there.

Challock is one of two villages in Kent with a church dedicated to the Arabian medics Saints Cosmus and Damian. The other is at Blean, near Canterbury. The church at Challock is well removed from the village – or, more correctly, the village is well removed from the church, for like several other villages in Kent and elsewhere, Challock was hard hit by the Black Death in the 14th century. The villagers moved away from the old plague-ridden centre of population and started again on a new site, a mile away, leaving their old church where it was.

They might well have lost it during the Second World War, when it was badly bomb damaged in 1943, but it survived to be largely rebuilt and rededicated in 1958. During rebuilding, a series of wall paintings were added. Roundels depicting scenes from the lives of the two saints were made in 1953 by two students, Rosemary Aldridge and Doreen Lister, and other paintings, in the chancel, were added in 1955 by John Ward RA, the book illustrator. They show scenes from the life of Christ, with the figures in modern dress. In 1982, a sanctuary chair was stolen from the church but local craftsman David Tomkins made a new one, carved from Kent oak, which will, in time, no doubt become a church antiquity in its own right.

Challock is yet another of several places in Kent that lays claim to being the birthplace of William Caxton. The evidence upon which the claim rests is very flimsy, especially since the father of English printing himself claimed to have been born in the Weald and Challock is 500 foot high in the North Downs.

A relatively new public attraction at Challock is the gardens of Beech Court. The present owners like to offer visitors the thought that Richard III's illegitimate son might have helped build the 15th century house. The man believed to have been the Royal offspring worked as a carpenter at Eastwell Manor at Boughton Aluph and is buried in the now ruined chapel there, so it is by no means impossible. Today, teas are served in the old oast house and the surrounding gardens are a delight for anyone who enjoys beautiful and some rare trees and shrubs.

🍁 CHARING

Heaven knows what Charing might have looked like today if it had become the Kentish Klondike some of the locals thought it might in George V's silver jubilee year, 1935. That was the year that gold and silver were found in them thar Charing Hills. But there was no gold rush. The quantities turned out to be too small to bother with at half an ounce of gold and 23 ounces of silver per ton of clay.

So Charing remained the attractive hillside village on the south slopes of the North Downs that it had been for centuries and still is today. This is despite the fact that it is bisected by the A20 Maidstone-Ashford and Folkestone road which separates the main village from a cluster of houses and the railway station on its southern side.

It has always been a much-visited village. It is on the route of the old Pilgrims' Way, which was old long before any Canterbury pilgrims trod it and the Roman London-Dover road. Before the arrival of the railway in 1880, both the Swan and the King's Head were coaching inns.

Archbishops of Canterbury used to stay at the manor house (now Palace Farm, just outside the churchyard) so that it became known as the Archbishop's Palace. It was probably the 14th century Archbishop John Stratford who built the Gate House, the great archway of which alone still stands. The former banqueting hall, where some of the 4,000 men and women who travelled with Henry VIII on his way to the Field of the Cloth of Gold in 1520 were entertained, is now a huge barn on the north side of the church.

In 1590, the 13th century church of St Peter and St Paul was very badly damaged by a fire caused, according to contemporary records, by the discharge of a gun by a Mr Dios while he was out bird shooting. The day was very hot, the wooden shingles on the church roof very dry and the hot shot started a fire which burned so fiercely that the bells in the steeple melted. Another possible victim of the fire (although it may have been carried off by Henry VIII's Commissioners during the Reformation) was the famous relic, the block on which John the Baptist was beheaded, supposed to have been brought back from the Holy Land by Richard the Lionheart himself.

When the church was rebuilt, it was equipped with only one bell, giving rise to the rhyme:

> Dirty Charing lies in a hole;
> It had one bell – and that was stole!

No one seems to know when it was 'stole', but today the church has six bells, given by Bishop Tufnell in 1878.

On Charing Hill, which rears above the village on the north side, was one of the several secret hideouts dug and fitted out for a proposed British resistance movement if the Germans had invaded England in 1940.

Charing takes pride in its history and draws attention to points of interest with plaques on the walls of several of the houses. In the High Street, for example, the former Swan Inn is identified as an early 16th century hall house and 19th century posting house while, opposite, another house recalls it was once the Venture Works, where Alf Cackett (1857-1947) made penny-farthing bicycles and, he claimed, the first diamond-framed cycle in Kent. He also built the Venture motor-cycle.

🍁 CHARTHAM

At the foot of the Chartham Downs, and just off the A28 south-west of Canterbury, Chartham boasts a nice mixture of old and new, from the roadside 18th century cottages beside the Artichoke Inn to the bungalows nearer the river.

The River Stour divides just outside the village to provide two courses through it. In the past, those streams were sources of water power for local mills and today one of them still provides some of the water for the Chartham Papers paper mill.

Paper-making has been a major occupation in Chartham for more than 600 years. In 1793 an advertisement in the *London General Evening Post* advertised the Chartham Mills for sale, as 'New-built by Peter Arder, lately deceased.' William Weatherly bought the mills in 1798 and it was a nephew of his who later introduced straw into paper-making technology for the first time. The mills were destroyed by fire in 1857, rebuilt in 1860 and rebuilt and re-equipped again in 1949 by Wiggins Teape. In 1939 the Chartham mill was a strategic war-time site producing all the tracing paper Britain needed.

The Artichoke Inn at Chartham is thought to date from the 14th century and the original medieval character of the building was revealed during restoration in 1994, when some of the old timbers were exposed. Thirteenth century St Mary's church overlooks the village green and from across the green so does timbered Bedford House, which flaunts the date 1420.

Since St Augustine's Hospital, which used to sprawl across the hillside above Chartham village, was closed in 1993, the buildings have been demolished and the site redeveloped with homes. On balance, it is a visual improvement to the local scene.

 CHART SUTTON

With Sutton Valence and East Sutton, Chart Sutton is one of the Three Suttons, triplet parishes occupying an east-west strip of countryside that tumbles down a steep hillside into the Weald.

It is a modest enough little village of some 800 or 900 souls, with nothing much to boast about except superb views and one or two interesting former inhabitants: Stephen Norton, 14th century bell-founder, who built Norton Court; Sir Edward Hale, who took part in the Royalist rising in Kent in 1648 and acquired Norton Court in 1660; and Sydney Wooderson, the miler who ran in the Munich Olympics in 1938.

In 1949, a little clay statue of Venus, a coin and some pottery were found, providing evidence that the ubiquitous Romans sojourned here. But when Coenwulf, King of Mercia, granted lands in the Weald to Earl Suithnode in AD 814, 'chart' simply meant open land. By the 11th century, the Domesday surveyors found a little stone-built Saxon church here, one of a string of churches built along the line of the ancient trackway by which traders travelled from the west of England to the shortest sea crossing to the Continent. The bureaucrats also reported that there were vineyards hereabouts, as well as two water mills. One of them was Chart Mill, the great wheel of which was melted down for war materials in 1914-18.

St Michael's church was struck by lightning and burned to ashes in April 1779, yet by November 1782 it had been rebuilt and was again being used for services, which says something for the resourcefulness of a small community and not a little about the resources of some of the wealthier members of that community. Although the fire melted the bells, the tower remained standing and the bells were later recast and rehung. There was another major restoration in 1897 and another in 1964-67.

The village was almost wiped out by the Black Death, leaving little besides the church, but it struggled back to existence a mile or so from the earlier site. In the mid-19th century, it might again have ceased to be because this was one of a number of places in Kent from which villagers emigrated to Canada to escape rural hardship.

🍁 CHESTFIELD

From a few houses and bungalows alongside the road linking Whitstable with Canterbury through woods and the little community of Tyler Hill, now near neighbours of the University of Kent at Canterbury campus, Chestfield has burgeoned into a recognisable village of some significance in the last 30 or 40 years.

Indeed, what rail travellers used to know as Swalecliffe Halt is now Chestfield & Swalecliffe station, relegating the older village on the other side of the Thanet Way and the railway line into second place. The new parish that was created in 1988 includes much of the older village and extends south into what remains of the ancient Forest of Blean.

Not that Chestfield is all that new. It was mentioned in a Saxon charter, although the Domesday survey recorded only eight cottages there. At that time it was held by a Norman knight and was known as Chestwill, remaining in the possession of a family of that name into the 1400s. It changed very little until the 1920s, when a developer called George Reeves moved into the Manor and oversaw the development of the place until he died in 1941.

Today, the little Tudor village is very much developed, with a large playing field area and many new homes. The story of the village is told on a lectern-like board on the village green, near the double-sided village sign. The first village sign was erected by Chestfield Society and passed to the parish council when that came into being in 1988. It was replaced in 1993 jointly by the society and the council and each of them is acknowledged on one of the two faces of the sign.

❧ CHEVENING

Apart from a few houses opposite the church, there is very little else to identify Chevening as anything more than a tiny hamlet. Even the 13th century church, St Botolph's, with its 16th century tower, seems to stand respectfully to one side of the lane leading to the house that is Chevening's reason for being.

The house, which stands in a magnificent park, was built in the first half of the 17th century for Lord Dacre, partly by Inigo Jones, although it was remodelled and altered in the 18th century. It was bought by ancestors of Earl Stanhope in 1717 and was left to the nation in 1967 by the 7th Earl on condition that it was occupied by the Prime Minister of the day, a Cabinet Minister or a descendent of George VI. The 115-room Georgian mansion was prepared as a home for Prince Charles at a cost of more than £1m but rumour has it that when he saw the decorations he declared: 'Good gracious no, how awful!' and declined the offer out of hand.

After the Prince's rejection, the house became the official residence of the Foreign Secretary and Lord Carrington was the first occupant in that office.

Probably the most distinguished – certainly the most distinctive – member of the Stanhope family was Lady Hester Stanhope. Born in 1776, she was the eldest daughter of Charles, Viscount Mahon, son of the second Lord Stanhope, and another Lady Hester, who was the daughter of Lord Chatham – 'The Great Commoner' – and sister of William Pitt the Younger. When Charles inherited the Chevening estate in 1786 he was regarded as something of an eccentric, although there was nothing very eccentric about the iron Stanhope printing press that he invented, nor his screw-propelled steamship. He was way ahead of his time with his mechanical calculating machine which just about set the seal on his reputation for eccentricity.

As though to justify what others thought of him, he removed the Stanhope coat of arms from Chevening's gates, renamed it Democracy Hall and called himself Citizen Stanhope – all at a time when most of the English upper classes were keeping an apprehensive eye on events in France.

After her mother died and her father remarried, the young Lady Hester grew up to be exceptionally free-thinking for a woman of her time. Neither Kent nor London nor even England could satisfy her lively mind and after her uncle William Pitt died she travelled in the Near and Middle East, where no European woman had ever before travelled alone. She dressed as a Turkish man and made several daring expeditions into the desert, where she became known to Bedouin Arabs as the Queen of the Desert.

She finally settled in a former monastery among the Lebanon mountains where, abandoned by family and friends in England, she surrendered her British citizenship and lived the life of an increasingly impoverished recluse. She died, almost completely alone, having been finally deserted even by her servants, in June 1839.

There is known to have been a church at Chevening in 1122 although the first known priest took office in 1262. The present church is 13th century, with a tower that was added later, in about 1500.

🍁 CHIDDINGSTONE

Perhaps Time never does stand still, but in Chiddingstone it has certainly slowed to a leisurely saunter. The village is unique in Kent. It is not only generally agreed to be the most perfect surviving example of a Tudor village in the county, it is also the only one owned, since 1939, by the National Trust.

The character of the place is wholly Kentish. Its little main street is overlooked by 16th and 17th century houses with half-timbered and tile-hung frontages and by lovely old St Mary's church, built of richly honey-coloured sandstone with a big 17th century timbered porch.

The church, which is not part of the National Trust property, is the third or perhaps the fourth to stand on this site. We know there was a Saxon church there, although no structural evidence of it now remains. It was one of those that the Norman Bishop Odo was made to surrender to the Archbishop of Canterbury in 1072. But the earliest identifiable masonry is among the rubble facing of the east wall of the chancel where 13th century windows can be discerned. In 1624, the church was struck by lightning and extensively damaged by fire. The repairs were not completed until 1629 and there were later alterations, too. The church owns one of the few surviving 'vinegar' bibles, in which the parable of the vineyard is mistakenly referred to as the parable of the vinegar.

The Bore Place Chapel commemorates the Tudor house that was said to have been built on the site of a monastery where Henry VIII once slept during his courtship of Anne Boleyn. There was also a legend of a headless horseman who rode through the farm once a year and a story that treasure was buried in the garden of the house. More recently, in 1998, it was the site of a remarkable example of outdoor art, which took the form of a Lilliputian maze made entirely of loaves of bread.

The Castle Inn, opposite the church, dates certainly from 1637 and probably a century or two before that. The main road used to continue straight past the inn, where the wrought iron gates are now, and past the 'castle', then known as High Street House. But the 19th century squire who fancied a castle rather than a mere house to live in had the road diverted so that the hoi polloi could be kept fashionably at arm's length.

Now the road bends to leave the village by skirting the grounds of Chiddingstone Castle, the old manor house of the Streatfeild family, remodelled into the present castellated mansion early in the 19th century. The first Chiddingstone Streatfeild was an Elizabethan ironmaster and the family remained squires and patrons of the village for 450 years. In the churchyard is the Streatfeild family vault, with a bust of the founder, Henry Streatfeild, who designed and built the vault in 1736.

At the other end of the group of High Street buildings which also includes the post office and general store, a clearly marked footpath leads off to the great boulder known as the Chiding Stone. It is variously believed to have been used as a Saxon land boundary, a Druidical altar and a place to which neighbours brought their grievances to be aired in public. Declared culprits were 'chided' and sent home with the proverbial flea in their ear as a warning to behave themselves better in future.

In 1977 Chiddingstone Castle was offered to the National Trust to become part of the village unit, but the offer was turned down. It remains one of the few examples of castellated Gothic Revival manor houses in Kent, set in picturesque surroundings that include a lake, caves and some very fine trees. It was on the verge of ruin when it was bought in 1955 by the connoisseur Denys Eyre Bower, who died in 1977. He was a passionate collector and his famous collection of art and curiosities can be enjoyed by visitors when the house is open throughout the summer.

🍁 CHILHAM

In an effort to preserve the attractions of Chilham village square, a spacious visitors' car park is provided at the bottom of Taylors Hill, which leads up into the square. It is only a short walk and very well worth the effort for the houses on either side, although you may well still find the square full of parked cars when you do reach it.

It is quite the most perfect village square in Kent. Facing each other across it are the church and the castle, which is just as it should be in a village that is wholly 16th/17th century in character and which, cars notwithstanding, has been treated very kindly by successive centuries.

Emerging into the square from the car park hill, past the Old Copper Kettle restaurant, the 15th century White Horse Inn practically promises buxom serving wenches and pewter pots frothing with brewed-on-the-spot ale. It is a promise it does not keep, although there is nothing wrong with the modern hospitality it extends to its visitors. Opposite, period cottages, including some shops, form one complete side of The Square.

The church, St Mary's, is of typically Downland flint construction, chequered with Caen stone and containing some very fine medieval stained glass.

But Chilham does not put all its attractions into The Square. Leading from it is School Lane, which after passing the memorably named Little Belke and Elephant House, introduces the pink-washed Woolpack Inn. It leads naturally into The Street and up past a wealth of beautiful brick and timber beams and white paintwork back into The Square.

The castle is said to stand where, in 55 BC, Britons gathered behind their fortifications to defy Caesar's legions and broke the Roman charge so that the conquest of Britain had to be postponed until a later date. King John gave Chilham to his bastard son Richard, who married a Dover girl. It was at the castle that John stayed when he came to meet Stephen Langton, the Papal choice for Archbishop of Canterbury against John's own favourite, John de Gray, Bishop of Norwich. Only the keep of the castle still stands today. It was Sir Dudley Digges, James I's Master of the Rolls, who built the present Jacobean house, reputedly designed by Inigo Jones, in 1616. The 300 acres of the castle grounds are terraced and feature a mile long avenue of Spanish chestnut trees, and the inner park was refashioned by Capability Brown in 1777.

The house was bought in 1940 and occupied by the 13th Viscount Massereene and Ferrard, a member of the Skeffington family that traced its origins back (although not without contradiction by some historians) to the Norman Conquest. But he died in 1996 and the property was sold to a Greek millionaire, ending 50 years of public access to the grounds. Some of the buildings in the grounds are currently being converted to form cottages and apartments around two period courtyards.

The famous Chilham Castle heronry in the deer park dates from the 13th century. It is said that if the herons do not return to nest there by St Valentine's Day each year, unspecified but dire misfortunes will befall the castle's owner.

The first bombs on England during the Second World War fell in Chilham, though not on the village itself and not on the house, either.

For those who can bear to tear themselves away from such a perfect time-warp village there is, on the east bank of the River Stour below the castle, the so-called Julliberrie's Grave. A long barrow, 150 feet by 7 feet high, some say it marks the burial place of one of Julius Caesar's captains, although it is almost certainly very much older than that.

🍁 CLIFFE-AT-HOO

There is little enough today to suggest that Cliffe was once a town of some size and importance, apart from St Helen's church, which is quite out of proportion to anything a casual inspection of the village might suggest was needed there. The 13th/14th century banded flint and ragstone building, the only church in Kent with that particular dedication, dominates the village, which clings to the very fringes of the North Kent marshes where the Hoo Peninsular sticks out its thumb of land into the Thames and Medway estuary.

On the seaward side, there is a kind of melancholy about the barren windswept acres beloved of wildfowl and their watchers, but inland the landscape is more garden-like, the richly fertile soil hosting orchards and crops of vegetables and cereals.

During the 16th century, Cliffe was a considerable town and may well have declined by then from earlier even greater size and importance. If this really were the Cloveshoo (or Cloveshoh) of Saxon times (and despite the often-repeated assertion that it was, there is no firm proof of it) then it was here that no fewer than seven Saxon councils were held between the years AD 742 and 824 and here that synods drew up the rules for better government of the Church, providing a framework for centuries to come.

It is claimed, too, that Magna Carta was drafted here in 1215 before the final document was taken to Runnymede for King John to sign.

Early in its career, Cliffe village was a farm of the monks of Christ's Church at Canterbury, with a 14th century population of about 3,000 people. But then in 1520 there was a great fire which marked the beginning of a decline until by the middle of the 19th century the population was only about 900.

Then, in 1824, the digging of the Higham to Strood canal brought labourers to Cliffe from far and wide and for a time there was no shortage of work for able-bodied villagers. Although the canal project flopped rather badly, all that digging was not wasted, because the same line was used by the South Eastern Railway, which opened in 1845 and brought a branch line to Cliffe in 1882.

The branch line came to meet the demands of the cement works which had brought another string to the bow of village prosperity during the 19th century. The first factory was built there in 1868 and after an explosives

factory was built nearby in 1901 the population again soared to over 3,000.

Today, the High Street is still picturesque with weatherboard houses, despite a lot of new building elsewhere. The old St James' Day (25th July) tradition of blessing the apples in churches has lapsed now and so has the apparently purely local tradition, referred to by Edward Hasted, that required the rector to distribute every year a mutton pie and a loaf of bread to as many as chose to demand it, at a cost of about £15 a year. Remembering what a mutton pie and a loaf of bread would have cost in Hasted's 18th century, we can assume that rather a lot of the local people turned up at the rectory to claim their hand-out.

Recent features of local interest include a bench hand-carved from sleepers reclaimed from the former railway, and an 8 foot high conker with proportionate oak and chestnut leaves, made of oak and cedar wood, designed by local schoolchildren to be set up in Cliffe Woods.

COBHAM

When Mr Pickwick and his friends walked from Rochester to Cobham, they did so 'through a deep and shady wood' from which they emerged 'upon an open park with an ancient hall displaying the quaint and picturesque architecture of Elizabeth's time, where large herds of deer cropped fresh grass.' That was Cobham park and today's visitors need not strain their imaginations too far to see it in a very similar light.

When, after half an hour's walking, the Dickensian trio came to Cobham village, Mr Pickwick was moved to exclaim that this was 'one of the prettiest and most desirable places of residence' he had ever met with. That, too, is an opinion shared by hundreds of tourists who seek out this very attractive North Kent village today.

Cobham has never forgotten that Charles Dickens was a frequent visitor himself and the old Leather Bottle Inn is self-consciously Dickensian in appearance and associations.

The village snuggles up to the gates of Cobham Hall, the former 17th century home of the Earls of Darnley but now, since 1957, a public school. The building is administered by the Cobham Hall Heritage Trust with the help of the National Trust and it is required to be open to the public for some days during the year. Much of the wooded deer park is freely accessible to all, as it was in 1843 when Richard Dadd and his father walked there one evening after booking into the Ship Inn at Cobham for the night.

The evening stroll ended in tragedy, for poor demented Richard killed his father in the wood and escaped to France, where he was eventually arrested and returned to Rochester. He was committed to a mental hospital where he spent the rest of his life, producing some of his best – and now most highly valued – art work.

Behind the 13th century church of St Mary Magdalene, which claims to have more memorial brasses than any other church in England, is 16th century Cobham College and almshouses. The Darnley Arms, reputedly of 12th century origin, has a tunnel linking it with the church. The Ship Inn is said to have been built with timbers salvaged from a vessel which sank off Sheerness and at the west end of the village, 17th century Owletts is another National Trust property.

A Darnley heir, the Hon Ivo Bligh, later 8th Earl, occupies a unique place in English cricketing lore. He was a cricketer of note in his youth and he played for Kent from 1877 to 1883. Ill-health ended his active career, although he was twice after that President of Kent County Cricket Club and also President of the MCC in 1900.

In 1882 England lost at home for the first time in a Test Match against Australia and *The Sporting Times* reported the event in the form of a mock obituary notice:

> 'In affectionate remembrance of English cricket, which died
> at The Oval on 29th August, 1882, deeply lamented by a
> large circle of sorrowing friends and acquaintances. RIP.
> NB The body will be cremated and the Ashes taken to Australia.'

Although not among the defeated English team at The Oval, Ivo Bligh soon afterwards led a touring side to Australia 'to recover the Ashes'. During the tour, some Australian ladies collected the ashes of a cricket bail and put them into a small pottery urn, which they presented to the English captain. One of the ladies was Miss Florence Morphy, who later became Ivo Bligh's wife. Bligh duly succeeded to the title and after his death in 1927 his wife gave the urn, with the Ashes inside it, to the MCC in whose safekeeping it remains, whether or not Australia wins a Test series.

Such a story deserves to have a twist in its tail and this one has. It is said that once, while the Ashes were still at Cobham, a maid accidentally knocked over the urn on the mantelpiece and the Ashes spilled out into the fireplace below. Quickly scooping up a roughly equivalent quantity of ashes from the fire she put them into the urn, which she replaced as though it had never been disturbed and it is those ashes that now repose in the custody of the MCC.

No one knows, now, if the story is true or not and there are different versions of it, anyway. Personally, I like this one.

In 1948, there were hopes – and fears – that Cobham might become a coal mining village after five men began mining there, despite National Coal Board experts' advice that there was not sufficient coal to make it worthwhile. But although mining continued for some time, local opposition to the enterprise and growing evidence that the NCB may have been right, after all, finally saved the beauty spot from a fate that might well have been worse than death.

🍁 COOLING

Does Cooling deserve to be included among Kent's villages? There is, certainly, very little of it, although it gives the impression of a tiny community that is stirring itself in its landscape of orchards and cornfields, with distant views of the River Thames where it begins to spread into the estuary, and waking up to the fact that there may be more to life than dreams of better days.

Once, of course, it existed to service the needs of the owners of Cooling Castle and the estate that supported it, and the village declined with the importance of the 'big house'.

Old St James' church was closed at the end of 1976 and declared redundant in 1979, although it is still well looked after. Its most famous feature is the group of 13 graves of members of the Comport family, which died out en masse in the 1770s. They inspired Dickens to have Pip, in *Great Expectations*, speak of 'five little stone lozenges, each about a foot and a half long, arranged in a neat row', the graves of five little brothers of his.

There is very little remaining of the fortifications that earned the name of 'castle' for the manor house that Henry de Yvele, one of the great builders of his day, completed for Sir John Cobham in 1385. At that time, French pirates were raiding the Thames and Medway coastlines, burning riverside villages like Cooling all the way to Gravesend. To protect the house and also to offer some resistance to the pirates, the king's permission was sought and given to fortify the house and the great gateway was built by a man called Thomas Comp, at a cost of no less than £8!

When Sir John died in 1408, the house was inherited by his daughter who survived three husbands before she married 'that warrior of renown' Sir John Oldcastle, a Lollard leader and, therefore, a kind of early socialist, believing that church wealth should be distributed among the poor. The Archbishop of Canterbury did not share Sir John's views and a summons for the Squire of Cooling's arrest was delivered to the castle. Sir John escaped but was eventually caught, tried in London, hanged and burned before a large crowd outside St Giles' Hospital in London on Christmas Day 1417.

Sir John is usually supposed to have been the model for Shakespeare's Falstaff. His widow married for the fifth time and in 1554 the castle was captured by Sir Thomas Wyatt. But it was not much used after about 1580 and the present house was built in about 1670, on the site of the original Saxon manor. Today, only the great roadside gateway and a few remnants of the walls remain as a crumbling but undeniably picturesque memorial to the fortifications, but the house remains in private occupation.

Immediately adjoining it is the 16th century tithe barn, a listed building which has been beautifully restored and is now available for functions of all kinds. Part of the building is equipped and licensed for the conduct of weddings. It is, certainly, a very pleasant venue for a joyful occasion, although it does seem a pity that only a few yards away the rather lovely old St James' church has to watch one of its traditional functions usurped in this way.

During the First World War the local pub, the Horseshoe, caught fire. Firemen from Cliffe galloped to the scene but there was not enough water in the nearby pond to save the building which had to be entirely rebuilt. Today, renamed the Horseshoe and Castle, it is back in the business of providing a cheerful centre for the little community. Perhaps, who knows, one day it will be necessary to bring the church out of retirement, too.

🍁 COWDEN

Cowden is pretty well as far west as it is possible to travel without leaving Kent. Indeed, parts of the parish straddle the Kent Water (further south it is the Kent Ditch) which forms the border with East Sussex and Surrey where the three counties meet.

It's an attractive little village, centred around the 13th century (although much altered in 1884) church of St Mary Magdalene with its slender, wooden shingled spire, bomb-damaged during the Second World War and since re-shingled. The spire is barely perceptibly out of perpendicular, but it is enough to have allowed some long-forgotten grudge to be expressed:

> 'Cowden church, crooked steeple,
> Lying priest, deceitful people.'

The church is, typically for this part of the county, built of sandstone, its tower and steeple massively timber-framed inside. The old bells were recast and rehung in 1911 to commemorate the reign of Edward VII and a sixth bell was added at the Coronation of George V.

One of the stained glass windows, given to the church in 1947, celebrates 'the remarkable preservation of this village during the years 1939-45' and features figures of St Bridget (representing the women of the parish), St Nicholas (for the sailors), St George (the soldiers and airmen) and St Mary Magdalene (the church's patron saint), all in the company of St Walstan (the farmer bishop of Worcester 1062-95, representing the local farmers). Below them are 20th century figures: a sailor, soldier, airman, a nurse and others making up a representative group of Second World War characters, all turned towards a Christ-figure whose protection they seek.

This is old Wealden iron country, recalled by the cast iron memorial slab in the church, to John Bottinge, dated 1622. This was a time when the area was producing guns for the Army and the Navy, as well as much more humble domestic and agricultural ware. Cowden had its own blast furnace in 1573 and during the 17th century it had two. The air of prosperity the place must have breathed in those days lingers still.

The Romans would have found British ironworkers plundering the local orestone when they built their London-Lewes road across what is now the garden of Waystrode Manor. The first owners of the manor received it from King John in 1208. Crippenden Manor, built in about 1607, was once the home of another ironmaster, Richard Tichborne.

Another member of the Tichborne family, Robert, presented a Londoners' petition to the House of Commons in 1649, in favour of the execution of Charles I. He was one of the Commissioners who, in 1651, prepared the way for the union with Scotland and he was knighted in 1655 by Cromwell and made a peer in 1657. After the Restoration he was arrested and sentenced to death, but he was reprieved, imprisoned in Dover Castle and died, in 1682, in the Tower of London. The family, however, did not die out in Cowden until 1708, when John Tichborne was buried there.

Today, there is almost no local industry at all, although that could be about to change. Planning permission has been given to prospectors to drill for gas and/or oil at Cowden and although similar permissions have been given elsewhere in the Weald of Kent during the last decade or so, all of which have led to the conclusion that commercial exploitation would not be worthwhile, the fact that exploration continues keeps open the possibility that the elusive 'gusher' will spout its precious mineral somewhere. If and when it does, it will change the local character completely, wherever it happens. The weight of local opinion quite emphatically falls among those who hope it never does.

 COXHEATH

It could be said that Coxheath owed its existence as a village to a war. Until 1756, it was still just open heath, one of the last true wildernesses left in Kent, frequented only by smugglers and highwaymen and other lawless refuge seekers. At the start of the Seven Years War, though, it suddenly became a huge military camp, with 12,000 Hanoverian and Hessian troops quartered there. Its former sinister reputation soon gave way to a new one – for the number of duels fought there, usually over the ladies of nearby Maidstone.

The county town had mixed views about the camp. The business community was inclined, on the whole, to be forbearing about the disadvantages, but feelings ran high once or twice between Maidstone Corporation and the military authorities about which should exercise the right to punish soldiers who misbehaved themselves in the town's confines.

The camp was the scene of several big reviews of troops by visiting dignitaries, including one by the king himself, George III, and his Queen Charlotte in 1778. The king made it an occasion to knight the Mayor of Maidstone, William Bishop, before he left, which probably did something to reduce the friction.

During the Napoleonic invasion scare, the heath was one of a network of sites for warning beacons, as recalled by the empty brazier on the top of the post that carries the village sign in the main street. After Waterloo and the defeat of Napoleon in 1815, Parliament closed the camp but by then it was too late for the heath simply to revert to its old wild state and the area was enclosed and the development of Coxheath village began.

Since then, there has been rapid growth which has almost totally overlaid any trace of the older buildings. The old workhouse, built in 1838 for a Coxheath Union that included 15 neighbouring or nearby parishes, became part of Linton Hospital but that, in its turn, finally closed in 1993. In the same year, Coxheath, which had been an independent civil parish since 1964, became a separate ecclesiastical parish too, and the workhouse chapel, which was built in 1884, was transferred to Rochester Diocese by the South Thames Health Authority for the nominal sum of £1. Now, as Holy Trinity church, it is Coxheath's parish church and what remains of the old hospital building behind the church houses the headquarters of the Kent Ambulance Service.

The old hospital site on Heath Road is now destined for housing redevelopment.

🍁 CRANBROOK

The author H. E. Bates, who lived in Kent during the Seconed World War and who knew Cranbrook well, said the village gave the impression of being a town trying to remember what once made it important. Certainly, it is a bit difficult to decide whether it is a town declining into village status, or a village aspiring to be a town.

It once had a railway station, but that has gone, leaving no evidence that there ever was a rail service. Several of the old pubs have given way to other kinds of trades and whether that represents a loss or a gain is a matter for argument in the bars that remain, no doubt. There is a car park now where once there was a tanyard and the old ropewalk is now a housing estate.

Yet this was once the capital of the 14th-16th century Wealden woollen industry and for 300 years it was one of the wealthiest and largest towns in Kent. When Queen Elizabeth I stayed at the George Hotel during her Royal Progress through Kent in 1573, the people of Cranbrook were able to present her with a silver gilt cup, and according to a dubious but persistent tradition, they rolled out a length of Kentish broadcloth a mile long so that Her Majesty could walk dryshod from Cranbrook to nearby Coursehorne manor.

Cranbrook itself is L-shaped, with the church at the angle. Another local tradition claims that the figure of Father Time on the side of the tower of St Dunstan's church comes down once a year to cut the grass in the churchyard, but reliable eyewitness evidence of the phenomenon is difficult to come by.

It was to Cranbrook, during the 19th century, that John Callcott Horsley RA came to live. With George and Frederick Hardy, Thomas Webster and George O'Neill, he formed the Cranbrook Art Colony, which produced many of the bestselling pictures of their day. Horsley himself was drawing master to Queen Victoria's children and is credited with the 'invention' of Christmas cards. Now the New Cranbrook Colony consists of artists of all kinds, dedicated to promoting art in the area.

In 1983 Whitstable historian Wallace Harvey published a small book about a certain Thomas Clark of Canterbury, who frequently visited friends at Cranbrook during the 1790s and who wrote hymn tunes with the help of John Francis, master of Shepherds House School there at that time. One of those tunes he called *Cranbrook*. It was first published in 1805 and it was to become more famous than all the others, though not particularly in Kent and not with the original words. The tune was adopted in 1877 to be sung with the words of *On Ilkley Moor baht 'at* by the Heponstall (Yorkshire) Glee Choir and it has since become one of the best-known of all English folk-songs and Yorkshire's own signature tune.

Village or town, Cranbrook is the only place I know for which a complete and very detailed guide book was ever written all in rhyme, called *Cranbrook:*

Cranbrook.

Containing Characteristic sketches in Verse, Descriptive of Local Scenery and the Manners and Customs of the Inhabitants of that Ancient Town, and published in 1819 by an author who gave himself the name of Tyro-Carmine. There is a hint of the great McGonegal about the style, especially when the author gets down to naming just about every tradesman and local character. Nevertheless, it is, in its way, a valuable reference source and it is certainly unusual and rather more entertaining than a great many less intimately knowledgeable guides.

Cranbrook advertises its presence with one of the most impressive windmills in the country. Built in 1814 for Henry Dobell by James Humphrey, the imposing smock mill, 75 feet high, stands on a three-storey brick base, topped by a Kentish cruck cap that looks a bit like an upturned boat. After it had fallen into disrepair, the mill was bought by Kent County Council in 1957. A major restoration by Dutch experts was completed in 1960, when the sweeps turned in the wind once more, for the first time since 1953. They still turn from time to time and demonstration grinding is one of the attractions of the milling museum that welcomes visitors.

Providence Chapel in Stone Street is believed to be England's first prefabricated building, built for visiting preachers, but the newest attractions are the Gardens of Gaia, privately owned but open to the public, and the 15 foot high Ring of Hope sculpture by Rick Kirby, which won the 1998 Rouse Kent Public Art award.

 CUXTON

> If you would see a church miswent
> Then you must go to Cuxton in Kent.

The old couplet refers to the curiosity of the Cuxton church alignment, on a south-west axis instead of the more usual east-west one. There could be several reasons for it, but one suggestion is that the church was built on the foundations of an existing Roman chapel or shrine which did not have the normal Christian church alignment.

There was certainly a Roman villa nearby. In fact, the area around the church was probably more or less continuously inhabited long before the Romans arrived. In 1962 archaeological excavations at Cuxton uncovered some 200,000 year old bones of an elephant that once stomped round these parts, together with a great many flint hand axes and the chips left over from their manufacture. There were some human bones, too, dating from about the first century AD.

The first known rector of the church at Cuxton was a man called Thomas who was appointed in about 1185, and it was from that date that the village numbered the years to its 800th anniversary which it celebrated with a nine-day festival in June and July 1985. Its most famous rector, though, was William Laud, later to become Archbishop of Canterbury under Charles I. He only stayed at Cuxton for a few months in 1610 and very probably, when he was executed by Cromwell's Parliamentarians in 1645, he was tempted to wish he had spent the rest of his life there in quiet obscurity.

For centuries the most notable building in the parish was Whorne's Place, built late in the 15th century by Sir William Whorne, who was Lord Mayor of London in 1487. It was subsequently enlarged and antiquary and historian Sir John Marsham had a particularly fine library in the old stable block. Only the old granary remains, now a private house, and the railway line runs through the site of the stable block.

Another lost curiosity of Cuxton is the grey marble pyramid that used to stand inside St Michael and All Angels' church. It was built by the wife of Richard Coosens JP, who was buried there in 1779. Margaret Coosens died in 1783, obsessed by the fear that she might be buried while in some kind of trance and not actually dead. So she had the pyramid built with a small chamber with a glass door covered by a green silk curtain. The door was locked, but the key was inside where Margaret lay in her unfastened coffin, dressed in scarlet satin ready to return to the world if her fear proved to be justified. By 1868, though, it was reckoned the lady really was well and truly deceased, and the coffin was removed and buried in the churchyard.

The 19th century cement manufacturing boom along the banks of the River Medway brought a population explosion to villages like Cuxton and there has been another, commuter-based expansion since the Second World War. From being home to something over 550 people in 1901, Cuxton had a population of twice that by 1961 and now well over twice that again. Cuxton marina is a popular centre for Medway boating enthusiasts.

 DARENTH

Many of the north-west Kent villages have succumbed to the pressure for homes for people who are not, and do not aspire to become in any traditional sense, villagers. They have sprawled over countryside well beyond any original village bounds, providing essentially town homes for families that look to nearby towns, including London, for employment and, as often as not, for most of the other elements of their chosen life-style, too.

Darenth is one of a number of such villages, a Darent Valley village with two distinct parts. South Darenth is the newer and much the larger, and barely distinguishable from its similarly distended neighbour, Sutton at Hone.

South Darenth is almost entirely purpose-built commuterland, conveniently close to the railway station at Farningham Road for trains to Swanley and central London and to the A225 road to Dartford and with easy access to the A2 (a motorway in all but name), the M20 and the M25.

The antiquity of the place is all but swamped now but the village was once given by King Athelstan (AD 925–940) to Duke Eadulf and later passed into the possession of Christ Church at Canterbury, to become one of the manors of the Archbishop of Canterbury. Archbishop Hubert Walter exchanged the church and manor of Darenth for the manor of Lambeth in 1195.

Two of the smaller Darenth manors, St Margaret Helle (or Helles) and Clequdon have since become lost. The chapel of St Margaret Helle was mentioned in the Textus Roffenses, where it was assessed at sixpence a year payable to Rochester Cathedral. In 1522 Archbishop Warham ruled that although it could baptise and bury local people, marriages could only be solemnised at the parish church, which was some distance away.

Nothing of the chapel remains today but the parish church continues to be dedicated to St Margaret, also. It dates from the 10th century and its fabric contains remnants of a nearby Roman villa on the banks of the River Darent which was excavated in 1894/95. One of the features of the church is the great sculpted Romanesque font which dates from about 1140. The church, which stands on Darenth Hill, is said to be the third oldest in Kent, having been built in about AD 940 although, of course, added to after that. It was largely destroyed by fire in 1710 and restored.

Darenth hospital was built as a lunatic asylum in the 1880s, one of the largest ever built. It continued to be a psychiatric hospital until the 1970s when demolition workers unearthed a very rare Anglo-Saxon glass bowl in the hospital burial ground. A new £100 million hospital was begun in 1997, and the old village of Darenth has the new Bluewater Park shopping complex virtually on its doorstep, too.

How can antiquity compete with modernity of that kind?

🍁 DAVINGTON

Davington has to delve pretty deeply into history to remember anything very much to say for itself. However, hints of the old Davington are still to be seen on the short sharp hill that carries the road up from creekside Faversham to what remains of Davington Priory and the hilltop village itself.

The Priory was founded by Fulk de Newenham in 1153; a small Benedictine nunnery for 26 nuns dedicated to St Mary Magdalene. There was already a church there, probably on the site of a pre-Christian site of some religious significance, and that was rebuilt, with twin towers. Faversham already had its Abbey, founded by King Stephen himself, and relations between the two houses were frequently far from harmonious.

Perhaps as a result, the Priory did not prosper. By the 1340s there were only 14 nuns there and by 1527 only the Prioress, one nun and a lay sister. The Prioress died in 1534, and after the last nun died in 1535 the lay sister decided enough was enough and left, so that even before the Act of 1536 that suppressed the smaller religious houses, the convent had passed into Crown ownership. The Crown promptly sold the lease to Sir Thomas Cheyne.

The old Davington parish church was either dismantled or fell down some time between 1534 and 1580 and after that the owners of the Priory allowed parishioners to meet in the Priory church. However, after the church was damaged in the gunpowder mill explosion of 1781, despite payment of more than £344 in compensation to the owners, it fell into disrepair. By the time the property was bought by Thomas Willement in 1845 very few services were being held in the church which was more used by smugglers as a warehouse and shepherds as a lambing pen.

Willement was heraldic painter to George IV and he did much to revive the ancient art of glass painting. He restored the Priory and lived there until he died in 1871. The Priory remains in private ownership, its most famous 20th century owner being Bob Geldof, the pop star who carved his own niche in history with a series of huge-scale fund-raising concerts.

It was not until 1931 that the church was restored and it reopened as the parish church of Davington on Sunday, 23rd October 1932. The church has only one tower now but the original two are said to have inspired the twin towers of the church at Reculver, after two nuns from Davington were shipwrecked on their way to the Isle of Thanet. One drowned but the other had the new church built, modelled on their home Priory church, as a thanksgiving for her own safety and a memorial to her less fortunate sister.

A picturesque feature of the Priory and one of the architectural attractions of the village is the little postern gate at the top of a short flight of stone steps set into the stone wall at the top of Davington Hill.

Nearby Davington Court, once the home of the Earl of Athlone, was demolished in the 1950s to make way for new homes, leaving only the old gateway incorporated into a modern wall to lend its name to Old Gate Road.

🍁 DENTON

This is the East Kent village, some seven miles from Dover and very different from the village of the same name that has been virtually swallowed up in the urban sprawl of Gravesend.

This one is fairly typical of its East Kent kind: snuggled into a heavily wooded valley, with a village green, half-timbered and tile-hung cottages, and a church a little distance along a grassy track neighbouring Denton Court.

Just outside the village is a Jacobean farmhouse known as Tappington Hall. This was the manor of Tappington-Everard built by Thomas Marsh in about 1628 and said to be one of the oldest continually inhabited houses in Kent. According to legend, Baron FitzUrse took refuge here for a time after his part in the murder of Archbishop Thomas Becket in Canterbury Cathedral in 1170, and it is also said to be where the Black Prince was knighted.

Later it was owned by two brothers, one a Royalist and the other a Parliamentarian. They shared the house, but they never saw each other until one day – so the story goes – they met by chance on the stairs, where they fought. The Roundhead killed the Cavalier, since when it has proved to be impossible to remove the bloodstain from the wooden stairs.

In 1796, Tappington Hall was inherited by the young Richard Barham who, later on, wrote many of his *Ingoldsby Legends* there. Barham was born in Canterbury in 1788 and he became particularly good at composing sharply witty verses, some of which were published while he was still at school. As a young man, he decided not to pursue the legal career for which he had trained, but instead took holy orders. He became a curate at Ashford and later rector of Snargate and curate of Warehorn on Romney Marsh. There he made something of a hobby of collecting old stories told to him by his parishioners and these formed the basis for many of the *Legends* later on.

The *Legends* were published as tales of the fictional Ingoldsby family of Tappington-Everard and one of them is called *The Spectre of Tappington*. In that, Barham described Tappington Everard ('generally called Tappington') as 'an antiquated but commodious manor house in the eastern division of the county of Kent.'

According to him, one of the owners of the mansion had been a certain Bad Sir Giles who once welcomed a stranger who disputed ownership of the house with him. After a night of feasting and drinking the stranger retired to bed and was found in the morning 'a swollen and blackened corpse.' Long afterwards,

Sir Giles haunted the grounds and, according to the *Legend*, was blamed for stealing the breeches of other residents.

Denton Court, next to the church, stands on the site of an original manor house, once the home of Attorney General John Boys who died in 1653. It was rebuilt early in the 19th century by the writer Sir Egerton Brydges and became the home of children's author and short story writer Mrs Mary Stephens-Smith. Her distinction was to have been one of the models, in her youth, for one of the most famous of all Victorian paintings, entitled *And when did you last see your father?*

The picture showed a fair-haired young Royalist standing before a Bench of Parliamentarians seated behind a table, and being questioned about his Royalist father's whereabouts. Behind the boy a pike-bearing Roundhead soldier has his arm round the shoulders of the boy's weeping sister, who was Mrs Stephens-Smith, niece of the artist William Yeames who painted the picture in 1878. Her brother James was the model for the young man being questioned.

Denton is one of several villages in the Dover district that displays an illustrated sign describing the village. It stands on the little village green opposite the Jackdaw inn, named for one of Barham's most famous *Legends*, *The Jackdaw of Rheims*. The sign explains, in English and French, that the village dates from Anglo-Saxon times and the name means 'valley farmstead'. The church of St Mary Magdalen was built in the 13th century and is said to have inspired 18th century Thomas Gray, who was a frequent visitor to the village, to write his famous *Elegy in a Country Churchyard.*

🍁 DETLING

Once, not all that long ago, all the traffic travelling between Maidstone and the North Kent coast around Sittingbourne used to have to go through Detling. Now it goes past it, thanks to the dual carriageway road linking the M20 on the south side of the North Downs with the M2 on the north side.

The Cock Horse Inn at the top end of the village main street recalls that here, once, carriers could hire an extra ('cock') horse to help haul their loads up the hill.

Detling earned early notoriety in 1252 after a local cleric called Hamon fell in love with a lady from Adisham, near Canterbury, called Juliana, who was the wife of a certain Ralph de Bubehurst. Their affair led to the murder of poor Ralph, whose dagger-hacked body turned up on a beach in Sussex and started a hunt for the killers.

The guilty lovers fled, but Juliana was caught and imprisoned in the Archbishop's gaol at Maidstone, from where she escaped and claimed sanctuary in Detling church. She could not stay there for ever, though, and eventually gave herself up, was tried and banished from the realm for ever. After that, history lost sight of her and Hamon, who disappeared without ever standing trial. Perhaps they met somewhere and lived happily ever after.

For the most part, though, Detling has gone about its business, century after century, without attracting very much attention to itself. It was one of those manors that Bishop Odo, half-brother to William the Conqueror, acquired illegally and was forced to relinquish to the Church at Canterbury. During the 18th century the topographer Edward Hasted found the place 'exceedingly unpleasant either to dwell in or to pass through', although it certainly is not that today. On the contrary, Detling is a pleasant, if not very distinguished, village with some attractive old architecture, including a Tudor gateway flanked by a mounting block built into the wall on the corner of the Pilgrims' Way.

During the First World War there were two Army camps and a Royal Flying Corps airfield in the parish, and even before 1939 the airfield at the top of Detling Hill was ready for the coming war. It was severely damaged by enemy bombers in 1940 and again in 1944 but it survived the war and was finally disposed of by the RAF in 1959.

Now part of the former airfield belongs to the Kent County Agricultural Society, which holds the three-day County Show there each July. Another part is now an industrial site. Detling remembers its links with the RAF, however, and in September 1998 the village unveiled the memorial which now stands opposite the inn.

The little church of St Martin of Tours at Detling has what is claimed to be the oldest and most ornamental 14th century carved oak lectern of its kind. It was once pawned by a churchwarden who couldn't balance his books and had to be redeemed in haste by a local benefactor.

🍁 DITTON

The village the church alone remembers now lingers vestigially around the ford where the stream crosses the road, but even there the memory is fading. Stream Cottage is a 15th century half-timbered former rectory and Old Mill House still stands – just – amidst the overgrowth of trees and bushes that almost hide it completely.

The village green, in three parts separated by footpaths and lined with trees, still spreads itself out in front of the ragstone church of St Peter ad Vincula, an unpretentious little church with a 13th century tower surrounded by its churchyard. But most of the rest of the village is 19th and 20th century, reaching out into the agricultural land south of the A20 and forming a pretty well continuously urban area with neighbouring Larkfield.

Even the green has been belittled by the larger recreation ground, where the Community Centre is, and the village sign stands on a little triangle of grass on the very edge of the parish, opposite the war memorial, where the road from Aylesford forms its fishtail junction with the A20. The sign, which was unveiled in November 1996, is an attractively colourful one, featuring the church with its red tiled roof, and the stream with ducks, with the name of the village enscrolled across a garland of traditional local crops of hops, cherries, apples, pears and strawberries.

Yet, for all the newness, by standing aside from the arterial A20, Ditton manages to preserve many of the characteristics of a traditional village and gives the impression of being, on the whole, a very pleasant little community.

🍁 DODDINGTON

The most distinctive feature of Doddington is the church, which has an unusual wooden tower and an even more unusual dedication, to the Beheading of St John the Baptist.

Why it should have a wooden tower, I cannot say. The reason for the dedication is, however, more well known. At least, local tradition has it that Richard I (The Lionheart) stopped overnight in Doddington on his way back to London from the Crusade in the Holy Land. Instead of a chip off the 'true cross' or a phial containing 'one of the tears shed by the Virgin Mary' (or any of the other 'relics' brought back by Crusaders to be cherished by their local abbeys and churches) the Royal souvenir hunter had nothing less than the stone on which John the Baptist was beheaded. He did not leave the precious relic at Doddington, but in 1467 the church adopted the dedication in commemoration of the stone's passage through the parish.

Doddington is still a very attractive village. The Chequers Inn, which claims 12th century origins, forms a welcoming focal point where the road through the Newnham Valley is joined by the road that crosses the M2 on its way from Lynsted. The most significant house is Doddington Place which although not particularly old (it was built during the 19th century) is well known for its beautiful gardens, open to the public throughout the summer.

Early in the 20th century, Dr Josiah Oldfield, author and penal reformer, came to Doddington where he built a little hospital in 1935. He was co-founder, with Mahatma Gandhi (the Indian independence campaigner who pioneered non-violent civil disobedience), of the Fruitarian Society to promote vegetarianism. After the house burned down, Dr Oldfield lived the rest of his life almost as a hermit in a converted woodshed, dying at the age of 89. The site is now occupied by a youth hostel.

A less visible curiosity of Doddington is the parochial library that was founded as a result of the will of a former vicar, the Rev Daniel Somerscales, who died in 1737. The library was added to by a 19th century successor, the Rev John Radcliffe, and by others and is one of the few surviving ancient libraries of its kind. It was formerly housed in the vicarage but in 1982 the Faversham Society arranged for it to be installed in the attic of its Fleur de Lis Heritage Centre in Preston Street, Faversham. It consisted of 400 volumes of theological, medical, natural history and geographical books in Greek and Latin, including one of the works of Erasmus, printed in Antwerp in 1535, and several books by the 16th century theologian John Calvin.

 DUNKIRK

There is still a Bossenden Farm at Dunkirk to recall that day in 1838 when the Battle of Bossenden Wood was fought by a rather pitiful little band of 'disciples' of the self-styled Messiah, John Nichols Thom. Or, as he preferred to call himself, Sir William Honeywood Courtenay, Knight of Malta and rightful heir to the Kentish estates of Sir Edward Hales.

Thom was born a Cornish publican's son in 1799 and had already led a fairly lurid life by the time he turned up in Canterbury at the age of about 35 – although he himself claimed to be 2,000 years old.

He offered himself as a candidate for Parliament and during the elections campaigned colourfully in a crimson velvet suit with gold lacings and tassels, carrying a sword which he did not hesitate to draw if harangued during an election speech. He won 374 votes and elevated himself to the peerage by assuming the title of Lord Viscount William Courtenay of Powderham. He was tried for perjury and spent the next four years in Barming Asylum, from which he was eventually released by Royal Decree after his father had petitioned on his behalf.

He went to lodge with the Culver family at Bossenden Farm where he decided he would champion the cause of the local farm workers who murmured against the 1834 Poor Law Act. This had ended outdoor relief of poverty for the able-bodied and required anyone unable to keep themselves to seek help in one of the hated Union workhouses. For several days he rallied followers to a home-made banner which he paraded round the surrounding countryside until a farmer applied to the authorities at Canterbury for the arrest of his truant workers.

The summons was issued and Constable John Mears with his brother Nicholas and another man set out to serve it. It was Nicholas Mears who confronted Courtenay and was killed by him. Many of Courtenay's disciples would have deserted him at this point if he had not rallied them with renewed promises of a share-out of confiscated estates of the gentry that would amount to 50 acres of land apiece.

The full story of the events of that year were told for the first time in full in P. G. Rogers' book, *Battle of Bossenden Wood* (OUP 1961). At about noon, a hundred men of the 45th Foot regiment came from Canterbury to arrest Courtenay. He shot and killed a young officer, Lieutenant Bennet, and another eight people died in the short, sharp battle, including Courtenay himself. Twenty-five of the rioters were arrested, some to be transported for life, others destined for terms of imprisonment.

The bodies of the dead were taken to the Red Lion Inn at Hernhill and an inquest was held, but not before relic hunters had ripped their hero's blood-stained shirt to shreds. Others broke their fingernails tearing bits of bark off the oak tree against which he had fallen. Thousands of sightseers came to see him in his coffin and for a time after he was buried in Hernhill churchyard a watch was kept on the grave to protect the body from grave-robbers. The grave was purposely left unmarked and is now lost.

The burials had to take place at Hernhill because there was no church at Dunkirk at the time. Events there focused attention upon the village and the Central Society for Education sent an investigator to find out what it was about life in Dunkirk that had led its people so tragically to follow a man like Courtenay.

The report of the investigation mentioned widespread smuggling in and around the village and 'nothing calculated to inspire any regard for order and law.' The report summed up: 'It is not to be wondered that people fell into pernicious courses.'

Perhaps Mad Thom (as he came to be called) did not after all fail the followers to whom he had promised a better life. In 1840, only two years after the battle, the little hilltop church was built, using flints from Canterbury's old city wall. However, by 1996 the church had been declared redundant and planning permission was given for its conversion into a private home.

Today, 610 acres of Church Woods are owned by a conservation consortium and form part of a continuous belt of 1,310 acres of woodland managed by the Royal Society for the Protection of Birds.

🍁 EASTCHURCH

There is a memorial on the corner of High Street and Church Street facing the 15th century parish church at Eastchurch, on the Isle of Sheppey. It is of Portland stone, flat on one face and curved like an aeroplane wing on the other, and carved with aeroplanes and other motifs as well as the names of aviation pioneers who first flew from here.

For this was where British aviation took off and moved from the minority eccentricity that it was in the first years of the 20th century towards the major industry it was to become. Stone Pett Farm was the site of the early airfield.

Some notable early aviators who first became airborne at Eastchurch included Winston Churchill, who learned to fly there; Charles Stewart Rolls, half of the famous Rolls-Royce team, who made an historic two mile flight from Eastchurch airfield round the church tower and back and later became the first man to fly across the English Channel and back again; and Cecil Grace, who was killed in a flying accident there in 1910. Lord Brabazon of Tara, who became holder of Pilot's Licence No 1, also flew from Eastchurch.

The Aero Club of Great Britain (later the Royal Aero Club) was founded at nearby Leysdown but then moved to Eastchurch. The Short Brothers bought 4,000 acres of Sheppey marshland and built the first British aircraft factory before they moved to Rochester and made their name with their famous flying boats and other aircraft.

Today, the roar of aero engines has left Eastchurch and the biggest single concentration of residents is inside the open prison at nearby Standford Hill. The village has grown into a seaside resort with several holiday camps as near neighbours.

But in the early 14th century, Shurland Hall was the home of the de Shurland family, of whom Sir Robert was surely the most memorable. Although perhaps not before that waggish cleric, the Rev Richard Barham, told the story of how the 12th century knight rode his faithful horse Grey Dolphin out to sea to petition the king for a pardon, for a crime for which he had been excommunicated by none other than the Pope. Arriving triumphantly back on shore with his pardon, he was met by an old woman who predicted that although the horse had saved his life that day, it would be responsible for his eventual death.

The knight took the precaution of beheading the horse there and then, leaving the corpse where it fell, but some time later while walking on the beach he stubbed his toe against the bleached skull of a horse. One of the teeth pierced his shoe, causing a wound which caused his death.

After the de Shurlands, the Hall passed to the Cheyne family, several of whom held important appointments, including Sir John who was Lord Warden of the Cinque Ports and who died in 1499. He was succeeded by Sir Thomas Cheyne who rebuilt Shurland Hall using stones from Chilham Castle, which the family also owned. In 1532 Henry VIII and Anne Boleyn stayed at the Hall when they were on their way to Calais but it was partly destroyed during the Commonwealth, by which time it was no longer owned by the Cheynes.

Now, all that remains is part of the gatehouse, which English Heritage wants to restore as a national monument when it has the money to do so.

🍁 EAST FARLEIGH

The 14th century ragstone bridge across the River Medway at East Farleigh is generally reckoned to be the finest medieval bridge in south-east England. Interesting and picturesque it may be. Convenient, however, it is not. At its southern end the road curves through 45 degrees which, together with the hump of the bridge itself which is not wide enough for two vehicles to pass on it, creates problems for approaching cars and long queues form, first on one side and then the other.

The railway line, with a level crossing, cuts across the approach to the bridge on the north side, so one way and another it is far from an ideal river crossing point for modern traffic.

The bridge featured prominently in the Civil War, when during the Battle of Maidstone the Royalists tried to hold the town against Parliamentary forces led by General Fairfax. The Royalists, who assembled on Penenden Heath (then just outside Maidstone but now part of it), knew the Roundheads were at Rochester and expected the attack to come from north or west of the town. Instead, Fairfax sent his men round the town, crossing the River Medway by way of East Farleigh bridge and then swooping up from the south to win the day.

The village is older than the bridge, though. Quite how much older we can't be sure but we do know that in the 9th century it was recorded as Fearn lege, probably meaning a clearing among the ferns. The manor was already well established when it was given, in AD 961, to Christ Church at Canterbury by

the Saxon King Edred and the church was listed by the Domesday clerks in 1086.

The East Farleigh village signs, one of which stands on a tiny triangle of land between the church and the Bull Inn, together with a flower-filled horse trough and a mounting block, features the bridge and the river and also three oast kilns and a fruiting hop bine. Once across the river, the road climbs steeply and from the top there is a splendid view across the valley, the sides of which were, until quite recently, thickly clothed in hop gardens, now like most others throughout the county, disappeared.

In St Mary's churchyard there is a cross to the memory of 43 hop-pickers who died of cholera at East Farleigh in 1849. Edith Cavell, the nurse who was accused of spying and was shot by the Germans in Brussels in 1915, nursed typhoid victims at East Farleigh during the time she was a young probationary nurse in Maidstone in 1896.

EAST MALLING

If the abbey had not been built where it is, no doubt East Malling would have remained the only Malling. As it was, the abbey gathered people around it into a separate village that became Town Malling (now West Malling) and left the older settlement to the east very much a junior partner.

What helped East Malling to retain its individuality in the shadow of its big brother West Malling was the stream that runs through the village. Once it turned no fewer than six water wheels, which powered the stones that ground flour for its own inhabitants and also for those of the abbey and their dependants. But as time went by, East Malling mills developed an economic importance as the flour was traded over a greater area than the immediate vicinity.

At one point the stream was diverted to create a moat round a house at East Malling. The moat has been filled in now and nothing is known of that house except that it was bought during the 16th century by Richard Manningham and razed to the ground in order that he could build for himself a far grander house.

That one we do know about because it was called Bradbourne, one of Kent's finest houses and now the headquarters of Horticultural Research International. It is still known locally by its old name, East Malling Research Station, and, among a great many things too technical to dwell upon here, concerns itself with improving and developing varieties of fruit of all kinds.

Manningham was a Bedfordshire man who made his fortune in the City and died in 1611. But after him the house was owned by a family that left a much deeper impression upon county history, the Twisdens. They rebuilt the house and altered the rebuilding until they had it more or less the way it is today, a pretty house at the end of a long drive; one of the best Queen Anne houses in England with a specially fine Jacobean oak staircase inside.

The Twisdens (Twysdens, Twysendens – depending upon the period) provided Kent with one or two notable sons. One, Sir William, the first baronet of Roydon, was a noted scholar, astrologer, book and manuscript collector, Member of Parliament – and buccaneer! He died in 1629 and it was his son, Thomas, who first changed the Twysden to Twisden when he became Baronet of Bradbourne in 1666.

The last baronet, Sir John, died in 1937 and the 200 acre estate seemed certain to be bought by developers and planted with new houses.

As it happened, though, the East Malling Research Station was already established on neighbouring land and was looking for more on which to expand. It bought the house and more than 500 acres of Bradbourne estate and made it a centre of international repute, which it still is.

The other major property in East Malling was Clare Park, which lay between the village and the London Road. Clare House was built in 1793 for banker and timber merchant John Larking, founder of the Maidstone Bank, but during the difficult times of post-Napoleonic Europe, the bank failed and Larking fled the country. Today, Clare Park is a council housing estate built around a secondary school.

East Malling was mentioned in a Charter of King Edmund in about AD 940 and in the Domesday survey in 1086. In about 1100 it passed from the ownership of the Archbishop of Canterbury to West Malling Abbey, which held it until the abbey was dissolved in 1538. The church, which had been St Mary's, was rededicated to St James the Great and is partly 11th century.

🍁 EAST PECKHAM

The Kent historian Edward Hasted, writing in the 18th century, described East Peckham as 'too deep and mirey to be pleasant on account of the stiff clay soil on which are bred and fattened some of the biggests beasts in any of these parts.'

That same clay soil, however, later made the parish one of the Wealden centres of hop growing and the former Whitbread hop farm at nearby Beltring was the last stronghold of large-scale, old-style hand picking of hops in Kent. It 'went mechanical' in 1969 and although the massed oast kilns – the largest group of its kind in the world – remain a major landmark, it is now a museum and leisure centre.

A century ago, East Peckham was one of nine separate hamlets, none of which was the village of that name. It was not until the 20th century that builders chose the existing community around the Pound as the site for the centre that became the village of East Peckham.

One of the hamlets was Hale Street, which grew up where the B2016 (known locally as Seven Mile Lane) meets the B2015 (Wateringbury-Pembury road). By the beginning of the 1970s residents were already campaigning for a bypass to give them some respite from the growing volume of traffic to and from the international rail depot at Paddock Wood. They finally got their bypass in 1998 and the parish council planted a tree to mark the great occasion.

The River Medway runs through the parish, fed by a skein of tributaries that also water the area. In 1997 a new weir was installed to replace the gate that had served river users for more than 60 years, as part of a plan to enhance the river generally.

St Michael's church stands well away from the village centre, on a hilltop where it was left after the village that once surrounded it moved away. The old church was redundant by the 1830s and in 1840 the new parish church of Holy Trinity was built, although it was not until 1972 that St Michael's was finally closed. The dredging of the river between Maidstone and Tonbridge in 1740, and the building of the wharf at Branbridges that created a little inland port for barges, offered new employment opportunities for people living close to it.

In the 18th and 19th centuries, East Peckham was one of the reception areas for London foundlings sent out from Thomas Coram's Foundling Hospital. The children were nursed here until they were old enough to be sent back to London to be apprenticed. Some later returned, married and became 'natives'.

In about 1504, Thomas Roydon came to East Peckham and enlarged a house called Fortune. It became known as Roydon Hall and later passed by marriage into the Twysden family which owned it until 1837. Since 1974, however, the house has been the headquarters of the Age of Enlightenment which encourages the practice of transcendental meditation.

 EASTRY

One of the treasures of Eastry is a brass Standard Winchester bushel measure, inscribed 'Hundred of Cornillo, 1792' which was owned by the former Eastry rural district council for many years and was given to St Mary's church in 1974. The Winchester measure dates from Saxon times and the Hundred of Cornillo once took in the towns and villages of Deal, Sutton, Ripple, Ringwould, East Langdon, Sholden and part of Northbourne.

It is, in its way, a surviving reminder that Saxon kings of Kent once had a royal palace here, astride the Canterbury-Sandwich road. The palace is generally supposed to have stood where Georgian Eastry Court now is and it was the setting for one of Kent's oldest legends.

The story is told that the 7th century King Egbert was persuaded by a nobleman called Thunor that his cousins Ethelred and Ethelbert coveted his crown. So the royal brothers were murdered and their bodies hidden behind the king's throne, where they were spotlighted by a divinely focused pillar of light that led to the discovery of the crime.

To atone, the king agreed that the princes' sister could have all the land her pet deer could cover in a day's coursing, on which to build an abbey. Thunor's arguments against the settlement lost ground rather literally when the earth

opened beneath him and swallowed him up. The very spot where it happened is known to this day as Thunor's Leap.

Perhaps he fell into one of the Eastry caves. Legends persist that these caves, access to which is privately owned, were once an extensive labyrinth with origins lost in the depths of pre-history. Others say they never were anything more than relatively limited 17th century chalk mines. Towards the end of the 19th century there were people who claimed to have walked from Eastry to neighbouring Woodnesborough through the tunnels. One was even said to reach all the way to Canterbury, some ten miles away, and another to Sandwich in the opposite direction. Traditionally, Archbishop Thomas Becket hid in the caves while he was preparing to flee England from Sandwich in 1164.

Before the First World War, Eastry seemed all set to find new prominence as one of the Kent coalfield villages. But although two railway stations were opened there in 1916 and 1925, and the East Kent light railway ran through the village, the line failed and was finally closed in 1987, leaving Eastry with a fairly serious heavy lorry traffic problem to take its mind off its prestigious distant past.

During the 19th century, the 18th century clock in the massive tower of the church of St Mary the Virgin was replaced. The church was given a telescope so that churchwardens could see the time ball at Deal, which dropped at exactly twelve noon every day, and so keep the village church clock on time.

🍁 ECCLES

Until the 1860s, Eccles was known as Bull Lane and was just a few cottages alongside the lane that is now the main road through the village. But the name is not new. Judith Glover, in her book *The Place Names of Kent*, traces it in its present form back to 1208 and suggests that it derived from the 10th century Aecclesse, meaning the meadow of the oak.

Whether or not the Romans knew the name or the meadow, with or without the oak, when they came we don't know. What we do know is that one of them liked whatever he did find there because he built the largest Roman villa yet excavated anywhere in Kent, quite close to the present village.

It seems he was some kind of pottery magnate – the Josiah Wedgwood of his day, perhaps – and his pottery must have paid for a pretty luxurious life-style because the villa had 140 rooms including an elaborate suite of baths, with several heated rooms and a cold plunge, that would have outshone many a private swimming pool today.

The site of the Roman villa was first discovered by local clergyman the Rev Beale Poste in 1848, who found a lot of Roman pottery during a walk across a field. The first buildings were uncovered in 1882 by historian George Payne but serious excavation did not begin until 1962, after the outlines of the buildings were seen from the air. Work was completed in 1976, after which the site, which is on land owned by Blue Circle Cement, was again covered with soil. Now a report on the dig is being completed for publication.

It was the building boom of the 1800s that brought the village out of its own extended Dark Age, as it did several other Medway valley villages. Thomas Buss, who was born in Aylesford in 1848 and moved to Eccles at the age of eight, wrote a pamphlet in 1908 in which he recalled the village as he remembered it during those years of growth.

According to him, the 'boom' began after Thomas Cubitt bought two farms near the river and opened a brickyard and a cement factory on the land. One of the local farmers, Thomas Abbott, foresaw the need for homes for workers in the new industries and he built a row of 22 houses and the Walnut Tree public house. Buss remembered the men who came to work in the new brick and cement works as a pretty rough lot, from all over the country, drawn by the promise of high wages. They earned £5 a week, which was very high indeed for those times and they spent most of it on gin and beer in the Walnut Tree. The young Buss used to go with his father to the public house with wheelbarrows to collect the drunks as they fell out onto the street and wheel them home.

Eccles church was built at the end of the 1880s but however well it competed with the Walnut Tree in the 19th century, it could not compete with the materialism of the 20th. In 1930 Eccles had its own cinema, as well as its pubs, the Working Men's Club and the recreation ground and in 1979 the church was sold for more new homes to be built on the site.

Today, Eccles is still one of the villages where there is more profit to be made from what comes out of the ground than from what is grown in it and the area is deeply scarred with quarry sites, some of which are still active.

🍁 EGERTON

The little village of Egerton is not one that very many tourists stumble across by accident unless they happen to be following the Greensand Way walk, which passes through the churchyard of St James' church.

For at least a thousand years the village has congregated round its church in the deeply rural East Kent countryside north-west of Ashford, roughly between Charing and Headcorn, with Pluckley as its nearest neighbour of any size at all. It is a village of about 1,000 people living in old and new red brick and white weatherboarded cottages around a little green, opposite which the George Inn extends its hospitality to such visitors as do happen upon it.

One of the oldest properties is Spring Cottage, part of a medieval hall house built in about 1400. It was bought for renovation in 1967 and some of the original wattle and daub cladding – clay, straw and animal dung mixed with horse and cow hair spread over a framework of woven hazel wattle walls – was uncovered. Part of the original thatch was found under the roof tiles, too.

The church, though, is a good deal older than that, and stands on the site of an even earlier one. The present building is mostly 14th century, restored in the mid-19th century, with some interesting internal features including the chandelier which was given to the church in 1699. It was later sold and then given back to the village and installed in the church again. It is said to be the oldest chandelier of its kind in England – possibly in the world.

The 15th century church tower is almost 100 feet high and from the hillside on which it stands it makes an impressive landmark.

ELHAM

They say the man upon whom Baroness Orczy modelled her fictional hero of the French Revolution, the Scarlet Pimpernel, used to stop and dine at the Rose and Crown at Elham while he waited for a fresh horse to carry him to the coast for one of his real-life dashes to France to rescue some doomed aristocrat from the guillotine.

Across the road the Abbot's Fireside inn, a brick and tile-hung building dating from about 1480, was built as an inn, but it was called the Smithies Arms when the Duke of Wellington used it as his East Kent headquarters when he was preparing for the expected Napoleonic invasion. There is a local tradition, too, that Prince Charles (later to be Charles II) hid there during his flight to the coast pursued by Roundhead troops in 1651.

Other buildings that contribute to the charm of the Square include The Master's House and Poor's House. Opposite New Inn is another timbered building housing the gift shop and post office and at one end the great slab of the Methodist church, which bears the date 1839 over its classical style frontage, puts a fairly ponderous full stop to the village.

The church of St Mary the Virgin was built in about 1180. It has been added to since then and today it is one of the most beautiful old churches in Kent, with a massive flint tower topped by a rather curious little spire. Nineteenth century stained glass depicts some of the notables of their day, including politicians Benjamin Disraeli and Lord Salisbury, writer Thomas Carlyle and singer Madame Patti, all portrayed as biblical characters.

Beside the church is the King's Arms and, across the road, The Old School House, which was built in 1620 and rebuilt in about 1700.

Elham was certainly known to the Romans because fragments of some of their cremation urns have been dug up nearby. It was found by the Domesday bureaucrats, too, by which time Bishop Odo of Bayeux had added it to his extensive Kentish landholdings. In the 13th century, the village was owned by the son of Henry III, later to become Edward I, and it was he who persuaded his father to permit a Monday market to be held in the Square. It became famous for its hides and leatherwork before it died out during the 19th century.

Probably the most glamorous 20th century resident was the late film star Audrey Hepburn, although she was only a schoolgirl here when her mother, who was a Dutch baroness, whisked her off to safety in neutral Holland at the beginning of the Second World War. In fact, of course, they would have been safer in Elham.

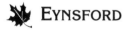 # EYNSFORD

Eynsford Castle.

Early in the 20th century, a man called Elliot Downs Till had some village stocks made and set up in Eynsford to replace the original ones that used to stand on the triangular green at Bower Lane's junction with the A225. He thought it would make a nice feature for the street scene.

Unfortunately, the new stocks awoke local memories of a man who had died in the old ones in 1838 and there were some villagers who wanted them removed. Mr Till felt sure the opposition would subside once people got used to the new stocks, so he put a fence round them instead of removing them. It was not enough. The fence was uprooted and the stocks burned where they stood.

He also founded Britain's Arbor Day and Eynsford was the first English village to celebrate it. Queen Victoria's diamond jubilee was one of several occasions celebrated in the village by the planting of trees, the species initials of which spelled out appropriate quotations. It was also Mr Till, himself a teetotaller, who bought the former Harrow Inn, renamed it the Castle Hotel and then restricted the sale of alcohol there.

He died in 1917, at the age of 82, of a bee sting on his ear and Eynsford sufficiently forgave him to put up a lychgate to his memory.

Eynsford really is a picture-postcard village, with its many architectural styles, including several timbered houses. The River Darent swarms very prettily over its ford where local children slake their insatiable fascination with running water. For older pedestrians there is a little gem of a medieval hump-back bridge with two low semi-circular arches separated by a bold cut-water on the upstream side where the river passes under as well as round the white weatherboarded Old Mill, with its barrelled roof of corrugated iron.

Across the river, the view is blocked by the 16th century half-timbered Plough Inn and its neighbouring jettied house, but the way leads to Lullingstone Castle and some of the finest excavated remains of a Roman villa in Britain, on permanent exhibition under cover by English Heritage.

St Martin's church, with its wood-shingled spire, has a tower clock surrounded by a quotation from Browning:

> Grow old along with me,
> The best is yet to be.

Nearby are the remains of Eynsford's old castle, one of the most complete Norman castles of its kind in England. Also looked after by English Heritage and open to the public, for some years it was used as kennels for the hunting dogs owned by the Hart-Dyke family of nearby Lullingstone Castle.

Lullingstone isn't really a castle at all, and never was, despite the impressive towered gateway which was built in the last years of the 15th century. Between the gate and the house is a wide expanse of lawn on part of which stands the ancient parish church of St Botolph, known appropriately enough as the Church on the Lawn. The church can be visited at any time, and there is public access to the 600 acre park but not to the house.

House and church were both restored by Sir Percyvall Hart in the 18th century in honour of Queen Anne, who often stayed there. A rather odd little story is told of his daughter, Ann. It relates how, on the night of the celebration of her betrothal to Sir Thomas Dyke of Horeham in Sussex, she slipped away to her bedroom where she made a rope of knotted sheets and climbed down into the arms of a young naval officer called Bluet, who was waiting for her in a boat in the moat. Together they ran away and were married. The jilted Sir Thomas swore he would never marry anyone else and, indeed, he did not. When Bluet died nine years later his widow found the faithful Sir Thomas still waiting for her and they were finally married.

A later member of the family, Sir William Hart Dyke, and two of his friends framed the rules of lawn tennis at Lullingstone in 1875 and first played the game there, using a ladder supported on two barrels instead of a net.

The house remained in the same family for 600 years. It was empty when Sir Oliver Hart Dyke married Zoe, who became Lady Hart Dyke and who started the famous Lullingstone silk farm in part of the house. After the Second World War, the enterprise moved to Compton House in Dorset and supplied silk for Lady Diana Spencer's dress when she married Prince Charles and became Princess of Wales.

Eynsford is a village that has much to boast about – and it does. Its village sign is held aloft on a post decorated with brass plates commemorating the number of times it has won the South-East In Bloom competition and Kent's own Best Kept Village competition.

🍁 Farningham

It is appropriate that Farningham should follow Eynsford alphabetically in a book like this because the two are such close neighbours it is difficult to say where one ends and the other starts.

Most of the historic and architectural interest of Farningham is near the brick-built 18th century bridge over the River Darent. Several of the older buildings, most of which are 18th century, are listed as being of architectural or historic interest and the whole area is designated one of great landscape value within the metropolitan green belt.

Hasted, in one of his more lyrical moods, described it in the 18th century:

'The River Darenth meanders its silver stream across the parish northward, in the midst of a valley of fertile meadows when the hills rise both towards the east and west. As you approach it from the hills on either side, it forms the most beautiful and picturesque landscape imaginable.'

Well, there have been changes since that was written, but it is still possible to go along with him, in general if not in every particular.

The village had its beginnings in Saxon times and its name derives from a description of a village near a running stream. Before it was bypassed by the A20 in the early 1920s, the old London road carried the traffic through Farningham where the Lion Hotel was once one of the stops for stage coaches and Sparepenny Lane once had a toll bar across the Eynsford end.

Between the two 20th century wars, sprawling development did nothing to enhance the landscape immediately round the old part of the village. It nevertheless retains several listed buildings which survived the claim that this was the most-bombed parish in Kent during the Second World War, although only twelve people were injured in the bombardment and none killed. Some of the stained glass in the parish church of St Peter and St Paul proved to be less durable but what remains includes the work of the son of a former vicar, Charles Winston, carried out in 1832 when he was only 18 years old. The replacement glass in the west window became the first in any British church to have a representation of Queen Elizabeth II.

In the churchyard is the tomb of Thomas Nash, of which it is said that anyone who can throw a pin through a hole in its side will be rewarded by sight of the Devil.

Nowadays, Farningham is right in the heart of the county's commuter-land, although still sufficiently rural to be much sought-after by such of London's work-force as can afford its relatively high prices.

🍁 FORDWICH

In May 1883, the *Kentish Gazette* carried a curious item of church news that leaves us yearning, more than a century later, to know more. The paper reported: 'Now that the Rev E. Brailsford, having been released from prison, has resumed his duties at Fordwich Parish Church, the good that has been done in his absence is melting away. He has dismissed the choir, so carefully got together by the Rev Stuart Robson, and has in other matters so thoroughly gone back to the "old lines" that whereas during his absence, the church has been crowded, the congregation has now fallen back to the half-dozen old women looking out for the charities.'

The little church of St Mary the Virgin at Fordwich stands at the heart of the village, keeping any such internal strife – if, indeed, there is any – very much to itself. The present building is mainly 13th century, with just the occasional hint of its older Saxon origins. Way back in the 12th century, the foundations were weakened by River Stour flooding and the church developed the list that is still evident today.

One of the more enigmatic treasures inside the church is the Fordwich Stone, a carved tomb traditionally claimed as that of St Augustine himself. Near the church are the remains of a monastery where, it is recorded, the bishop (later archbishop) who established Christianity in Kent in AD 597 expressed a wish to be buried. The Abbots of St Augustine's Abbey at Canterbury certainly owned land at Fordwich. Augustine died in AD 604 and the stone, whoever it commemorates, has travelled about a bit since then for it was once in the nave of the church and, after that, in the churchyard. Then it went to a Canterbury garden before travelling back to the church at Fordwich in 1866 and finally being taken back inside the church in 1892.

Latter-day historians have debunked both the 'legend' (which they say is of modern origin based on nothing more than a conversational remark) and the stone itself which, although undoubtedly very old, is now thought to be most likely a memorial to some local notable, possibly the founder of the church at Fordwich.

Historians can be such spoilsports!

After it was granted self-government by a Charter of Henry II in the 12th century, Fordwich became a proud borough and a major East Kent inland port. As a corporate member of the Cinque Ports and later a non-corporate member it paid Ship Money to its Head Port of Sandwich. The new status was deemed deserving of a bridge, so that travellers to and from the town could cross the River Stour dry-shod. The first bridge was a wooden one, but that was replaced by a brick-arched one and the present one is 18th century, like much of the rest of the village.

There is a tradition that local custom once decreed that if the good people of Fordwich elected as their mayor a man who declined the honour, for whatever reason, all the freemen of the town were empowered to pull down the unfortunate man's house.

In those days the river was much wider than it is today and barges were still trading up to Fordwich late into the 19th century. The trade was killed by the opening of the Canterbury-Whitstable railway, which made sea-side Whitstable, rather than river-side Fordwich, the port for Canterbury.

Today, Fordwich is a pretty riverside village, but it remained a borough until as recently as 1886 after a Royal Commission in 1876 recommended its demotion to the status of parish. It still has its picturesque little town hall – sometimes known as the Court House and reputedly the smallest in England, rebuilt in 1555 – to remind it and its many visitors of its former importance.

Outside the town hall one of the curiosities of Fordwich used to be the old ducking stool, a chair on one end of a beam which swung out over the river. Unruly wives were strapped into the chair by their husbands and 'dunked' in the river to dampen the heat of their tempers a bit. Such political incorrectness could not, of course, be encouraged today and the relic is now safely inside the building where it is less likely to arouse the nostalgia of visiting husbands or the retrospective indignation of local wives.

GODMERSHAM

Godmersham earns a mention mainly because of its association with the 19th century novelist, Jane Austen. Her brother was squire at Godmersham Park and some of her novels probably described the red-brick mansion and nearby vicarage, although with different names. Some say that the rectory of the Rev Collins in *Pride and Prejudice* was modelled on the vicarage occupied by the Rev Joseph Sherer, Vicar of Godmersham from 1811, and that Mansfield Park was, in fact, Godmersham Park.

In 1935 the house was bought by Robert and Elsie Tritton. Mrs Tritton was a New Yorker whose first husband, Sir Louis Baron, made a fortune from the famous Black Cat cigarettes. Robert Tritton was a noted collector and during their ownership, they were the hosts of many famous people, including the writer Somerset Maugham and artist Rex Whistler.

In 1985, the foundations of Court Lodge were uncovered on land next to Godmersham church. The Lodge was demolished 30 years before but it was once the centre of an estate that was owned by Canterbury Cathedral for a thousand years. It began life in 1270 as a great hall house and was said to have had the finest windows of any manor house in Kent. One of those windows was believed to have been removed by Dr Hewlett Johnson, the notorious 'Red' Dean of Canterbury, before the house was demolished but no one now knows what became of it.

The village is in the Stour valley, just off the A28 between Canterbury and Ashford, in wonderful walking country. The bridge across the river was built in 1698 and the donkey wheel which survived the demolition, in 1828, of Georgian Eggerton Manor is very early 17th century. The 15 foot diameter by three foot wide wheel was once used for drawing water from a 120 foot well and it was in use until 1923. Sir Charles Igglesden, in his *Saunters Through Kent with Pen and Pencil*, thought the wheel was 'a great sight which will repay anyone for the walk up to Eggerton.'

The church of St Lawrence the Martyr at Godmersham stands on rising ground near the River Stour. It has an 11th century north tower and the nave and west end of the chancel are also Norman, although the east end of the chancel is 13th century. The south transept, aisle and porch were added in 1865.

 GOUDHURST

Locals will tell you that if you climb to the top of Goudhurst church tower you will be able to see no fewer than 51 other churches, from Romney Marsh to the North Downs. Some say it's 68 churches, but perhaps that was before the tower was rebuilt, less loftily, after the older one was struck by lightning in 1637.

There was certainly a church in Goudhurst in 1119, and probably long before that. By the beginning of the 14th century, the village had a weekly market and two annual fairs. This was the period during which the Weald generally enjoyed considerable prosperity and, opposite the church, a group of weavers' cottages are a reminder that this was one of those Wealden villages that prospered greatly after the arrival of the Flemish weavers that Edward III encouraged to come and teach their skills to Englishmen.

The village was in the Kentish Weald ironworking region, too. The nearby manor of Bedgebury, better known today to many thousands of visitors for its forest and pinetum, had a quite famous 16th century foundry, owned by the ubiquitous Culpeper family, which cast guns for the fleet that fought the Spanish Armada in 1588.

Bedgebury is one of the oldest estates in Kent, having existed since at least AD 815. It was owned by the de Bedgebury family until about 1450 when it came into the Culpeper family. They lived in a house where the Great Lake now is and Queen Elizabeth stayed there in August 1573 when she knighted the owner, Alexander Colepeper. The Culpeper (the family spelt its name in various ways down the centuries) memorial is the most prominent one in the church, commemorating four generations, but the painted wooden effigies of the ironmaster Sir Thomas Culpeper and his wife form a rare monument of its kind. The estate was sold in 1680 when the house was demolished and a new one built, which became a girls' school in the 1920s.

Bedgebury forest was acquired by the Forestry Commission in 1924, when

London pollution made it necessary for the Royal Botanical Gardens at Kew to create the pinetum and its splendid collection of rare trees and shrubs.

As long ago as 1341 Goudhurst had begun to influence Kentish traditions. Then, the Archbishop of Canterbury decreed that the annual tithe due to the vicar of Goudhurst should include '... onions and all other herbs sown in gardens ...'. That led to a long legal argument about whether hops should be included among 'all other herbs'. The vicar and his supporters believed they should and the argument went their way, with the result that, ever since, Kent hops have been said to grow in gardens rather than in fields or yards as they are in other parts of England.

In 1747, a hastily recruited militia under the leadership of an ex-Army corporal called William Sturt took on and defeated, in what became known as the Battle of Goudhurst, a hundred or so of the most vicious outlaws of the day. They were members of the notorious Hawkhurst Gang of smugglers, including the three Kingsmell (or Kingsmill) brothers, Thomas, Richard and George, who were Goudhurst natives. They treated much of the High Weald countryside around Hawkhurst as if they owned it, riding in to take whatever they wanted and discouraging any opposition with ruthless thoroughness.

When the gang heard about the militia he had formed, its leaders sent a message warning that they would burn every house in Goudhurst and murder everyone in it. They even announced the exact day and hour when they would do it. But when they came, during the morning of Monday, 20th April 1747, the villagers were ready for them and beat them off in a pitched battle in which one of the leaders and two others were killed. The other leaders were later arrested, tried and executed.

Things are quieter in Goudhurst these days, although that is not to say it has not had its explosive moments. During the Second World War the church was damaged and all the glass blown out of its windows when a land mine fell on the village. The church tower was used as a Home Guard observation post and one of the men who manned it was Richard Church, the Kent author who lived in a converted oast house at nearby Curtisden Green.

The war was still not quite over for Goudhurst in 1959 when a local hotelier nearly blew himself up when he tried to use some old piping for electric cable ducting. The piping had been used as tethering rails in the village for some years but before that, unremembered locally, it had been stuffed with explosives as an anti-invasion device in 1940. When the cable wouldn't go through the piping, it was thought it must be blocked with beeswax and it was held over a fire to melt it out. There was a fortunately fairly minor explosion, which led to the discovery that the pipes were still full of nitro-glycerine which could have exploded with disastrous consequences at any time during the previous 20 years.

The former prosperity of the area is vouched for by the wealth of fine old houses that surround the village. Pattyndene Manor dates from 1470 and was once the home of the standard bearer to Henry VIII and, later, to Elizabeth I. Finchcocks is Georgian in a parkland setting, and is internationally famous for the collection of historical keyboard instruments it houses. The timbered Gatehouse at nearby Kilndown was once the home of actress Dame Edith Evans.

Late in the 19th century, James Fegan, founder of Mr Fegan's Homes, made it possible for orphan boys to learn farming on local farms to fit them for emigration to Canada. He died in 1925 and is buried in St Mary's churchyard, with his wife who was killed by a German bomb in 1943.

But Goudhurst is much more than a relic of past glories. It remains one of the more lively, flourishing villages in the High Weald, with a fair share of new building. The new primary school was built at a cost of £1.5 million to replace the overcrowded Victorian building and partly paid for by developers building homes on part of the site.

🍁 GRAIN

The Isle of Grain, rather like the Isle of Thanet, is no longer a discernible island as the result of the silting up of Yantlett Creek, but it is still the furthest extremity of the Hoo Peninsular and the village of Grain is the furthest extremity of the Isle. To describe the approach road to it as rather like an avenue is more accurate than fair, since the word does not suggest chain link fencing with KEEP OUT notices prominently displayed and a general air of inhospitable dereliction even where current activity is keeping actual dereliction at bay. One of Kent's beauty spots this is not, but it is, nevertheless, one of those that helps to pay the bills.

However, people have found it appealing, for changing reasons, for at least 2,000 years. There is Roman tiling built into the fabric of St James' church, which also has a fairly grotesque pagan fertility symbol over one of its doors. Most of the church, which once belonged to a nunnery on the Isle of Sheppey, is 13th century although there was a church there in the 8th century. Repairs were carried out by Dutch sailors who dishonoured Kent's claim to be the Bastion of Britain when they breached the Medway defences and sailed into the river in June 1667, having already taken Sheerness. It was afterwards asserted that the invaders behaved a good deal better, during their intentionally brief and mainly nose-thumbing occupation, than the English militiamen who arrived to 'liberate' the area after the Dutch had made their point and gone home again.

In 1823 the Lord Mayor of London ordered a ditch to be cut to allow boats to pass between Stoke and Grain again, as they could before the silting-up. Local people objected and a special jury at Surrey Assizes ruled that the Corporation of London had committed a nuisance and ordered the road and the causeway that carried it to be restored.

Queen Victoria took a rather curious fancy to Grain as a chosen departure point for trips to Germany. Port Victoria was built essentially as a railway station at the end of a line from Windsor, via Gravesend, and a little jetty from which Her Majesty could embark. The 'port' continued to bask in Royal patronage until 1911, when the Kaiser returned to Germany after attending the coronation of George V. After that, although various members of the Royal Family contributed towards the restoration of the church, the 'port' fell into disuse. The railway line was abandoned, the station rotted away and now only Port Victoria Road, which wanders off in its perpetual search for any skeletal remnants of the jetty, remains to commemorate the days when Royal voyages began and ended here.

But Grain was not permitted similarly to decline into oblivion. Royal patronage was succeeded by industrial development and 19th century prestige was replaced by 20th century commerce when an oil refinery was built here. In 1944, petrol was pumped to Allied invasion forces in France, via the pipeline under the ocean (PLUTO), and in 1953 the sprawling 750 acre British Petroleum Co's Kent oil refinery came into use, processing up to ten million tons of crude oil a year.

That was followed by the building of Grain power station, at the time the largest oil-fired power station in Europe and possibly in the world. Fuelled by oil from the adjacent BP refinery, as was nearby Kingsnorth power station, it was capable of producing enough electricity to meet all the needs of cities the size of Birmingham, Manchester and Liverpool.

But the refinery closed in 1982 and when, in 1987, British Gas unveiled plans to create the UK's second largest deepwater container port on the site, local conservationists feared for the future of rare marshland habitats. They were not at all reassured to be told that it could be at least 20 years before any such development was complete. Today, the Thamesport site is a significant employer and a relatively low-profile contributor to the local landscape of tall chimneys and squat gas and oil storage tanks.

There are plans for yet another power station, the fifth in this part of Kent, to be built at a cost of £400m on part of the former oil refinery site.

🍁 GRAVENEY

The road that follows the coastline from Faversham to Whitstable takes its travellers through Graveney, over the North Kent railway line and past the 12th century church of All Saints, before plunging across Graveney Marshes towards Seasalter. It is a functional village: a pub, a shop and post office, a primary school and a variety of farm buildings and cottages.

In 1971, during the widening of a drainage ditch on the low-lying meadow land behind the sea wall, nearly a mile from the sea now, the village found itself thrust a little reluctantly into public notice as a result of the discovery of what came to be known as the Graveney Boat.

Archaeologists fussed about the old timbers for weeks, guarding their precious find from untutored eyes with a great tent of plastic sheeting. They decided that it was probably a Saxon boat rather than a Viking one as they had at first thought, and that it had, therefore, lain there in the mud for about 1,000 years. They took it out piece by piece and carted it off for reassembly at the National Maritime Museum at Greenwich, leaving Graveney to return to slumb'rous anonymity once more.

This part of Kent has never been in the forefront of the county's history. The local economy was once eked out with a spot of salt panning, though always on a relatively small-scale. It was mentioned in the Domesday survey, when sea brine was collected in pans and transferred to coppers in which the water was boiled off, leaving the salt which was used mainly as a preservative for fish and meat. Salt panning died out certainly before the mid-16th century, when efforts were made to re-establish it to reduce British dependence on imports from France and Spain, made necessary by the population growth in London and other towns. But mined salt from Cheshire proved to be more economically viable, the North Kent coast 'panning' never did revive and Graveney settled into an agriculture-based life-style, with a bit of smuggling now and again to keep the wolf from the door.

The agriculture was seriously threatened by the disastrous flooding in February 1953, which devastated much of the east coast of England. When the water was finally absorbed, the land had to be reconditioned and a great deal of new drainage put in place behind the new sea wall that was built to prevent a recurrence of the disaster.

But Graveney church survived and today it is an attractive little edifice on the very edge of the village, overlooking open countryside beyond. It was probably built during the 12th century and is unusually light inside, most of the windows being of clear glass, only two of them displaying stained glass of the first half of the 14th century. Unfortunately, it is a little way out of the village centre and consequently very vulnerable. In 1998, 730 of its clay tiles, now much sought after and worth about £1,000, were stripped off its roof by thieves.

The neighbouring hamlet of Goodnestone also has a church, St Bartholomew's, which lies back from the road at the end of a narrow lane or causeway where it seems actively to discourage visitors of any kind.

GREATSTONE

In her book *The Gift of the Sea*, Anne Roper says Greatstone took its name from the larger pebbles scoured up-Channel, in contrast to the smaller ones which came from the Dover direction and which gave their name to neighbouring Littlestone.

Between the wars, this was one of those coastal areas where all sorts of holiday homes went up on often totally unsuitable sites and led, too late to save some places, to the Town Planning Acts of the 1940s.

In fact, Greatstone was one of the first places to be regulated by a town plan, so that instead of developing into a haphazard and ramshackle collection of beach huts, it was laid out rather well. The result is one of the happier results of post-war property-owning prosperity, with a resident population well-served by shops and other facilities to meet their everyday needs. But it is also a popular holiday resort, with caravan camps the legendary 'stone's throw' from the beach, where gently sloping sands make it ideal for young families.

During the Second World War some of the bungalows were requisitioned by the Army and used as camouflage for the pumps that were part of the PLUTO (Pipe Line Under The Ocean) installations that supplied fuel to forces taking part in the Normandy landings in 1944. Greatstone holiday camp was taken over, too, but after the war all was returned to residents and holidaymakers and more were built.

St Peter's church is particularly ship-shape because when the growing number of churchgoers baulked at travelling to nearby churches to worship, the community's own church was built – in the shape of a ship.

GROOMBRIDGE

Groombridge teeters on the very borders of Kent and Sussex. In fact, part of it actually spills over into the neighbouring county and there is some local controversy about whether it should remain thus divided or be absorbed wholly into one county or the other.

At one corner of the triangular green the Crown Inn keeps a friendly eye on the 17th century brick church of St John the Evangelist. This began life as a chapel built by a Protestant owner of Groombridge Place in thanksgiving for the failure of Charles I's plans to marry the Catholic Infanta of Spain. The church overlooks the green from across the B2188, from which an access to the Burrswood Centre slices the green into two.

The Burrswood Christian Centre for Health Care and Ministry, established in 1960, includes a church, a conference centre and a tea room. It offers physiotherapy, hydrotherapy and other treatments for physical and spiritual ills in 220 acres of some of the most beautiful countryside in England, itself a balm to both heart and soul.

Two sides of the green are framed by tile-hung and weatherboarded cottages behind pollarded lime trees, creating a picture-postcard scene that is both peaceful and, at the same time, oddly lifeless, in spite of the fairly constant stream of traffic that passes it.

There is, though, nothing lifeless about moated Groombridge Place, which advertises its welcome to paying customers to explore the wholly delightful gardens and grounds. The house, although not open to the public, can still be admired from across the moat. It boasts a 700-year history, beginning in 1239, when Henry III gave his permission for a fortified and moated castle to be built. In 1286, a Charter of Edward I permitted the founding of a weekly market and annual fair at Groombridge. The fair died out in the early 1900s but the market was still being held every week until the middle of the century.

Through the centuries, Groombridge Place has been owned by some of Kent's most distinguished families, including the de Cobhams and that Sir Richard Waller who, after the Battle of Agincourt in 1415, found the wounded Duke of Orleans, half-brother of the French King, and brought him back to Groombridge. Here he was nursed back to health while waiting for the ransom that was demanded for his return to be paid. Unfortunately for Sir Richard, word got around and the prisoner was claimed by the Crown, as was the huge ransom that was eventually paid for him.

After the Wallers, the castle was owned by the Sackvilles (of Knole, at Sevenoaks) but it was the 17th century owner, Philip Packer, who rebuilt it pretty much as it is today. After 1734, the house lay empty and falling into dereliction for 20 years, during which time it may well have been used by the notorious Groombridge Gang of smugglers as a 'hide'. The gang was finally broken up and one of its leaders, John Bowra, who turned land agent and map-maker, was commissioned to draw up an estate plan, which is still preserved at Groombridge Place.

The new owner, William Camfield, restored not only the house but St John's church and the village generally. After the Camfields, the estate was inherited by the Rev John James Saint and his family, who are commemorated pretty prominently in the churchyard.

The diarist John Evelyn, who was a friend of the Packers during their ownership and stayed at Groombridge Place more than once, described it as 'a pretty melancholy seat, well wooded and watered' and he confided to his diary his opinion that the new house would have been far better situated south of the wood. Nevertheless, there is some reason to believe he helped design the gardens although he probably did not envisage such features as the Enchanted Forest, Sacred Pools, Draughtsman's Garden with its giant chess and draughts sets, and much else besides, all designed to help Groombridge Place compete with other major visitor attractions.

 HADLOW

The Medway valley does its best to camouflage its villages in lush woodlands, but there is no hiding Hadlow, thanks to Walter Barton May. About 150 years ago he added a 170 foot tall tower to the Hadlow Castle his father had built and now, despite having had the 40 foot high octagonal lantern on the top removed for safety reasons, the tower still soars above the village and commands attention from miles around.

It is, in fact, one of the largest follies in Britain. Some say May built it so that he could see over the surrounding countryside to the sea. Others believe it was built as a folly, inspired by Beckford's tower at Fonthill Abbey in Wiltshire. The most popular, though the least likely, story is that he built his tower purposely so that he could keep an eye on his wife after she left him and went home to mother, just down the road at Fishall!

The May family came to Hadlow in 1647, but the village was already well established by then. Stone Age men had used flint tools nearby and the church celebrated a thousand years in 1975 although it was rebuilt in the 12th century, the steeple was added in 1568 and there have been other restorations and alterations since.

King John gave Hadlow to the Order of Knights Hospitallers of St John of Jerusalem. They held it until 1540 when Henry VIII sold it to the Fane family, who built Hadlow Place.

The 'castle', which was never anything of the kind, was saved from demolition in 1951 by portrait painter Bernard Hailstone, but only after part of it had already been demolished. The tower and the lodge gateway that gives access to the castle from the A26, which is the village main street, were protected by a preservation order and what remained of the rest was adapted for private ownerships. New homes were built in the grounds, creating a very pleasant and exclusive little private estate.

Walter Barton May was an eccentric man. In a corner of the neighbouring churchyard is the decaying grandeur of the May mausoleum, which he ordered to be built so that he could be buried, seated, above ground. His wish was not carried out. He was, in fact, buried quite conventionally, but the mausoleum remains as his memorial.

Also in the churchyard is a 19th century memorial to 30 hop-pickers who were drowned when the cart in which they were crossing the Hart Lake bridge fell into the water, taking them with it.

Today, Hadlow has a neat and tidy look. Its main street is attractively brick paved and passes by several old and attractive buildings, including the Old Bakery and two Tudor inns. The conversion of The Maltings into luxury apartments and penthouses has retained the old kilns with their white cowls to remind us that this was in the very heart of the Mid Kent hop-growing and brewing country no more than half a century ago. Hadlow College, on the southern edge of the village, keeps alive the farming traditions of this part of Kent and invites visitors to the various gardens and garden centre maintained by the students.

🍁 HALLING

During the 19th and early 20th century, the River Medway, which had been a major Kent thoroughfare for many centuries before that, assumed new significance as the demand for building materials encouraged more excavation of chalk and clay for cement making.

The river winds through the North Downs, which are virtually all chalk, and many cement works were opened and enlarged upstream almost as far as Maidstone, bringing employment and prosperity to riverside villages like Halling. Cement became the dominant industry and, according to Donald Maxwell, writing in 1921: 'From Halling to Snodland, the river is literally walled on one side or the other with kilns and loading barges.'

By that time, in fact, the industry had passed its peak and many of the kilns and towering chimneys were falling into ruin. The first half of the 20th century was a period of depression for the whole area, mainly because of the decline of the cement and brick industries in the Medway valley which mirrored the decline into which the construction industry fell during the same period.

New production methods concentrated cement manufacture into larger works, like the one at Northfleet, which had an effect on the smaller factories along the Medway. However, production at Halling and neighbouring Snodland continued. In fact, in 1998 battle was joined between the Blue Circle cement company and local conservationists over plans to open a new works on land between the two villages, which gives a hint of how much less importance the industry has to the local economy now.

But at least one man knew Halling, even if he had no name for it then, 4,000 years ago because his remains were found just behind the railway station in 1912. His only means of transportation, of course, were his own two feet and dug-out canoes like the one – his, for all we know – that was found when the foundations were being dug for an electricity pylon on Halling marshes. Even he was no pioneer in these parts, as evidenced by the discovery of a much earlier skeleton, surrounded by flint chips and the bones of a horse and a sheep, all of whom lived 25,000 years ago.

Long after all these early inhabitants were dead, Romans were charactistically careless with their small change hereabouts, but Halling's history can be said to have begun when Bishop Gundulph of Rochester built a palace there in 1077. By that time, there was already a church on land given to the church of St Andrew at Rochester by King Egbert of Kent during the 8th century. The palace was the last sanctuary of Archbishop of Canterbury Thomas Becket's successor, Richard, in 1184.

Richard was at the palace at Wrotham when he had a vision in which he was accused of destroying the Church and warned that he, too, would be destroyed. Next day, while on his way to Rochester, he was taken, sick and shaking, to Halling, where he died in the bishop's palace that same night. Some said he was poisoned but perhaps there was something about the place that did not agree with visiting bishops, because after that several Bishops of Rochester died there.

One who did not was Bishop Fisher, whose involvement with Elizabeth Barton, the so-called Holy Maid of Kent, led him to the Tower and execution in 1535. His death ended the connection between the bishops and the palace at Halling, part of which was, however, later to become the home of William Lambarde, the man who is remembered as the author of the first county history, *A Perambulation of Kent*, published in 1576.

Lambarde had three wives. The first was a teenager from Ightham. It was the second, a widow called Sylvestre Dalison, who brought him to Halling, her home. They were married in 1583 but she died shortly after giving birth to twins in 1587 and is commemorated in Halling's St John the Baptist church with a memorial that shows her sitting up in bed with her six children, including the twins, around her. Lambarde married for the third time, another widow, in 1592 and lived on in Halling until 1598. He died in 1601.

There is a local story that William Caxton, 'The Father of English Printing', also married a local girl and set up a printing press in the village, but there is little hard evidence that it is true.

The bishop's palace survived into the 19th century as a farmhouse but was finally demolished when the cement works were built on the site. All that remains today is a bit of wall around the churchyard.

The village, which shares its bypass with Snodland, grew considerably during the 1990s, with many new homes. It is, in fact, still growing and in 1995 a new primary school was built in the High Street, to replace the 19th century one in Vicarage Road.

🍁 HARRIETSHAM

For anyone with the time and be-bothered-ness to explore a little, there is much more to Harrietsham than meets the eye of the A20 traveller.

The village is split into two parts by the road and both parts veil themselves from the frenzied traffic behind some fairly unlovely roadside development. But on the south side, in East Street for instance, there is the old Bell public house and nearby Bell Farmhouse has been called the most complete example of a traditional Wealden house remaining in Kent.

Newer, but also attractive in their different way, are the terrace of almshouses that Mark Quested built in 1642. He was a local man who became a member of the City of London Fishmongers' Company, which paid for the rebuilding of the almshouses in 1770.

On the north side of the village, a row of white painted cottages dabble their footings in the little Len stream that flows under West Street behind the Roebuck Inn. Harrietsham's church of St John the Baptist is on the north side, too, somewhat aloof from the rest of the village. Parts date from Norman or possibly Saxon times, although much of it today is 14th century with a 15th century tower.

Just below the Pilgrims' Way on Stede Hill is Stede Court, a house that has had many different owners and several different names during its 400 year life. Just before the beginning of the Second World War it was restored by architect and author Robert Goodsall, who gave it back its old name.

It was in 1575 that half the original Harrietsham manor came into the ownership of William Stede. He bought the other half as well in 1579 and for 200 hundred years successive members of the family were the most prominent of local landowners. The house was forfeited by Dr William Stede, a lawyer who was charged with helping the Kent Royalist rebels in 1648 and had to sell the house to pay his fine. However, his son, Edwyn, who was born in Barbados and became Lieutenant Governor there, came home in about 1693 and restored the family fortunes. The house was finally sold out of the family by a later Edwyn, grandson of the first one, whose fondness for cricket cost him more lost wagers than he could afford.

During the war the house served several purposes and it was for a time an Army officers' mess where Field Marshal Montgomery and Lt-Gen Brian Horrocks were just two of a number of war-time VIPs to be entertained.

In 1948 there were plans for a holiday centre and homes at the top of Stede Hill itself. Owners of land there, who stood to profit substantially from such a development, were highly indignant when the new Town and Country Planning Act prevented it.

A Harrietsham legend tells of Nicholas Wood, a local lad in the early 1600s, whose enormous appetite earned him a somewhat freakish reputation. He dined out – so to speak – on his appetite, which enabled him to consume, at one sitting, no fewer than 84 rabbits and at another a whole hog followed by three pecks (equivalent to six gallons) of damsons. It was said that he would grease his belly with butter to stretch the skin in order to be able to eat more.

🍁 HAWKHURST

Hawkhurst is sometimes described as two villages in one because of the difference in character between the older area around The Moor and the newer at Highgate. The individuality of the two areas is underlined by the fact that each has its own church, even if the later one is now redundant.

The village clusters round the crossroads formed by the Rochester-Hastings A229 road and the road up from Rye (A268) that joins the A21, and the east-west cross-Sussex route.

It is one of the largest villages in Kent, comparable with Cranbrook and, like Cranbrook, it has the origins of its prominence in the great days of the Wealden woollens industry, in the 14th, 15th and 16th centuries. When the Weald surrendered its industrial pre-eminence to coal-rich areas further north, it experienced periods of hardship during which smuggling supplemented the incomes of many local families and Hawkhurst became the operational headquarters of the infamous 18th century Hawkhurst Gang. Several of the local buildings, including Hawkhurst Place, the Tudor Arms hotel and Tickners, claim associations with the gang.

But although it was wool and smuggling that wrote some of the most memorable pages of Hawkhurst's history, the village was well established long before either of them. Although not mentioned in the Domesday survey, the village was known to William the Conqueror. When he founded Battle Abbey, to commemorate his victory over Saxon Harold, he gave the Royal Manor of Wye to the new abbey and Hawkhurst was one of the Wye 'dens' that went with the gift. A century later, Abbot Odo of Battle

Hawkhurst.

confirmed for Hawkhurst undisturbed possession of their holdings for a yearly rent of £10, 20 hens and 250 eggs. A century after that, Abbot Henry of Aylesford reduced the rent to £8, without amending the number of hens and eggs.

St Laurence's church, beside The Moor, was certainly founded before the Norman Conquest. It is much the older of the two Hawkhurst churches and, like so many in this part of Kent, it is built of the local sandstone which ages into warm honey-coloured hues. A flying bomb (V1, or doodlebug) fell in the churchyard in 1944 and did a great deal of damage. The restoration work was not completed until 1957, when the church was re-dedicated by the Archbishop of Canterbury. The great east window, dating from about 1350 and said to be one of the finest pieces of architecture in the county, fortunately escaped serious damage, although all the glass was lost. It was replaced in 1956. One casualty of the bomb was a memorial to astronomer Sir John Herschel, who lived in Hawkhurst from 1840 until 1871.

An interesting sidelight is thrown upon church-going in former times by an entry in Hawkhurst church records for 1842, when it was resolved that 'the urinaries be removed from the sides of the entrances to the church and that a Necessary with urinaries attached be erected adjoining to the parish stables building, contiguous to the churchyard.'

Highgate is the part of the village most visitors know best. That is where the famous Victorian colonnaded parade of shops is. It is almost unchanged since it was first built and forms an eye-catching centre-piece for this part of the village. The Royal Oak was a row of three 16th century cottages before it was converted to a posting inn and All Saints' church dates from the 1860s, designed by the architect Sir George Gilbert Scott. It is redundant now and at the time of writing a small battle is being waged over whether it should be converted into flats or used as a community centre.

William Rootes set up shop in Hawkhurst as a cycle trader before ambition and opportunity conspired to take him and his two sons, William and Reginald, into the more lucrative production of Hillman, Humber and Sunbeam cars and so into English automobile history as founder of the Rootes car empire. In 1886 the famous Babies' Castle, the largest country home of the Dr Barnado organisation, was opened by HRH Princess Mary Adelaide, Duchess of Teck, and her daughter Princess Mary, later George V's Queen Mary. The home became an adult care centre in 1963.

🍁 HEADCORN

Headcorn is one of the county's larger villages, just far enough from Maidstone to encourage independence and with enough history to support a robust identity of its own. A railway village, with its own railway station, it is an attractive part of Kent's commuter belt, as is evidenced by the amount of new building in and around the village.

The main street is flanked by some attractive half-timbered houses, including the Old Cloth Hall, a reminder that this is yet another of those Wealden communities that shared in the boom in woollens production that followed the 14th century arrival of Flemish immigrants and lasted until the industry moved north during the 17th and 18th centuries.

The Old Vicarage, now Headcorn Manor, is a Wealden hall house and there were once four windmills serving the village and the surrounding countryside. Now there is one – and that is only to be found on the village sign which stands in a corner of the village green, well-screened among the summer foliage of the trees.

For several centuries the Headcorn oaks were more famous than any of its buildings. But then, in the mid-20th century, Authority decreed that they must be felled because they had become unsafe. Villagers protested vigorously, and even formed vigilante groups to protect their trees, but they lost out to Authority's insistence and trees that, according to local legend at least, had left their acorns in the days before Headcorn emerged as a village in the great Wealden forest, were sacrificed to a new sewerage system.

One, however, remained: a gnarled and riven veteran, said to be more than a thousand years old, still growing in the churchyard. Local tradition claimed the tree was already well-grown when visiting monks preached beneath its canopy before the church was built. It was also said that King John sat in its shade while he enjoyed a spot of 13th century bull-baiting when he visited the village once. In *The Annals of Headcorn* in 1878, Robert Furley wrote that the tree's girth at its base was 46ft 8ins and in 1966 a local photographer proved – well, the camera cannot lie! – that no fewer than 27 children could cram into its hollow trunk.

As it grew old, the tree was thought to be in need of support and wooden props were put against it. But after a while it was found that the props had rotted away and only stayed in position because they were held up by the tree. However, time and the vandals who lit fires in the hollow trunk, had their inevitable wicked way with even so famous a tree, which was pretty well destroyed by fire in April 1989 and was finally felled, like all the others. Today, only its noble stump, overgrown with weeds, remains, marked by a plaque which relates that far-seeing villagers in 1940 recognised that the old tree's days were numbered and planted one of its acorns which grew into the very fine chip off the old block 50 yards away, where it looks ready to keep an eye on Headcorn for another thousand years.

The approach to the church of St Peter and St Paul is by way of an avenue of horse chestnut trees planted to commemorate the diamond jubilee of Queen Victoria. There has been a church on the site since 1100 and probably some time before that although most of the present building is 14th and 15th century. The church guide claims that the roof is perhaps the finest in Kent and the greatest single glory of the building.

In 1224 the first Priory of the Friars of the Holy Trinity was founded at nearby Moatenden by Robert Rokesley. Also known as the Crutched Friars, they were granted tenancy of the manor in 1249 on condition that they provided a priest for the local people, which they did for more than 200 years, until the Black Death reduced their number to two.

Just outside the village, at Lashenden, a Second World War airfield reverted to private ownership after the war was over and is still used for private flying and parachute jump training. In 1985 owner Chris Freeman won an award from the Civil Aviation Authority for having the best privately owned airfield in the country, but for most of the past 50 years he has warded off the antagonism of some of the local people who object very strongly to the take-off and landing noises of aircraft that punctuate the Wealden peace.

🍁 Herne

There is a sort of sad inevitability about the way the little village of Herne is losing its individuality to the encroachment of surrounding development. Its white weatherboard houses still make a pretty enough picture, but it is a fleeting one that tends to be blurred by the much more strident impressions left by the nearby town of Herne Bay and its still growing suburban estates.

Chronologically, it is the town that is the satellite of the village. Herne has had its unexpectedly grand church of St Martin of Tours for all of 600 years, since it was founded during the 14th century. A few years ago evidence of an earlier church on the same site was discovered. It was at Herne's flinty church that Nicholas Ridley, when he was vicar there, allowed the Te Deum to be sung in English for the first time in England. Ridley went on to become a Bishop and supported Archbishop Cranmer in what Queen Mary called 'corrupt and naughty opinions' about who should be Queen of England, which earned him martyrdom at the stake in Oxford in 1555.

John Ruskin, the 19th century art critic and author, is supposed to have declared that Herne church tower was one of the three most perfect things in the world. Modern historians have proved, to their own satisfaction at least, that he said no such thing – at any rate, not about Herne church tower. A pity. Such a commendation would not embarrass the tower of Herne church in the least.

In the 1960s, workmen pulling down a row of cottages uncovered an oblong black metal plate engraved with a picture of a boy and girl in early Stuart or possibly Tudor costume. It proved to be a long-lost piece of a memorial brass to John Atte Sea and his family. He lived at Herne from 1575 until 1605, with his first wife Martha until she died in 1586 and after that with his second wife, Sara. He had eleven children. The family home, Strode Park, is today a residential home for disabled people.

A notable landmark in Herne is the 18th century smock mill on Beacon Hill, a direct descendant of a mill first mentioned on the site in 1511. The present building dates from 1781 and was falling into disrepair when members of Herne Society took it in hand in 1971 and raised money for its restoration.

In his book *Reminiscences of a Country Parson*, the Rev Giles Daubeney recalled that when he came to Herne from Benenden in 1905 there were three men in the village still who had been smugglers all their lives. The old associations are commemorated today in the name of one of the village inns, The Smugglers.

Today, Herne Common is the home of Brambles wildlife park, one of the largest wildlife sanctuaries in Kent.

🍁 HERNHILL

On a high point looking northwards towards the coast west of Whitstable over the Graveney marshes, Hernhill hovers in a thoroughly acceptable way round its rectangular village green. John Newman, in his book in Nikolaus Pevsner's *The Buildings of England* series, commented that Hernhill green is all it should be and, really, it couldn't be better expressed today.

The Red Lion Inn, across the green from the church, is a Wealden hall house that is almost as delightful to look at as it is to go into. The date on the wall is 1364 and there is a wall sundial, too. Behind the inn, Walnut Tree House is 16th century but with Saxon foundations, clearly proud of the Historic House of Kent badge it wears on its wall.

Along the back of the green the central facade of a picturesque row of 19th century cottages on the site of the old vicarage and tithe barn is interrupted enticingly by a central arch. Local lore claims there is church treasure buried beneath them. Manor House with its half-timbered north end wing and its brick crenellated addition encroaches upon the churchyard.

Across the road that passes the green, Church Farm buildings include a round kiln oast which, since hops are no longer grown locally, has been converted into a very attractive private home.

One approach to the village, from the Faversham end, passes the very old Three Horseshoes pub, which can trace its landlords back 300 years. At the other end is The Dove, a former Victorian beer-house, and 200 year old Bessborough Farmhouse, which once housed the parish paupers. Tourist attractions include the gardens and vineyard of Mount Ephraim, which are open to the public.

Orchards cover much of the surrounding countryside and, one way and another, Hernhill is a very attractive little village indeed. Very understandably, it is a designated conservation area, over which the 15th century church of St Michael presides with a kind of lofty pride.

There was an earlier church on the site, dedicated to St Stephen, and even that may well have been on a site of pre-Christian religious significance. The present building is one of relatively few Perpendicular style churches in Kent and has been little changed during the last 500 years. Some of the stained glass in the windows is thought to be 16th century, possibly from Northern Europe.

An oak tree planted on the green in 1935 to commemorate George V's silver jubilee has seats on both sides, one of them provided to mark the coronation of his grand-daughter, Elizabeth II, in 1953.

It was to the churchyard at Hernhill that the body of the man they called Mad Thom, but who took for himself the name of Sir William Courtenay (to which he was not entitled), was brought. His brief career as a Parliamentary candidate, self-acclaimed Messiah and small-time rabble-rouser ended in 1838 at the battle in Bossenden Wood (described in the entry for Dunkirk), when he was shot down by soldiers sent to arrest him. No one can show you the grave site because it was not marked, so that the morbidly curious should not disinter him for relics. The grave is said to have been dug only four feet deep, four paces north of the north chancel door, but there is no evidence of it there now.

Six others who were killed with Thom in that battle were also buried in the churchyard during a two-hour service that was conducted without any psalms or hymns being sung because the choir men were all either among the dead or in prison awaiting trial for their part in the affair. The names of the dead, however, are recorded on a plaque against a sundial in the churchyard.

Robert Goodsall, in his *Fourth Kentish Patchwork* published in 1974, claimed it was Hernhill (which, incidentally, he never did spell correctly, without a middle 'e') and not the more commonly assumed Herne, near Herne Bay, that Somerset Maugham used as his model for Ferne in *Of Human Bondage*.

HEVER

There is more to Hever than just the castle – but not a lot more. There is St Peter's church, the Henry VIII inn and a short street of houses, some old and some not so old, and that really is about all there is to the village. Yet this must surely be one of the best-known and historically most significant villages not only in Kent but throughout England.

The castle is old, no doubt about that, although it has been pretty thoroughly renovated during the last hundred years. The huge gatehouse, the outer walls and the moat were all built in about 1270 and it was the Bullen family (it did not become Boleyn until after they went up in the world and before they came back down in the world again during the 16th century) that added the Tudor house inside the walls.

The family fortunes were at their height when its most famous daughter, Anne, caught the Royal eye. Poor Anne. How different might have been the history of England if Henry VIII had not lost his heart to her and she her head to him.

There must have been something about the Bullen women that particularly captivated the king. Elizabeth Howard became the king's mistress after she had married Sir Thomas Bullen. One of the daughters of the marriage, Mary, comforted the royal heirlessness for a while until her young sister, Anne, usurped her in the king's affections.

When a king went a-courting in those days he did so with a considerable retinue that had to be entertained by the lady's family while the lady entertained the monarch. It was no small expense to have the king dropping in at all hours, although Sir Thomas was mollified if not actually recompensed with a succession of titles. No doubt he made his guest as welcome as that guest thought proper until, at last, Henry was able to divorce his Queen Catherine in defiance of the Pope and Anne was duly crowned Queen of England on May Day 1533.

The marriage saddled her with a reputation of having seduced the king away from his faith as well as his wife. The reformation was begun that founded the Church of England and paved the way for some of the most cruelly bloody religious persecutions the country would ever know.

In September that year, the royal couple's first child was born; a girl they called Elizabeth (later, of course, Elizabeth I) and not the son the king craved. That was Anne's first misfortune. Her second was a miscarriage in 1534, followed by a still-birth and then another miscarriage. It was too much for the volatile Henry, whose disappointment boiled over in rage. He ended the marriage by having Anne executed by a specially commissioned French swordsman on Tower Hill, for the High Treason of adultery with five men, including her own brother.

So ended the Thousand Days of Boleyn glory. Her father, disgraced Sir Thomas, died two years later and was buried in St Peter's church at Hever, where he is commemorated by one of the finest church brasses in England. His wife and his heir, Anne's brother George, were both already dead, so the king claimed the Hever estate for himself. He later gave it to his divorced fourth wife, Anne of Cleves, who lived there until she died in 1557 – surely one of the most insensitive gifts of all time, even for a man whose sensitivities were very much more his servants than his masters.

After that, the castle began a slow decline. During the 18th century it was a private house and notorious as a centre of the Kent and Sussex border country smuggling trade. A century after that it was no more than a humble farmhouse.

But then in 1903 the house was bought by William Waldorf Astor, the New York millionaire and one-time American Ambassador in Rome, who became a naturalised Briton and was later created Viscount Astor of Hever. Like many another convert, he became more English than the English and he chose Hever upon which to lavish his investment in his chosen life-style. He employed the architect Frank L. Pearson and, it is said, 2,000 workmen to undertake a four-year programme of restoration of the building and the creation of magnificent gardens. Most of what Hever Castle is today is the result of his work.

William Waldorf Astor died in 1919 and his younger son, John Jacob VII, MP for Dover from 1922 until 1945, became the first Baron Astor of Hever. It was his son, the second Baron, who became chairman of the board of The Times Publishing Company and later Life President of Times Newspapers, and who first opened Hever Castle to the public. He and his wife, Lady Irene, lived there from 1962 until 1982 when he resigned as Lord Lieutenant of Kent and retired to Scotland, where he died soon afterwards.

Despite an income of nearly £400,000 a year from the visitors who came to Hever, the cost of maintaining such a national monument privately was more than the family wanted to continue to bear. In 1981 they decided to sell the castle and the 3,500 acre estate, and it was offered for sale at £10.5 million, plus £3 million for the contents which were sold separately. The house and estate were bought by Yorkshire-based Broadland Properties, but the castle and grounds remain open to the public, both day visitors and longer stay residents, as a conference centre as well as a stately home.

The old gateway is the finest remaining at any castle in England and two of the three portcullises are original, the outer one probably the only one in England still capable of being lowered to keep out unwelcome guests.

❧ HIGHAM

In fact, there are really two Highams, Upper and Lower, forming one long parish that includes the hamlets of Upshire, Gads Hill, Chequers Street, Gore Green, Church Street and Lillechurch. The parish church of St John, built in 1862, is in the main village which is just off the A226 Gravesend-Rochester road.

Lower Higham is further north and Higham Church Street is as far north as a vehicle can take you. It is at the end of a very minor road that doesn't so much end as fray out into farmland which spreads itself out across Cliffe Marshes until it, too, frays out on the southern bank of the River Thames, looking across to the Tilbury Marshes on the Essex side.

Higham Church Street is certainly remote, but on a fine, warm summer's day, it is a very pleasant little haven of peace and tranquillity. Only the very few people who need to would be foolhardy enough to visit it on any other sort of day, anyway. It was once an important trading and religious centre at a point where it was possible to cross the Thames by a causeway that linked Essex with Kent.

Then, there was an abbey hard by the church, which was known as St Mary-at-the-Abbey. The church, which is built of ragstone, with bands of flint, (similar to that of St Helen's church at nearby Cliffe) was remodelled in the 14th century, but there is still evidence of Saxon and Norman work. Early in the 18th century the boarded belfry and shingled spire were added and in 1863 the church was thoroughly restored and further added to. One of the remaining original features is the splendid medieval carved door.

Its churchyard is the last resting-place of many of the navvies who lost their lives during the building of the canal tunnel through Higham towards Strood. The canal was never completed and the tunnel was used for the railway that linked Port Victoria, on the Isle of Grain, with Gravesend.

Today, the few farm buildings of Abbey Farm are the only near neighbours and there is very little trading done at Higham Church Street. What religion survives there, only the handful of residents will know. The church has been supported by the Redundant Churches Fund since 1987.

The Benedictine nunnery that left Abbey Farm its name was founded by King Stephen in 1148. His youngest daughter, Princess Mary, was Prioress and the nunnery was still there in 1512 because it was then that the vicar of the church, one Edward Steroper, was reprimanded by his bishop for keeping company with one of the nuns, a certain Lady Anchoretta Ungelthorpe.

Perhaps he was not the only one who 'kept company' with the nuns, either. It surely was not necessary for the Prioress, a year later, to petition the bishop for a wall to be built round the nunnery, 'for the increase in virtue and observance of the rule', in order to fend off the attentions of just one vicar?

On the other hand, though, in 1520 – by which time the Lady Anchoretta had become Prioress and admitted she had taken money from the Common Chest of the nunnery in order to pay debts owed to her sister – two other nuns were said to have borne children fathered by the vicar, so perhaps the wall was needed after all.

Anyway, the nunnery was closed in 1522 and scarcely a breath of scandal has emerged from what survived of the old village since!

It was to Chequers Street that the Gravesend-Rochester railway came in 1845 and there that Higham Station was built, just about halfway between Lower Higham and the former hamlet of Higham Upshire, which is now the larger centre of population. The railway tunnel between Higham and Frindsbury, two and a quarter miles long, was designed for the Thames and Medway Canal by William Tierney Clark, who also built an iron bridge over the Danube at Budapest. But when canals began to give way to railways, the route was adopted by the Gravesend and Rochester Railway, which later became part of the South Eastern Railway network.

Upper Higham began to emerge as the main centre of population during the 18th century, after river traffic declined and rail and road became the magnets for trade and residence. Gad's Hill was a notorious place for highwaymen who waited until the travellers had slowed their pace on the hill and then relieved them of such encumbrances as their purses and other valuables.

The Sir John Falstaff inn recalls that it was here where Shakespeare's great comic character had his own taste of highway robbery in company with Prince Hal. Here, too, began the Dick Turpin legend after a gentleman was robbed on the hill early one summer morning. He afterwards identified his robber who, however, was able to prove he was with the Lord Mayor of York at 8.30 pm that same day and was acquitted of the robbery by a jury that could not bring itself to believe a man could be in Higham and York on the same day.

Later the robber was convicted of other offences and admitted the crime, telling how he had ridden to Gravesend, forced a ferryman to take him and his horse over the river, and had then ridden across Essex to Cambridge and so to York. He went to a fete in the York tea-gardens and deliberately engaged the Mayor in conversation for some minutes to establish his alibi. The hero of this exploit was not called Dick Turpin, who was a different character altogether, but a well-known Kent highwayman called Swift Nick.

Almost opposite the Sir John Falstaff inn is Gad's Hill Place, built by a man called Stevens, a barely literate ostler at an inn who was canny enough to marry the landlord's widow, became a brewer and reached the pinnacle of social achievement by becoming Mayor of Rochester. Now the house is a school, but once it was the home of Charles Dickens, who lived there from 1856. It was in the garden of this house that the author had his famous Swiss chalet workroom, in which he was working on the story of Edwin Drood the day before he died in June 1870. His daughter, Katey, married Charles Allston Collins, younger brother of the writer Wilkie Collins, at St Mary's church in 1860.

 HIGH HALDEN

High Halden is on the edge of Romney Marsh and has been an inhabited spot for many, many years. Tiffenden Manor, south of the village green, claims to have been farmed continuously for more than a thousand years.

The village was the original Kent seat of the Hales family which played a significant part in county history for centuries and stemmed from Nicholas Hales, who lived at Hales Place, on the Woodchurch road, in about 1330. Sir Robert Hales was, among other things, Lord Treasurer to Richard II at the time of the Peasants' Revolt in 1381, an office that made him a target for the rebels' resentment and got him killed.

Edward Hasted, in the 1700s, did not think a lot of High Halden. He spoke of it as being 'situated very obscurely, in as unpleasant a part as any within this county.' William Ireland did not find it a lot better when he wrote of it in his *History of Kent* in 1830. He described it as 'very retired, damp and as unpleasant as any I have seen in the county.'

Today, the village has a rather open look about it and there seem to be more new than old houses. There used to be a railway linking the village with Tenterden and Headcorn, but that was closed in 1954.

In the 19th century, Henry Latter built a house on the site of Harbourne Hall, which featured in G. P. R. James' novel *The Smuggler*. In fact, the house in the novel was a fictitious one, although on the real Harbourne Hall site. It is said that when Mr Latter read the novel he became so dissatisfied with the old house that he had it pulled down and another built on the pattern of the one in the book, using bricks made from clay dug on the site and timber felled on the estate.

The old house was linked with some of the leading smuggling families of these parts and the Ransleys, one-time leaders of the notorious 18th and 19th century Hawkhurst and Aldington Gangs, rented land on the Harbourne estate. George Ransley began life as a farmer, prospered as a smuggler and built the Bourne Tap at Aldington in which to settle as an innkeeper and master smuggler.

During the Second World War the house was an Army headquarters where some of the details of the D-Day invasion were planned. Although several bombs were dropped in the area, the house itself was never hit, despite the fact that in 1944 the local Home Guard captured a man in Harbourne woods while he was in the very act of signalling to enemy aircraft to help them pinpoint their Harbourne House target. Since then, the old house has been demolished and the site is now occupied by a new one built in 1980.

High Halden was one of the villages where the sport of goal running was played. This seems to have been a uniquely Kentish sport, popular during the late 18th, 19th and the first half of the 20th centuries, when it was played with robust enthusiasm by several teams engaged in knock-out competition. Surviving reports suggest that some of the teams took the knock-out part rather too literally and what rules there were seem to have been wholly inherited and subject to local variations. Yet players wore their own colours and travelled quite widely in order to compete against other teams. Teams seem to have been anything from 10 to 20 strong, with spectators recruited on the spot if one team turned up with fewer members than its opponents were fielding.

As far as can be gathered from surviving reports, the object of the game was for each member of a team to make a 30-yard dash to circle the opposing team's 'point' flag without being 'tagged' by his opponents. Some of the 'tagging' could be very robust indeed and sometimes resulted in retaliation and a free-for-all in which supporters joined with equal enthusiasm.

🍁 HIGH HALSTOW

In no sense a twin of its Lower namesake, some seven miles away on the other side of the River Medway, High Halstow is a high and airy place with a wide-awake and generally modern look. The pub, beside the church, is 16th century and was originally the parsonage but there are few other signs that this is, in fact, a long-settled place.

The local Women's Institute celebrated its 25th anniversary in 1982 by erecting a village sign on the signpost in the tiny triangle of green opposite the church, where the road branches off down towards Hoo. The sign features a standing heron, a reference to the Northward Hill nature reserve. Today, the village has another, more elaborate double-sided sign in two mosaic discs built into a wall in front of the village medical centre.

St Margaret's church is an unusually low-profile building, with a very squat tower, capped by a low pyramid of a spire, entirely rebuilt in the 18th century. The age of the church is confirmed by the 14th century brass memorial to one of its priests, although otherwise the interior is curiously bare of memorials and the churchyard is similarly bereft. It suggests that no one important enough – or (by no means the same thing) rich enough – to warrant permanent remembrance has died in High Halstow during the past 600 years.

The bells of St Margaret's have been ringing out over the Hoo Peninsular since 1675, but early in the 20th century the vibration they caused threatened to bring down the church tower. They were no longer rung in the old way, but instead were equipped so that they could be chimed by one man. The system enabled the great tongues to swing rather than the bells themselves, which was quieter and safer, too. Then, in 1983, the five bells were restored at a cost of £9,000 and a certain amount of volunteer labour and rehung on metal supports which replaced the old wooden ones first built into the church in about 1350.

The village is one of the oldest in the district and from its prominence on a low ridge of ground among the surrounding reclaimed marshes enjoys a view of probably the greatest variety of scenery of any on the Hoo Peninsular. There is excellent grazing on land that may have been claimed originally by Romans but was certainly very much improved by Dutch engineers during the 17th century and English farmers since then.

Like so many villages all round the Kent coastline, and especially, perhaps, on the North Kent marshes, High Halstow admits to having been a resort of smugglers right up into the 19th century. It was probably never more than a fairly local trade on a small scale and nothing like that which went on along the south coast and up into the High Weald.

High Halstow is a big village that is getting bigger. There has been a lot of new building during the 20th century and a major new estate at the Grain end of the main street will increase its size still further.

 HOATH

Some of the East Kent villages are very small indeed; mere pinpricks on even quite large-scale maps. Hoath is one of those.

It is almost an intrusion upon the prairie-like countryside in which it sits; a sort of thin crust of human settlement on either side of the road that seems to have lost its way in an unpeopled landscape south of Herne Bay. Yet it has been there certainly for 500 years, if the date, 1440, on Clayhanger Farm is to be believed.

The little flint church of Holy Cross even keeps its dedication to itself. The wayfarer will look in vain for any outward admission to the name. Yet it, too, has been there since the early 14th century, although most of the building today is Victorian, with a vaguely incongruous-looking wooden bell-tower and steeple. Next to the church is Hoath Court – and that, together with the pub, just about sums up Hoath village.

A little further along the same road, however (if you happen to be travelling from west to east) is the hamlet of Marshside – appropriately named, since it is as far as it is possible to go without plunging into the Chislet Marshes that border the vestigial Wantsum Channel which once made Thanet a true island. Marshside is no greater a metropolis than is Hoath, but it has a more lived-in look and it does have a very pleasant pub, the Gate Inn, which features a pond-side garden and a somewhat raddled old pillory just outside the front door. Inside, there is a gallery of photographs recording local social activities which seem to confound any assumptions that this is the dead-and-alive corner of Kent that casual acquaintance might suggest.

HOLLINGBOURNE

I always think of Hollingbourne as a kind of peanut of a village because it has two centres of population, each different from the other in character, separated by a sort of no-man's land of council houses, school and playing fields and the railway station.

At the upper end, where Hollingbourne Hill curls up the lower slopes of the North Downs, the Pilgrims' Way emerges from its Downland meanderings just above the warm red-brick welcome of Hollingbourne Manor and the Dirty Habit. This pub with a memorable double entendre of a name was formerly the Pilgrims Rest.

At the opposite end, near where the B2163, the village main street, joins the A20, are the shops and some very picturesque old half-timbered and brick buildings, including the Sugar Loaves and 16th century Windmill Inn. In 1997, Maidstone Council approved plans for a new £250,000 village hall to be built behind the Windmill. Just before Eyhorne House, where Musket Lane joins the village street, the village sign stands on a very small grassed area.

It is a very happy arrangement, in fact, because it means that anyone who travels through the village from either direction has a first and last impression that lingers long after the middle section is forgotten.

There is, of course, a reason for this separation. There used to be two manors, Hollingbourne and Alnoitone (nowadays rather whimsically contorted into Elnothington). There was a church at Elnothington, on the southern boundary of the parish, but that is long gone, leaving only a faint echo among local lore of the late 13th century scandal that rocked (but, human nature being what it is and always was, also no doubt delighted) the village with its revelations of adultery by William the chaplain with a local girl called Emma Horseman.

Eyhorne Street is lined with houses dating from the 16th century, but the red-brick Georgian Eyhorne House was condemned to demolition in 1976. However, it was saved and is now privately owned. At the opposite end of the village, 16th century Hollingbourne Manor is also privately owned. On the wall immediately outside the gates, a stone set into the wall describes the boundaries of those lands owned by the Rectory and those belonging to the inheritance of Sir Thomas Culpeper.

All Saints' church is probably 14th century, although it succeeded a much older church on or near the same site. Evidence of that was found in 1969 when workmen digging outside the church walls found a number of chalk blocks, below ground level, which when uncovered were found to have traces of red paint and gold leaf on them. The general belief was that these were remains of one of those earlier churches. A list inside the church claims the first vicar of Hollingbourne held office in 1282. The six bells, which are among the heaviest in Kent, were rehung in 1897 to commemorate Queen Victoria's 60 years on the throne and the church was completely restored in 1965–71.

A brief history of the manor, also inside the church, tells how Athelstan bought it from his father, Ethelred II of Kent, in AD 980 and gave most of it to the church at Canterbury.

The great treasure and curiosity of the church is the famous 300 year old Culpeper Cloth, usually described as an altar cloth even though it is improbably large for that purpose. According to Hasted, the Kentish historian and topographer who lived in Hollingbourne and whose son was vicar there, the cloth was embroidered by the four daughters of Sir John, afterwards Lord, Culpeper of Greenway Court. The cloth is not on display but can be seen on application.

The story is told that it took the four girls almost twelve years to complete the work, while their father was abroad sharing the exile of the future Charles II. During that time, one of the sisters actually went blind through working by candlelight on the cloth, which is of purple velvet decorated with applique fruits of all kinds, including Kentish hops and hazel nuts, worked in gold thread.

The Culpeper (or Colepeper) family crops up all over Kent at just about all periods of history, but the first Hollingbourne Culpeper was Francis. The family chapel in the church, however, was built specially to contain the tomb of Lady Elizabeth, wife of Francis' son, Sir Thomas. It is a particularly fine example of the work of the 17th century sculptor Edward Marshall: a white marble effigy of Lady Elizabeth, her head on a pillow and at her feet a curious mythical creature described as a Thoye – an animal with a dog's head, cloven hooves and covered in leopard-like spots. No wonder it is chained! The much-quoted inscription, in Latin, can be translated to describe Lady Elizabeth as 'Best of women, best of wives, best of mothers.' The paragon died in 1638, aged 56.

Among other interesting monuments inside the church is one, with a bust, to Dame Grace Gethin, who died in 1697 aged 21. She was another member of the Culpeper family who seems to have died of a broken heart shortly after marrying an Irish baronet. It is said that, after receiving Holy Communion, she was 'vouchsafed in a miraculous manner an immediate prospect of her future bliss for the space of two hours.' She is buried, with nearly 60 other members of the family, in Hollingbourne church and has monuments in Westminster and Bath Abbeys, too.

🍁 HOO ST WERBURGH

Here we have another of those Hoo Peninsular villages distinguished from its neighbours by the name of its 13th century church, one of the wonders of which is the yew tree in the churchyard which is said to be anything from 600 to 1,000 years old.

In fact, the parish became formally Hoo St Werburgh only as recently as 1968. Before that, although the name was used, most of the local people simply called it Hoo – as, indeed, they still do. Originally Hoo, or Ho, indicated a promontory or peninsular so, really, to speak of the Hoo Peninsular (as we all do, nevertheless) is tautologous and grammatically incorrect.

When Richard Church wrote about Hoo in 1948, he referred to it as cut off from the mainstream of life. Since then the mainstream has broadened out a bit in this part of the county and today Hoo St Werburgh is no longer small and not specially remote although it is bypassed by the A228 spine road.

It is the principal village of the Hundred of Hoo, surrounded by farming land and a good deal of 20th century development, including the great Kingsnorth electricity generating station, which dominates the local riverside scene and is a more prominent landmark than the tall shingled spire of St Werburgh's church ever was. The oldest parts of the large ragstone church date from the 13th century, with later additions and alterations, and it stands in a prominent position on the north bank of the lower Medway, at the southern end of the village.

Its dedication commemorates the daughter of Wulfhere, 7th century King of Mercia, who founded a nunnery at Hoo which was destroyed by Viking raiders. Her body was removed from Hoo to Chester. She was venerated locally because once, when the nunnery neighbours appealed to her to help them stop geese flying in and ravaging their crops, she called the geese to her and gave them a good talking to, after which they never touched the villagers' crops again.

The artist William L. Wyllie (1851-1931) lived at Hoo Lodge from 1887 to 1907 and painted many local views, some of which are held in Maidstone Museum.

In the late 19th and early 20th centuries, the village was thrust into that mainstream of life when land that had been wholly agricultural until then began to be valued more as an industrial raw material. Gravel was dug there; bricks were made and so was pottery. The barges that carried away the local products busied the river frontage until the 1930s, after which these industries declined.

The embarrassing Dutch raid on the Medway in 1667 brought soldiers to Hoo, to man Cockham Wood Fort, but the fort was never needed and very little of it remains now. Hoo Fort, like its twin, Darnet Fort, was built in the 1860s as part of the defences against the expected Napoleonic invasion. Both were originally intended to mount 25 guns on two tiers, but while the forts were still being built it was obvious they were going to sink into the marsh under the weight of that much ordnance. In the end the Hoo fort was armed with only eleven 9in rifled muzzle loaders, with stores and accommodation for the gunners. They were never fired in anger but both forts remained operational until before the First World War when they were abandoned by the Army, although Hoo Fort remained Ministry of Defence property.

HORSMONDEN

One of the things Horsmonden is known for is the invention, by one of its former residents, John Read, of the stomach pump. I know stomach pumps have been used to lifesaving effect many times since Mr Read first demonstrated his on a dog in 1823, but I still can't help wishing that a village like Horsmonden could have been spared that particular association.

It stands at the crossroads of the Brenchley-Goudhurst and Maidstone-Lamberhurst roads, its fairly large green overlooked by the Spitroast and Gun inn on one side, the Highwayman pub on another side and the Working Men's Club with its Victoria clock turret, erected by parishioners in 1887, at the top end. The fourth side has shops and the post office.

Horsmonden was one of the centres of the old Wealden ironworking region and its Furnace Pond is one of the largest and finest of the artificial lakes made to provide water power for the great hammers that once made all this part of Kent as noisy as the traffic does today. It was here that John Browne had his famous forge and foundry where, in 1616, he was employing 200 men in making great guns for the Army and the Navy.

Furnace Pond.

Browne had the monopoly on manufacture of royal guns and in 1625, after the outbreak of the Spanish War, his foundry at Horsmonden made 500 guns for the British ships. King Charles I visited the foundry in 1638 to watch a cannon being cast: a bronze four-pounder 42 inches long, now preserved in the Tower of London. Not long after that, though, Browne found himself in trouble because despite his previous royal patronage he sided with the Parliamentarians in the Civil War and would not make guns for the Royalists.

The famous foundry closed in 1685 and is now remembered both by the Gun and Spitroast, formerly the Gun, so named after it became an inn round about 1750, and by the cannon on one quarter of the village sign. The inn, too, sports a replica cannon on the flat roof of its porch.

After John Browne and John Read, Horsmonden's most noted son was Simon Willard who was born there in 1605 and grew up to become that Major Willard who founded the town of Concord in Massachusetts Bay in America. He is commemorated in St Margaret's church with a stained glass window and a framed copy of the page of the register recording his baptism in 1605. There is also a commemorative tablet outlining his life, which was placed in the church in 1890 by the World's Women's Christian Temperance Union, whose founder, Frances E. Willard, was a descendant of his.

St Margaret's church is more than a mile from the village, which moved away from it, perhaps because of the Black Death in the 14th century or perhaps in order to be nearer the employment offered by the iron foundry. In 1870, a new church, All Saints, was built to serve the new village but it became disused and was sold to Roman Catholics who still use it.

St Margaret's is more than 650 years old and well worth a visit. It has for its sole neighbours in the open countryside in which it stands the very attractive Church Farm Barn, now converted to a private home, and a four kiln oast house which is being converted into a very des res complex. The church steeple was damaged during a storm in 1990 and has not been replaced.

A brass wall plate to John Austen, who died in 1620, has been defaced, but his wife Joanne, who died aged only 36 giving birth to their tenth child in 1604, is remembered with a floor slab. He was a weaver, credited with having introduced the manufacture of Kentish broadcloth to Horsmonden, and he was an ancestor of Jane Austen, the author. The family built Capel Manor, which was demolished in the 1960s, and also bought the old Drum and Monkey public house, now a private home, which they closed to prevent their workers spending too much time there.

Another 'brass' (actually it is of a kind of imitation brass) commemorates Henry de Grofhurst, who was rector at Horsmonden for 50 years and died in 1361. It was restored in 1867 but it is very unusual and one of the best of its kind to be found anywhere.

Horsmonden also claims to be where the most famous of all the Kent hop varieties, Fuggles, was first found growing in a flower garden belonging to George Stace in 1861. Traditionally, the plant grew from a seed emptied out of a hop-picker's dinner basket with the crumbs at the end of the day's picking. Its qualities were recognised and the strain developed commercially by Richard Fuggle of Fowle Hall, Brenchley, in 1875.

The memorial that might best have kept alive the memory of the Rev Sir William Smith-Marriot was a Victorian building known as Scott's Tower – actually two towers erected as a memorial to Sir Walter Scott. Smith-Marriott was parson of Horsmonden parish for almost 40 years and a great fan of Sir Walter. Having built the tower, he filled one room with a collection of the works of Scott and over the twin doorways was inscribed:

> The Poet's mind can add a grace
> Into the charms of Nature's face.
> Turn from the tower if you came to scoff it -
> Or deem him fool who does not build for profit.

The structure was used by the Observer Corps during the Second World War – was there any eminence, natural or man-made, in Kent that was not, I wonder? – although it had been badly vandalised before that and has since disappeared altogether. The Smith-Marriott family will not be forgotten, however, while the various memorial tablets in the chancel of the church remain.

HOTHFIELD

It is said that Sir Arthur Sullivan's most famous composition – after, of course, his work for the Gilbert and Sullivan collaborations – *The Lost Chord* was composed and first played on Hothfield parish church organ by the man himself. Apparently, he was a guest of Lord and Lady Hothfield at their mansion, Hothfield Place, when the inspiration prompted him to pop across to the church and try the new piece out on the organ there. The rest, as they say, is history.

The church still stands, but Hothfield Place does not. The church was struck by lightning and pretty well burned to the ground in 1598, but it was rebuilt some five years later by Sir John Tufton, whose marble tomb, complete with effigies of Sir John, his wife and family, is one of the more magnificent of the church's monuments.

Away from the village, alongside the A20 in a field just behind the roadside fence is a small granite pillar which tells its own story in the inscription, which is headed simply TITHE:

> In memory of Roderick Morris Kedward, President of the
> National Tithepayers Association 1931-37, MP for Ashford
> 1929-31. Born 1881. Died 1937. This stone is a token of

gratitude for the splendid service he rendered in the tithepayers' cause and of admiration for his character. This site forms part of Beachbrook Farm where he was born and where he suffered repeated distraints for Tithe.

The stone and its inscription are a reminder of the bitterness of the days when farmers, not only here but all over the country, campaigned bitterly against the system that required them to contribute regular sums towards the maintenance of the clergy.

During the Second World War, scores of the distinctive barrel-roofed Nissen huts were built on Hothfield Common for the use of troops. When the war was over, the huts were used for ten years to house people during the time the post-war housing shortage was at its worst. Ashford MP Bill Deedes campaigned for them to be demolished as a health hazard to the people, particularly the children, who lived in them and eventually, in 1955, the occupants were all rehoused and the huts finally cleared away.

The proposed Channel Tunnel rail link will thrust through Hothfield parish and necessitate the demolition of Yonsea Farm buildings beside the A20. The buildings are late Georgian, built soon after the Battle of Waterloo, and lottery money is being sought to help pay for them to be dismantled and re-erected elsewhere as a working museum.

🍁 ICKHAM

The little East Kent village of Ickham has left very few permanent marks on past centuries and might very well have left none on the 20th if it had not been for 'Mini-Jaws'.

That was the name local journalists gave to a rogue perch which, in 1977, somehow got in among the goldfish in a pond owned by ex-trawlerman Alf Leggatt. The perch had helped itself to about 2,000 of Alf's goldfish before he called in the Army to deal with the creature. He had already tried to net it and others had tried to catch it with rod and line. But the golden plenty among which it lived disinclined the perch to vary its diet with barbed bait. So the Army was called in and tried to blow up the voracious perch. The attempt failed. Mini-Jaws champed on.

A second attempt was made by none other than the resourceful explorer and big game hunter Lt-Col Blashford-Snell. He set about the problem with characteristic directness, increasing the amount of explosive and confidently asserting that 'that must have done the trick'. A grateful Alf restocked the pond with another 800 goldfish – which began to disappear at once. Mini-Jaws was still at home and as gluttonous for goldfish as ever.

In the end it was Southern Water Authority experts who ended the predatory perch's rampage with a comparatively high-tech weapon called a stun-rod, which knocked out all the fish with an electric charge. The shocked perch surfaced amid his equally stunned prey and was pulled out, his days of easy pickings over.

Local pressmen had a lovely time reporting the successive highlights of this little saga, which has all the makings of a true village legend for a century or two hence.

Which is very much as it should be. Ickham deserves such a story to relate to its visitors. It is an attractive village, with a rectangular green that carpets the approach to the 13th century church of St John the Evangelist. Thomas Cranmer's brother, Edmund, was rector in 1547 but was deprived of the benefice in 1553 because he was married.

The first Ickham church was a wooden Saxon building that was there in AD 791. That was replaced in 1090 by a Norman church which, in turn, was extended and altered during succeeding centuries until the shingled spire and clock were added in 1870. The clock is unusual in having a mechanism like that of Westminster's Big Ben and a face with pointers carved into the stonework instead of figures.

The single village street is fronted with mostly 19th century cottages of brick and weatherboard and the green is flanked by a long black weatherboard barn. The Duke William public house has Forge House next to it.

The village was once the home of the 17th century scholar Meric Casaubon, who is buried in Canterbury Cathedral.

🍁 IDE HILL

West Kent has a wealth of picturesque villages and Ide Hill is one of them. There is no nearby town to encroach upon its hill-top remoteness and the buildings all round its sloping green have the well cared for look of a village fully appreciated by its inhabitants. Standing on one of the highest points of the Kentish sandstone ridge, it offers views south over the Weald and north across the Holmesdale Valley to the North Downs.

Nearby Bough Beech reservoir, completed in 1969, is a resort of bird-watchers and, of course, birds. Fifty acres is leased to the Kent Trust for Nature Conservation as a nature reserve and there is an oast house visitors' centre. The reserve distinguished itself very early in its life as the inland water chosen by the first large flock of eider duck to come to England.

This has been a prosperous farming area for centuries and this prosperity has left some very fine old buildings. One that might have been lost beneath the reservoir waters was 15th century Bayleaf, but instead it was carefully dismantled and moved to the Weald and Downland Open Air Museum at Singleton in Sussex. There it was reassembled and is now one of the museum's most outstanding acquisitions.

There has only been a church at Ide Hill since Bishop Beilby Porteus of London had a chapel built in 1807 to make it unnecessary for residents to go down the hill (and, of course back up again afterwards) to Sundridge. The present St Mary's church was built in 1865, and although designed for only 250 people it has the distinction of being the highest church in Kent. The blue and gold decoration of the chancel ceiling was the gift of an American family in memory of assassinated President John F. Kennedy, dedicated in 1963.

A popular local walk leads from the village green, alongside the churchyard and over the crest of the hill to where a stone seat was placed to commemorate Octavia Hill, one of the founders of the National Trust. Ide Hill was one of the first acquisitions of the Trust.

Nearby Emmetts Gardens boasts a Wellingtonia sequoia tree that stands over 100 feet tall. Sometimes erroneously described as Kent's tallest tree, its top does, nevertheless, reach a higher point than any other in the county simply because it is growing on the highest point in Kent.

The village itself includes several attractive old buildings, including 18th century Cock Inn.

🍁 IGHTHAM

It was at Ightham church, in 1570, that William Lambarde, author of the first English county history, *A Perambulation of Kent*, married his first wife, Jane.

The couple had met and fallen in love during that perambulation of his and the marriage took place on the day before Jane's 17th birthday. Tragically, it was not to last long. She died only three years later, childless, of smallpox. There is a monument to her in the church.

In 1643, Ightham's rector, the Rev John Gryme, provoked a Royalist rebellion in the village by refusing to take the Oath of Allegiance to Parliament or to impose the same oath upon all his parishioners. Soldiers were sent from London to arrest this rebellious Kentish cleric, but when they rode into the village they were confronted by villagers ready to fight for their rector if need be. There was a bit of a skirmish, from which the soldiers withdrew after one of the local men had been killed. The incident threatened to spark off a serious Royalist rising, very promptly quelled by a larger body of troops who rode with all haste to the village.

Although some distance from the village centre, Ightham Mote bears its name and is easily the most notable local building. The house is one of the finest moated houses in England, built by Sir Thomas Cawne who died in 1374, and is the object of a long and on-going restoration by the National Trust. Its name has less to do with the moat that surrounds it than with the fact that the house stands on the site of an ancient meeting place (mote).

The house was bequeathed to the National Trust by Charles Henry Robinson, an American businessman who bought it in 1953. Visitors who go in search of it today are led there by signs pointing the way, but it is not difficult even now to believe the old story that a party of Cromwellian soldiers sent to seek out this Royalist refuge during the Civil War got lost in the maze of lanes that all seemed to lead past rather than to the house, and never did find it.

The house was owned by the Selby family for almost 300 years. The most celebrated member of the family was Dame Dorothy, a lady in waiting to Elizabeth I and renowned for her specially fine needlework. There are various stories about how she foiled the Gunpowder Plot in 1605, one of which tells how she sent an anonymous letter to her cousin, Lord Mounteagle, warning him to stay away from the Opening of Parliament that year.

She didn't say why he should do that, but he recognised his cousin Dorothy's handwriting and began the inquiries that led to the discovery of the plot. The story owes something to a popular interpretation of the inscription on her memorial in the church, although some experts believe that refers only to a needleworked representation of the plot that she made.

Another memorial in the church commemorates Benjamin Harrison (1837-1921), the local grocer. He lived in the house, still to be seen, called Old Stones and earned an international reputation as an archaeologist for his finds and identification of very early flint tools.

Buried in the churchyard is Adelaide Kemble, who died in 1879. She was one of the great opera singers of her day, the younger daughter of the English actor Charles Kemble and niece of Sarah Siddons. Also in the churchyard is the double-sided headstone that records the death of Caroline Luard on one side and that of her husband, Major General Luard, three weeks later. Mrs Luard was found shot in local woods and although there was no clue to point to her murderer, suspicion fell upon her husband, who took his own life. The mystery of who killed Mrs Luard was never solved.

It was not the first murder in the village. William Wooding was murdered on Oldbury Hill in 1750 and a man called Ogilvy was sentenced at Maidstone to be hung in chains on the site of the crime. The wife of William James, who owned Ightham Manor at the time, kept a diary in which she recorded that the execution was carried out 'before a great number of people' and a later entry records that nearly two months later, 'Ogilvy dropped from his chains in the night.'

Samuel Pepys, the famous diarist, knew of Ightham through the reputation of Sir Charles Sedley as 'the lewdest fellow of his age'. He was once fined £500 for running, drunk and naked, through Fleet Street, in London. Nowadays, of course, he would be paid more than that to do it for the tabloid photographers. When he found himself in trouble for another drunken frolic five years later, the king himself intervened on his behalf and, it is said, got drunk with Sedley and his friends, just to show where his sympathies lay.

There is a local tale that it was a Mrs Hubbard, an inmate in Ightham's village workhouse in 1784, who inspired the Old Mother Hubbard nursery rhyme, although it has to be added that the claim is contested in other parts of the country.

🍁 IVYCHURCH

It is a rather odd thing about marshland anywhere. It is the flattest, most open landscape there is, yet always there is an air of mystery about it, as though the very openness were hiding secrets that only lifelong residents could reveal.

Ivychurch is not specially redolent of this secretiveness, but it is there, just as it is in all the other Romney Marsh villages, though more subtly, perhaps, today than it was in times past.

When the Rev John Streating was looking for another parish to serve after 19 years at Ivychurch 300 years ago, he wrote that he lived in 'an unhealthfull place and among rude and ill-nurtured people for the most part.' (I rather like that endearingly fair-minded 'for the most part'.)

I suppose the single incident for which Ivychurch is best known, because it has been taken up and quoted and repeated by almost everyone who writes about the place, was that Sunday a couple of hundred years ago when the rector arrived at the church to take morning service only to be met by the sexton who barred his way.

'Bain't be no service, parson,' that worthy told the rector firmly. 'Pulpit be full o' baccy and vestry be full o' brandy.'

As a matter of fact, it probably was not an isolated incident, even in

Ivychurch. Certainly it was nothing unusual in the Marsh churches generally. Smuggling was respectable, even though it was unlawful, and highly lucrative, too. There is many a family fortune still being enjoyed today that was begun when a humble labourer or (literally) moonlighting artisan first turned his hand to a bit of free enterprise smuggling.

Daniel Defoe, when he was riding in these parts, saw dragoons riding about 'as if they were huntsmen beating up their game' and when he inquired the reason he was told they were 'in quest of the owlers, as they call them'. He was told that sometimes the owlers were caught, but that often the smugglers operated in such numbers that the law enforcers could only stand and watch the contraband goods being carried off, not daring to meddle.

When Cromwell's soldiers had occasion to show the Parliamentary flag on Romney Marsh, it was in the church at Ivychurch that they stabled their horses. When the Second World War brought its threats of German invasion, it was in that same church that one of several secret stores of food was stacked away. Lookouts used the centuries old beacon turret on the corner of the church tower to watch the coast for the invaders that did not, in the event, arrive.

Ivychurch featured in Richard Barham's *Ingoldsby Legend*s story of Jerry Jarvis's Wig as the home of the 'reputable grazier' Humphry Bourne, who was found robbed and murdered on the Marsh after a visit to an Ashford cattle show.

The village is pretty well in the middle of Romney Marsh, a pleasant enough handful of cottages, an inn – the Bell – and a church that hints at a much greater congregation than could be recruited from the village today.

🍁 IWADE

This is the last village on the mainland before the Kingsferry Bridge carries travellers across the Swale and on to the Isle of Sheppey.

There has been a village here for centuries. The present church, All Saints, is 14th century. But the 20th century very nearly extinguished Iwade before it changed its mind and overlaid its antiquity with a huge estate-style development that has left the church looking more like a poor relation than a venerated oldest inhabitant.

For decades the villagers demanded a bypass for the A249 which carried increasing volumes of traffic right past its church as the industry of Sheppey grew. Today Iwade is bypassed by a dual-carriageway road and the Sittingbourne-Sheerness traffic no longer trundles through the village centre.

The changed character of old Iwade is not without its own attractions, one of which is the bright new sign which, although an unsubtle advertisement for the developers, guides visitors to the various amenities on offer and succeeds in making the WELCOME it extends feel genuine and warm. I sometimes think that Kent's fully justified pride in its antiquity could be better complemented than it is by a few more contemporary contributions that posterity will be proud to venerate.

Nearby Chetney Hill once had England's only lazarette, a quarantine colony for carriers of contagious diseases. Work was begun on building an isolation hospital in 1801, mainly for seamen and passengers arriving at Sheerness aboard ships that anchored in the Medway as a precaution against the plague. Ten years and £20,000 later it was abandoned, unfinished.

🍁 KEMSING

Set amidst West Kent countryside that looks like one great park, Kemsing is centred around St Edith's Well, which is surrounded by a little walled garden behind the village war memorial. A spring bubbles up to feed a tiny stream and a tablet on the wall explains:

> 'St Edith of Kemsing 961-984. This well lay within the precincts
> of the convent where St Edith, daughter of King Edgar, passed
> her childhood. Hallowed by her presence, the water became a
> source of healing.'

Although Edith was born in Kemsing, she lived most of her life in the Abbey of Wilton in Wiltshire. She was only 24 when she died and became venerated as a miracle worker. A shrine was built at Kemsing which prospered from the resultant visits of pilgrims.

There is a statue of the saint, surmounted by a clock and a bell, on the front of the most eye-catching building in the village – St Edith's village hall, which was given to the village in 1911. An inscription over the statue and beneath the clock tells all who care to read it:

> 'Tis mine each passing hour to tell;
> 'Tis thine to use it ill or well.

And, indeed, the bell above the clock does chime every hour.

Kemsing is a pretty village that has a well cared for look, particularly in the area around the well, which includes the post office, two inns – the Bell and the

Wheatsheaf, which eye each other covetously across the road – and several attractive old houses and cottages.

As well as being the birthplace of the 10th century saintly princess Edith, Kemsing is also noted as the birthplace of Women's Institutes in Kent. The county's first Institute was founded here in December 1915.

Every ten years, since 1961 when the village celebrated the 1,000th anniversary of St Edith's birth, a festival has been held on her feast day, 16th September. The church (no, not St Edith's, but St Mary the Virgin's) treasures the Kemsing Embroidery which was worked by 44 villagers and depicts village features in a series of roundels on a linen ground. It is exhibited in a glass case on the church wall.

There is a welcoming air about the village that is missing from some others. The spacious free public car park contributes significantly to that, and a nice touch is the invitation in the church porch to visitors to use the push-button that illuminates features of special interest inside. There is a great wealth of them, from the very elaborate rood screen with its crucifixion tableau with angels, the ornate heraldic canopy above the altar and the only remaining Domesday Tiles, designed by author Donald Maxwell in the 1930s to be a permanent record of local scenes.

 KEMSLEY

Despite the similarity of names, and the alphabetical proximity, it would be difficult to imagine two more different villages than Kemsley and Kemsing.

Kemsley is of no great age at all, having been built as a 'model' village on the marshes beyond Sittingbourne for employees of the local paper mill. Still today, the Sittingbourne and Kemsley Light Railway runs steam train excursions along the line linking the town with the village, which is dominated by the sprawling UK Paper mill and consists mainly of regimented estate development.

The village itself is centred around the square which, with its social centre, was intended by the original builders in the mid-1920s to fulfil the role of the traditional Big House in older villages. The Kemsley Arms public house and its neighbouring, rather grandly-named, Kemsley Concert Hall exhibit none of the characteristics of traditional village features at all.

I have seen Kemsley described as 'more like a forces' married quarters than anything else' and there is some justification for that. It has a utilitarian look about it and a feeling that successive developments have stopped caring about things like scale or form and put sheer quantity ahead of quality.

Kemsley is not a lovely place to look at, although for all I know it may be an ideal place to live in; but it is a big and growing village and, in its own way, a warning of what can result from the relentless pressure for new homes in Kent.

🍁 KINGS HILL

Kent likes to boast that it has more buildings listed as of historic and/or architectural interest than anywhere else in Britain outside London. But what, it is often asked, will be today's bequest that successive centuries will similarly prize?

Well, one development that may very well become a cherished example of late 20th century planning is the Kings Hill community on the site of the former West Malling airfield, which was one of those that featured in the Battle of Britain during the Second World War.

For years after the war no one was quite sure what to do with the old airfield. The Ministry of Defence wanted to sell it but the Air Ministry wanted it to be used for civil flying. Local people opposed such use, protesting that the noise of aircraft landing and taking off from the runway would be unacceptably intrusive. Various ideas were suggested but in the end Kent County Council, having failed to enlist the collaboration of local borough councils, took the plunge and bought the entire airfield in 1973.

The council then brought in American developers who formed a new company, Rouse Kent, to develop a showpiece business village. It was to be complete with three on-site 'village' housing developments of 1,500 homes in all, with a school for the children living there. Today, the development is still going on, and there are already more homes than was originally intended. It has now become an independent parish in its own right and some fear that it will spread to engulf neighbouring West Malling, Mereworth and Wateringbury which would then lose their separate identities. Nevertheless, the low density, low-rise business premises which house the headquarters of several nationally – indeed, internationally – known companies, part of the University of Greenwich, and offices of both Kent County Council and the Tonbridge and Malling Borough Council, all snuggle into sympathetically landscaped surroundings completely different from anything else anywhere in Kent.

The entrance to the village – for such it really is, however different from any other village in Kent – is off the A228 and is marked by a fairly dramatic piece of sculpture that is actually a series of blocks of shaped stone set one on top of another to make a lofty column. The brick paved roads leading to the various parts of the site curve gently through a tamed rural landscape of grass and shrubs. A central lawned roundabout features one of the most distinctive examples of outdoor art in Kent: three sculpted figures all pushing, from different directions, a huge polished metal ball.

The sculpture stands in front of the gateway leading to the golf club and some of the more up-market housing. The whole impression is one of tended parkland which, while very different from the rural setting of most of the county's long-established villages, still suggests a very pleasant environment in which to live and work.

🍁 LADDINGFORD

It is doubtful if Laddingford would have won a mention in this particular book but for something that happened in 1997.

It is one of Kent's more modest villages, little more than a group of roadside houses and some farm buildings – oh, and the Chequers public house, of course – set in that relatively unpeopled tract of Wealden countryside between Yalding and Paddock Wood. The little River Teise flows past Laddingford, under the 14th century bridge that, presumably, accounts for the village's existence, on its way to join the Medway at Twyford Bridge in Yalding. The little traffic that uses the road flows through the village without, for the most part, noticing it has done so. That's the sort of place Laddingford is.

The 'something' that happened in 1997 which thrust little Laddingford into word-wide prominence and, indeed, gave it a claim to kinship with the Biblical Garden of Eden, no less, was – an apple.

Local farmer Alan Smith of West Pyke Fish Farm grew an apple which weighed 3lb 11oz. He exhibited it at the annual Marden Fruit Show in October, where it amazed all who saw it. It won an entry in the *Guinness Book of Records* as the world's largest apple. The world's press carried the story of the Howgate Wonder, which brought its grower letters from all over the world, including some from people who recalled the man who first bred the variety on the Isle of Wight in 1929.

After its brief bask in the full glare of publicity, the monster apple might have ended up like the four and twenty blackbirds of the nursery rhyme, baked in a pie, but someone had a better idea. The paragon was rendered inedible by the process that immortalized it in bronze to astonish all posterity – until somewhere else grows an apple that weighs in at 3lb 12oz and

Laddingford yields up its moment of glory and slumps back into obscurity again.

🍁 LAMBERHURST

It was the price of hops that made Lamberhurst a Kent, rather than a Sussex, village. Until 1894, the Kent-Sussex boundary ran through the village, but then the two counties decided that it must become wholly part of one or of the other.

Lamberhurst was in the Wealden hop-growing region, where the price a farmer was paid for the hops he grew really mattered. For some reason, hops were regularly fetching higher prices in Kent than in Sussex at that time, so the canny folk of Lamberhurst voted to pay their rates in Kent, too.

Easily the most dominant local feature hereabouts is Scotney Castle, which was built in 1358 and for which the River Beult (pronounced Belt) was diverted to create a moat. That caused problems, too, because it meant the moat actually crossed the county boundary. When a maid at the castle was drowned in it, the coroners of Kent and Sussex argued over which of them should properly preside at the inquest.

Scotney was the local headquarters for Jesuit missionary work late in the 16th century. It is one of the local traditions that a certain Father Richard Blount once hid in a priest hole at Scotney Castle while searchers hunted for him. While the search was on, the lady of the house noticed that the priest's girdle was caught in the secret door, betraying its whereabouts and his. Crouching close to the door, she warned the priest of the danger and he pulled the giveaway girdle out of sight.

But you can't whisper through a stone wall, even if it is only a door disguised as a stone wall, and she was overheard by some of the searchers who at once began to pull down the whole wall in their efforts to find the secret door and its priestly hidey-hole. Before they succeeded, however, it began to rain heavily and the search was called off until next day by which time Blount had escaped.

When Edward Hussey built the new house and laid out its gardens in 1837-43, he carefully reduced the old castle to the picturesque ruin it is today. He was not the first of the Hussey family to arrive in Lamberhurst, however. That was Thomas, whose business interests included iron smelting and who bought the existing Lamberhurst furnace, known as Gloucester Forge after a visit by the Duke of Gloucester, eldest son of Princess (later Queen) Anne.

The forge became one of the most famous of the many Wealden ironworks. It was the main contractor for the supply of railings for St Paul's Cathedral.

Scotney Castle, near Lamberhurst.

Although parts of the railings were sub-contracted out to various other ironworks throughout the Weald, it was to Lamberhurst that a small part of them was returned by the Dean and Chapter of St Paul's in 1976, to be preserved in Lamberhurst's main street beside the village hall.

Other nearby features include Bayham Abbey (English Heritage), one of the most complete monastic ruins in Southern England, and also Bewl Water reservoir, the first sod of which was lifted in 1973. It now attracts thousands of anglers and other visitors to its water and the twelve mile walk avoiding the surrounding nature reserve which is not open to public access.

Lamberhurst vineyard, too, is one of the largest in England and St Mary's church is worth the dangerous walk alongside the busy A21, which has no footpath on the hill, to the road that stops dead at the churchyard gate. A small car park overlooks typical High Weald countryside. The yew tree in the churchyard is known to have been growing there for 1,500 years although the church itself is of Norman origins, with later alterations and restorations. It was rededicated after restoration in 1964.

The Owl House, just outside the village, is so named because of its association with smugglers (owlers). Today its Trust Farm produces bottled apple juice – 150,000 litres in 1997, not all of it from apples grown on the farm itself.

🍁 LEEDS

Probably throughout history Leeds village has been very much over-shadowed by the castle. Once, the castle would have shared the local limelight with the abbey, but that was one of the victims of Henry VIII's sweeping Reformation and is only remembered now by Abbey Farm. In 1846 the complete foundations of the abbey church were uncovered, including the crypt. They are still there, covered up again for safekeeping.

The village wanders up a hill that carries the B2163 and its traffic, from which the villagers have been clamouring for bypass relief for years. At the bottom of the hill, St Nicholas' church has a curiously squat tower with a relatively puny little spire capping it. It is a very massive structure – the second largest church tower in Kent – that has stood for 800 years or more and was added to the older Saxon church that was there before the present building. The church was once the abbey church of St Mary and St Nicholas and underwent major restoration in 1971.

The castle has long enjoyed the reputation of being the loveliest in all Europe. Now that it is, late in life, open to the public, the justice of that reputation is appreciated by thousands of visitors each year. It shares top billing among Kent's tourist attractions with Canterbury Cathedral and Aylesford Priory.

Leeds Castle has been the home of kings, queens and noblemen for almost all its history and for 300 years during which it enjoyed the status of 'The Ladies' Castle' it was home to no fewer than eight of England's medieval queens. Its last private owner was Lady Baillie, daughter of Almeric Paget, Lord Queenborough, whose grandfather commanded the British cavalry at Waterloo. It was Olive Baillie who restored the castle and its grounds to their present condition and then bequeathed the lot to the nation to be administered by the trustees of the Leeds Castle Foundation.

The castle in its open hillside countryside, with golf course and vineyard, is a romantic building and a perfect setting, floodlit and reflected with mirrored clarity in the still water of the artificial lake which moats it, for the open air concerts, ballet and other performances that are held there now.

Leeds Castle was built for defence more than a thousand years ago and it seems to have lost none of its security in the intervening years. It was chosen in 1978 as a safer alternative to a London hotel for the Middle East summit talks and has hosted other similar occasions since. Its moated fastness, amid wide open lawns and countryside, with the M20 practically passing its portcullis and putting London or the Channel Tunnel less than an hour away by car, makes it a security chief's dream.

🍁 LEIGH

However the spelling is pronounced in other parts of the country, here it is 'Lie' and it must be a strong contender for the title of the most attractive village in Kent.

The large village green is surrounded by trees and houses and there is a rather pretty village sign in the shape of a shield quartered with local scenes framed in decorative wrought iron.

Across the road from the green are the grounds of Hall Place (once Leigh Hall), part of an ancient deer park, with a lake and a some fine trees and shrubs. The house is Elizabethan red-brick in appearance, although in fact it and its impressive gateway were built in 1876 for the Nottinghamshire merchant and philanthropist Samuel Morley by the architect George Devey. Part of the house was demolished by fire in 1976.

Thirteenth century St Mary's church, beside the 19th century mock-Tudor Hall Place gates, has one or two curious features, including a pulpit with a

16th century wrought iron hour-glass stand and a most unusual brass in memory of an unknown lady who died in 1580. It depicts a woman on her knees apparently having been raised from the dead by an angel blowing a trumpet and is inscribed: 'Farewell all ye until ye come to me.'

The name of the village is said to mean 'sheltered place', which it certainly is. Cricket is played on the village green which was owned by the lord of the manor, Lord Hollenden, until he handed it over to the parish council in January 1948.

🍁 LENHAM

Lenham Square has been used as a film location more than once, and it is easy to see why. Take away the cars, introduce a few extras appropriately costumed and you have a corner of old Kent very much as it would have looked a century or more ago. The Dog and Bear on one side of the square was a coaching inn and parts of it are at least 300 years old.

From its earliest beginnings, certainly during Roman times and probably before that, Lenham has been a trading village. The major inheritor of Lenham's trading reputation is the international Freightflow depot which accepts goods brought in by TIR juggernauts for redistribution.

It grew up around the local springs that bubble out of the ground and trickle away to become the little River Len which joines the River Medway at Maidstone. It was those springs and the streams that flowed from them that gave Lenham its early reputation for growing fine watercress. At one time the village was noted as much for its luxuriant watercress as for its quarrelsome women – although whether or not there was any connection between the two is not known.

Today, the main motif of the more armorial of the two village signs alongside the nearby A20 London-Folkestone road is the watercress plant. The other, newer sign is more ornately pictorial and shows the village scene below the white cross on the hillside.

The cross, cut into the chalky hillside above the village, is a noted local landmark. The turf was first cut from it in 1922 as a memorial to 42 local casualties of the First World War. In 1939 it had to be covered up lest it should provide enemy aircraft with a navigational aid, but it was uncovered again when peace was restored, by which time 14 more names had to be added to the great granite memorial stones beside it. In 1960 villagers acknowledged that it was becoming too much to expect future generations of villagers to climb the steep hill to tend the memorial and the granite stones were brought down to the churchyard. The cross remains, though, still gleaming white on its green ground.

Evidence of Saxon occupation came to light in 1946 when Robert Goodsall, the Kent writer who lived at nearby Harrietsham, bought and began to restore the 15th century hall house on the corner of Lenham High Street and Maidstone Road. When the floor was taken up, the remains of three bodies – two men and a woman – together with a small collection of weapons, were found. Archaeologists judged them to be about 1,200 years old. The house is now the Saxon Warrior Pharmacy.

Lenham's most celebrated inhabitant lies at peace in the church, although it is difficult to imagine that she had much peace in her lifetime. Mary Honywood, wife of Robert Honywood of Charing, died in 1620, leaving 367 descendants. She had 16 children of her own, 114 grandchildren, 118 great-grandchildren and nine great-great-grandchildren. She lived through no fewer than six reigns and somehow or other found time to earn a reputation for prison visiting.

Despite its antiquity, Lenham is no museum piece. It is still growing, with many new estate homes. The former Lenham Hospital, built before the First World War as a tuberculosis sanatorium on the hill overlooking the village, later became a psychiatric hospital but was empty and disused after 1986. The latest plans for the site are to redevelop it into yet another housing estate.

❧ LEYBOURNE

The ruins of Leybourne Castle barely hint at the importance of the building and its owners in days long gone. Today, the remains are little more than a few walls onto which the manor house, behind the church, has been built. Yet Leybourne was a significant manor before the Normans arrived and 700 years ago the castle belonged to one of the most powerful families in Kent.

The manor came into the de Leybourne family during the reign of Richard I and Sir Roger de Leybourne was one of the barons who forced King John to sign the Magna Carta in 1215. That led to his being imprisoned in Rochester Castle, from where he was only released after he had paid a hefty fine. His son, another Sir Roger, was killed during one of the crusades and, following a custom of the time, his embalmed heart was returned to his family, who installed it in a unique (in Kent) heart shrine in Leybourne church.

He left a son, yet another Roger, who fathered the Sir William de Leybourne who enhanced the family fortunes no end by marrying Juliana, daughter and wealthy heiress of Sir Henry de Sandwich. It was that enhanced family fortune that enabled Sir William to play host to Edward I and Queen Eleanor at Leybourne Castle on St Crispin's Day (25th October) 1286. Two iron crowns in the church are believed by some historians to have been left as Royal mementoes of that visit, although it must be said others have found reason to doubt that.

Sir William had two sons. One, Sir Henry, grew up to be one of the most violent and lawless men of his day and he was finally outlawed for felony and disinherited in 1329. The other son, Sir Thomas, died young, leaving his father to be the last baron to live at the castle. His grand-daughter, Sir Thomas' daughter, another Juliana, inherited so much property and was so rich that she became known as the Infanta (Princess) of Kent.

But she was the last representative of the family into which she was born and from her the Leybourne estates passed to her husband, the Earl of Huntingdon, and later to the Crown. When she died, childless, in 1367 she was buried at St Augustine's Abbey in Canterbury and the family was extinct. The castle became the property of an abbey and fell into ruin after Henry VIII's dissolution. It was some time later that the house was built on part of the site.

Leybourne church is, in fact, older than the castle. Parts of it are 900 years old, although it has been added to and altered over the years. One of its rectors, John Larke, was hanged, drawn and quartered in March 1544 for denying Henry VIII's new title of Supreme Head on Earth of the Church in England.

Today's Leybourne village is almost entirely modern in character. Vastly expanded by estate development, its Old Rectory has been converted into a restaurant, its countryside crossed by new roads and gouged by sandpits that have become water sports centres and nature reserves.

Leybourne Grange, a 270 acre site between the A20 and the M20, was a home for 1,200 handicapped people until it closed in 1992. It now houses the Grange Park College for 16-20 year olds with severe learning difficulties and plans for much of the rest have included a 700-home housing estate. Among Leybourne's latest features is the 22 acre RSPCA animal rescue centre in Castle Way, which was opened in 1996.

 LEYSDOWN

The Isle of Sheppey is a place of sharp contrasts. In the south, the marshes are today much as they must have been centuries ago: low, flat, and dotted with sheep too busy fattening themselves on the plentiful grazing to look across the Swale to the mainland of Kent beyond.

The north-west corner of the island is relatively densely built up, with the towns of Queenborough and Sheerness now barely distinguishable, one from the other, and both dominated by the port industries that support their considerable populations. Much of the rest, though, is open, undulating countryside that appeals strongly to holidaymakers and, therefore, to providers of holiday accommodation, and everywhere there are caravan parks, chalet villages and holiday homes.

Leysdown is the most blatantly 'seaside' village on the island. The long, almost straight approach road bursts into a mini-Margate sea-front type main street, where shops flaunt all the traditional wares of sun hats and T-shirts, ice cream and comic postcards, fish and chips and kebabs.

A short distance further on, however, the natural character of the place makes some effort to regain control. The road, thus far disguised as a good, main highway, suddenly changes its mind at its extreme north-east end and becomes a cliff-edge cul-de-sac. Even here, though, the broad grassy clifftop has had to offer itself as a large car parking area where visitors can throw frisbies at each other or, if the prevailing wind is in a bad mood, sit staring through the windscreen at the Thames Estuary and the ships of all sizes that plough to and fro across their line of vision.

Very few of them know – or care – that long before this became the holidaymakers' playground village it is today, Leysdown was where British aviation began. It was from one of the neighbouring treeless fields that J. T. C. Moore-Brabazon (later Lord Brabazon) made the first circular flight in Great Britain, which won him a £1,000 prize. Later, in the 1920s, flying moved to nearby Eastchurch, leaving Leysdown with just a couple of farms, a pub, post office and general store and a few bungalows.

🍁 LINTON

You might travel the A229 out of Maidstone by car many times and never realise that it took you through Linton. St Nicholas' church is only a few yards back from the road, but it is on top of a bank and above the motorists' eye level as they go down the hill, concentrating on the approaching bend.

The colourful village sign, sturdily framed in timber, embellished with wrought iron and topped by the Kentish White Horse badge, is equally easily missed. In fact, it bears a shield with the name of the village very prominently across the middle and the rest quartered with representations of local features: a group of oast kilns, a deer (to remind us of Linton deer park), a cricket bat, ball and bailed stumps, commemorating the great days of Kentish cricket when Linton Park owners were enthusiastic patrons of the game.

Across the road from 13th century St Nicholas' church, the reeling timbers of the old Bull Inn and its own very lively inn sign do tend to catch the eye, but the few roadside cottages alongside it do not suggest a village.

Linton was born of a need to house the employees of the Big House, Linton Place, which was built in the park early in the 18th century by Robert Mann. The big white house on the hillside enjoys views right across the Weald and fully justifies the description given to it by Horace Walpole, who called it 'that Citadel of Kent, with the Weald as its garden'. Travelling along the A229 back into Maidstone, you see the house gleaming among the trees from miles away.

One member of the family was Sir Horace, who was known as the King of Cricket. He lost a considerable fortune gambling on the game and he sold Linton Park to Galfridus Mann to pay his debts. Galfridus gave the estate to his daughter, who married the 4th Earl Cornwallis, Bishop of Lichfield, which was how the property came into the possession of the Cornwallis family.

The last member of that family to live at Linton was the Lord Cornwallis they called 'The Spirit of Kent', Wykeham Stanley, 2nd Baron Cornwallis of Linton. He, too, was a talented cricketer who played for Kent from 1919 to 1926, captained the county side three times (1924-26) and was President of MCC in 1948. He was a member of Kent County Council and its chairman from 1928 to 1935, and as Lord Cornwallis he held an astonishing number of important offices in the county, including that of Lord Lieutenant of Kent from 1944 until 1972. The family moved away from Linton in 1937 but Lord Cornwallis outlived two wives and died in his 90th year at Ashurst Park, Fordcombe, near Tunbridge Wells, in January 1982.

The house in Linton Park has been sold several times in recent years and has had a number of uses including as a private school, a masonic headquarters and offices. Outwardly, it has remained essentially unchanged and still looks out across the Weald, just as it has since the early 18th century.

A fairly elaborate 17th century pink alabaster memorial in Linton church shows Sir Anthony Mayne and his wife, Lady Brigett, kneeling opposite each other. The Maynes were one of Kent's great families for many generations.

They moved to Linton from Biddenden and Sir John Mayne, a great-grandson of the memorial couple, led Royalists against General Fairfax's Parliamentary army in the Battle of Maidstone in June 1648. During conservation work in 1998, the two alabaster figures had to be separated in order to be removed and restored but they were reunited when the work was finished and should now be able to continue their stony devotions for a few more centuries, at least.

 LITTLEBOURNE

Quite what St Vincent of Saragossa, Spain's first Christian martyr, is doing patronising a very English little church like the one at Littlebourne, I don't know. I have seen it suggested that, since he was regarded as the patron saint of winedressers, he may have been adopted by the monks of St Augustine's Abbey at Canterbury who tended vines in this part of the abbey lands. The great barn that flanks one side of the churchyard is thought to have been their 14th century grange.

The village stands beside the Little Stour (the 'little bourne' from which it takes its name) and although the church dates its foundation from the 13th century, the 20th century has imposed itself fairly relentlessly upon its surroundings. There is still a core of quaint timbered houses but bungalow development in the 1960s, especially south of the church, expanded the original village which now seems to be under imminent threat of absorption into greater Canterbury.

Like so many villages, Littlebourne has experienced a considerable increase in traffic in recent years. The A257, the main route through the village, is the Canterbury-Sandwich and Deal road and the inevitable traffic tends to be relentless and fast.

Littlebourne has pretty well lost what claims it once had to be numbered among Kent's more attractive villages, despite the few individually eye-catching features that survive, including Littlebourne mill at the northern end of the village and the group of oast houses where the road bends in search of Howletts, itself a major local attraction, at nearby Bekesbourne.

🍁 LITTLESTONE

By no means a twin of nearby Greatstone, Littlestone has been described as 'a resort that never quite took off.' It is at one end of the Romney Marsh shoreline sea wall, a place of Edwardian and Victorian villas, landmarked a trifle self-consciously by the 120 foot loftiness of the red brick water tower built in 1890 and never embellished with the four clock faces it was designed to carry.

The pattern for the development of this hitherto tiny coastal community was set in the 1880s when Sir Robert Perks and surveyor Henry Tubbs built a home for Sir Robert and a terrace of houses to go with the new Grand Hotel and the church.

The two men also laid out Littlestone golf course, which became very popular with Government ministers and Members of Parliament generally. In 1913, the *Strand Magazine* told the story of how a day's golfing at Littlestone led to a wager being taken up by T. H. Oyler that he could drive a golf ball the 26 miles (as the crow flies) from Linton Park at Linton to Littlestone in under 2,000 strokes. He actually covered 35 miles in the three days and 1,087 strokes it took him to win the bet, losing 17 balls on the way. Modern traffic makes it unlikely that the feat will ever be repeated; certainly not by Mr Oyler who died, aged 91, in May 1941.

Littlestone was a lifeboat station from 1858 until 1928 and the old coastguard cottages are still there in St Andrews Road. In her book *The Gift of the Sea – Romney Marsh* (1984) Anne Roper recalled former times when the lifeboat was called out. A 'knocker-up' went to each of the cottages in turn and pulled the 'knocker-up cord', which was attached to a metal device that tapped on the window to wake up the sleeping coastguard within.

🍁 LOOSE

All villages are unique, but Loose does seem to have gone over the top a bit to distinguish itself from other Mid Kent villages. It has been encroached upon by the continuing outward sprawl of Maidstone, but the old core clings to its hillside slopes, each building seeming to hold hands with its neighbour, each preventing the others from slipping down into the stream at the valley bottom.

That stream powered mills and watered cress beds on the way down from Langley to the River Medway at Tovil since Saxon times. On its way it crosses the main road into the village opposite the old Chequers Inn and spreads out, gathering tributes from several local springs, on either side of the causeway that gives pedestrian access to the road up to the higher parts of the village, around the church.

It is, in fact, something of a tourist attraction to be able to walk on this causeway along the middle of the stream in which local children paddle in

The causeway, Loose.

hot weather. During the winter adults who use the causeway sometimes have to paddle as well, when the water washes over the footway.

All Saints' church is part 13th century and part – the greater part – Victorian, as a result of a serious fire in 1878. A yew tree in the churchyard is said to be 2,000 years old and measures 33 feet round its girth. It is one of the largest in the country although in July 1998 a report said it was in a poor condition and its future is in some doubt.

When (if) it goes, it will take with it a curious local legend, one of several versions of which promises that anyone who sticks a pin in the tree and then runs round it, in an anti-clockwise direction (naturally!) twelve times at midnight will be able to look through a small tower window and see a vision of a woman killing a baby. Quite why anyone should want to conjure up such a shocking spectacle at that or any other hour I don't know and not even the most eager researches have led me to anyone who has ever actually tried it so I can't vouch for its effectiveness.

The half-timbered Wool House at Loose, which dates from the 15th century and is now owned by the National Trust, is privately occupied and available to view only upon special request. It was probably once a fleece store for the local water-powered woollen mills and there is a local belief that it was once used by Cromwellian forces as a headquarters during the Civil War.

Loose is bypassed by the viaduct that carries the road from Maidstone out into the Weald. It was built in 1829 as an aid to troop movement during the Napoleonic Wars, having been designed by Thomas Telford with a 50 foot span between piers.

The Alpine character of the village might justify the local scout group being known as the Loose Swiss Scouts, which celebrated 90 years of scouting in Loose in 1998. In fact the name derives from the troop's foundation in 1908 by Jack Barcham Green, who had a Swiss wife and who lived in Swiss Cottage in Loose Road.

Members of the local Women's Institute were so wearied by the nods and winks inspired by its full title that it is now known as the Loose Valley WI, which has allowed another group to adopt the name and its inevitable, if not necessarily entirely appropriate, connotation and become known as the Loose Women.

The design on the village sign, which was erected in 1982, includes four roundels showing the church, a watermill, the Kent White Horse holding a chequers board, and a fish in the stream, all garlanded with hops.

🍁 LOWER HALSTOW

There are few reminders today of Lower Halstow's hey-day as an 18th and 19th century brickworks village, except the brickworkers' cottages. Even they have been outnumbered in recent years by new building that has increased the size of the village and changed its character, too.

Lower Halstow is on the edge of the Medway marshes, those 'lost lands' of Kent, once sufficiently above sea level to support possibly the largest area of potteries in Roman Britain.

The church of St Margaret of Antioch looks a bit as though it had hunkered down against the winds that beat against its old walls. It looks quite small from the front, but from the seaward side it is seen to be much larger. There is only the churchyard wall between it and a short creek wharf in which barges would once have moored to load the local bricks but which is now unused and derelict.

The church walls are an incredible hotch-potch of flint, stone and brick rubble and, with the old cottages almost immediately beyond the churchyard wall and the old creek giving access to the Medway estuary just a short stroll away, it is perhaps not surprising that the village has featured in more than one film over the years.

During the First World War several anti-aircraft batteries were located around the village as part of the Thames defences and when they were fired the houses here were more badly shaken than anything at the skyward end of the guns. However, it is an ill wind that blows no good at all – or, in this case, an ill barrage. One morning, after the guns had been firing heavily during the night, the wife of the Lower Halstow parson went into the church and found pieces of the old font lying in fragments on the floor. When she overcame her horror, it was found that the font was not a stone one, as everyone had supposed for centuries, but a rather lovely 12th century lead one, decorated with figures of kings and angels, which had been plastered over. It has been suggested that the plaster camouflage was provided to save it from Civil War army plunderers looking for lead for their bullets.

In the 1800s, several barges were built at Lower Halstow by John Woods, brickmaker, before his business was taken over by Eastwoods in 1880. In 1912 the Lower Halstow brickworks employed 120 men and boys and produced between 17 and 18 million bricks a year. The works closed in 1966 and the buildings were later demolished.

🍁 LOWER HARDRES

There is an Upper Hardres (pronounced, like its nether neighbour, Hards) as well. They are both just east of the distinctively Roman Stone Street which, except for a rather curious kink around Horton Park at the south end, runs arrow straight due south from just outside Canterbury to within a couple of miles of Hythe.

But despite their origins, the two are separate and distinct villages. Lower Hardres is perhaps less visually favoured than Upper Hardres, with a 19th century church I have seen described as 'ugly', although perhaps 'modest' would be kinder. Pevsner described it as 'conceived, outside anyway, as a humble village church, an imaginative leap before Pugin's example made such attention to appropriateness commonplace.'

Lower Hardres featured in the first reported case in Kent of the wrecking by farm labourers of steam threshing machines during the 'Captain Swing' disorders in the 1830s. Two magistrates and a posse of constables backed up by 30 dragoons were sent out from Canterbury to try to catch the gang of about 400 wreckers, but without success.

It was at Lower Hardres, too, that a rather curious little incident was reported at Christmas 1859 that had to do with the old East Kent custom of hoodening. Percy Maylam, in his book *Hooden Horse*, published in 1909, said that in bygone days it was probable that the hooden horse was to be found at Christmas in every village and hamlet and on every large farm in East Kent. By his time, however, it had died out almost everywhere, surviving only in Thanet and at Walmer.

The custom was to go from house to house collecting (demanding with menaces might well be the term we would use today!) money or goodies for a Christmas feast. The band was made up of a Waggoner with a whip who led the Horse; the Rider, who tried always unsuccessfully to get upon the Horse's back; and Mollie, a man in 'drag' who went behind the Horse with a besom broom.

The Horse was a man, known as the Hoodener, who held a usually rather crudely carved wooden horse's head on a stick. Attached to the head was a sort of hood of coarse sacking which more or less hid the man. The head itself was made so that the man could jerk a piece of string to make the loosely hinged jaws open and shut with a vicious clacking sound. Sometimes the jaws were lined with nails to represent teeth and altogether the creature was pretty fearsome. The whole performance was known as hoodening and it was accompanied by some fairly licensed horse-play and rustic ribaldry.

Maylam himself dismissed suggestions that the ritual was descended from Saxon Woden worship rites and thought it had more to do with morris dancing. However, the custom came under censure from the Church, which saw it as a pagan survival that ought not to be encouraged, and it lost a lot of support from ordinary people, too, when it became rather too robust a frolic for comfort. There were reports of one woman being so scared by the importuning horse that she died, although the story that Maylam quoted about Lower Hardres had a rather less tragic result.

His story concerned the visit in 1859 of a group of hoodeners to Lower Hardres Rectory, where a German and his wife were spending Christmas with the rector. The German lady was an invalid and had not walked for seven years. She was wheeled out onto the lawn in her invalid chair to see the hoodeners' performance and when the Horse (a man named Henry Brazier) pretended to jump at her, the jaws snapping viciously close to her face, the lady was so frightened that she sprang out of her chair and ran indoors. She was able to walk perfectly well from then on. Her husband was so delighted that when the hoodening season was over he bought the Horse and took it back with him to Germany.

The hooden horse is still very much an East Kent custom today and enjoying something of a revival, not just at Christmas time but as an accessory of morris dancers at summer fetes.

🍁 Lᴙᴍɪɴɢᴇ

The area around Folkestone has changed a great deal since St Ethelburga the Queen founded Kent's first monastery at Lyminge in AD 633. But this is still a very pleasant part of East Kent and Lyminge was, in fact, judged Kent Village of the Year in 1998.

Ethelburga was the daughter of King Ethelbert, the first Christian King of Kent, who made Augustine and his monks welcome and allowed them to make Canterbury the headquarters of their mission. She was married to the pagan Edwin of Northumbria and when he died she returned to Kent and founded the monastery and nunnery of which she became abbess and which took her name.

She built on the site of a Roman settlement which took its name from the Roman name for the river, the Limen, nowadays the eastern Rother. In its turn, Lyminge gave its name to one of the original seven (later reduced to five) Saxon lathes into which the kingdom and later the county was divided. It became the lathe of Shepway, which remained one of the five, and the name survives as that of the district council today.

Ethelburga died in AD 647, after which part of the monastery was given to St Augustine's at Canterbury. In AD 804 the nunnery was transferred to Canterbury. The monks remained in the monastery at Lyminge until about AD 965, then they, too, moved to Canterbury. The church of St Mary and St Ethelburga, however, remained and was rebuilt by Archbishop (later St)

Dunstan. Today, together with the old railway station, it is at the heart of a busy and generally pleasant village.

The Elham Valley Railway opened in 1889 and Lyminge had a railway station which encouraged development into a small market town. But the line was closed in 1947 and is now a public walk and the station houses the local branch of the county library.

In 1997, Lyminge Forest became the chosen site for major development as a Rank Group leisure park. The plans aroused a great deal of controversy and attracted protesters who made camp among the trees, determined to prevent the scheme from going ahead. In fact, it was an unforeseen fall in the Rank Group profits that did most to jeopardise the development which, by 1998, looked as though it might be abandoned.

 LYMPNE

Lympne has to get a mention if only for the fun of untangling a few tongues. The name is pronounced Lim – and why it needs all those redundant consonants, not to mention the final vowel, I do not know. It was the name of a Celtic town even before the Saxons had their way with it and no doubt it seemed to them a perfectly proper way of spelling it.

The Romans called it in their forthright fashion Portus Lemanus, and built one of their main Saxon Shore forts there to discourage raiders from sailing up the River Limen (now the Rother) and indulging in their piratical taste for the old Nordic pursuits of pillage, rape and arson.

After the Romans left, the port silted up and the once major town declined to become a very minor village indeed. *Sic transit gloria mundi* (as the Romans would probably have said if they had known about it). However, in AD 892 the channel was still open and a great Danish force of 250 ships sailed into the River Limen and rowed up into the Weald, stopping only to overcome very inadequate opposition at Appledore and make that their own base for a sustained campaign.

Today's memorials to the great days of Lympne include the Shepway (shipway) cross on top of Lympne Hill and, lower down, the remains of the old Roman fort, now called Stutfall Castle, which lie in tumbled ruins where centuries of landslides of the old shoreline cliff face have left them.

Lympne Castle and church are still there and no doubt both played their part in secreting smuggled goods brought up under cover of darkness from the Romney Marsh beaches below. Once, when an old pew was removed from the chancel inside the church, a chamber was uncovered which was at once identified as a hiding place for tubs of Hollands or other un-Customed wares.

The castle today owes much to the restoration carried out by Sir Robert Lorimer, the Scottish architect, at the beginning of the 20th century. He rescued it from threatened ruination and made it into the single large house it is today. Visitors to the castle can climb up to the concrete room which was built as an observation post during the Second World War, and also go up to the ramparts and enjoy the view over the Marsh. The ramparts are supposed to be haunted by the spirit of a Roman soldier who cannot bring himself to desert his look-out post and there are other ghosts reputed to be associated with the old castle, too.

More popular than either the castle or the church is lovely old Port Lympne, where John Aspinall keeps open house for the thousands of paying visitors to the mansion and its 300 acres of parkland wildlife sanctuary and 15 acres of gardens. The house is set into the steep slope of the old shoreline, from which the terraced gardens drop away, giving splendid views across Romney Marsh and, on clear days, across the Channel to the coast of France.

🍁 LYNSTED

Some old villages are marred by new building, but some seem to want to show it off almost as people show off new clothes.

Lynsted is one of these. It lies between the old A2 (Watling Street) and the newer M2, south-east of Sittingbourne. That it is old is obvious from the number of fine old buildings in and around the village. Half-timbered Lynsted Court, for instance, and Lynsted Park, part of an Elizabethan house that was built by Sir John Roper, later Lord Teynham, in about 1599, although it underwent major alterations in 1829. Jeffries is another 15th or 16th century timber-framed house and there are others, as well as several more modest old houses and cottages.

The church of St Peter and St Paul was very badly damaged during the Battle of Britain in August 1940 when a 50kg bomb fell through its roof into the north aisle, but it has been restored and now dares any other vandals to repeat the outrage. Another bomb from the same stick damaged several old houses nearby.

This is a village with a duck pond, which does much to enhance the cul-de-sac of new houses beside and behind it. There is a school, too, and the Black Lion pub and altogether it comes as no surprise to learn that Lynsted has been several times a winner of the Kent's Best Kept Village title.

There is a particularly fine collection of memorials inside the church, including those to members of the Roper family. In 1377 John Roper stumped up £50 towards the cost of a ship to fight the French and in 1588 another John was knighted for his financial contribution towards the cost of fitting out a ship to fight the Spanish Armada. It was Margaret Roper, daughter of Sir Thomas More, who, after his execution in 1535, brought his head to Lynsted on the way to Canterbury to be buried in the family vault in St Dunstan's church.

Another local family remembered in the church were the Hugessons, merchant adventurers and Royalists who raised armies to fight Cromwell's Parliamentarians.

🍁 MARDEN

When the 18th century Kentish historian Edward Hasted rode through Marden he was moved to record that it was a place with three streets, 'the houses of which are but meanly built'. The village has changed a bit since then. There are still, basically, three streets, but the 'meanly built' houses have aged into picturesqueness and although the village straggles a bit raggedly out into the Wealden countryside, the centre has that bustling, lively look that identifies it as anything but a mere picture postcard museum piece.

The village is in two parts: West End, where the school is, and Church Green, where the church and the Chequers public house are. The old village stocks in the churchyard were brought there from the village centre where they were in danger of being vandalised. Still in the centre, though, is the old timber-framed Court House, recalling days when Marden was part of a Royal Hundred and exempt from the jurisdiction of the county sheriff.

It inherited that status from even earlier times when it began as a den – a part of the original Wealden forest – claimed by the Royal manor of Milton Regis, near Sittingbourne. There was probably a Saxon church on the site, but the present church of St Michael and All Angels was built at the end of the 12th century, although it has been added to several times since then. One of the additions was the chapel built by Flemish immigrants who made their homes here in the 14th century and gave Marden a share in the prosperity created by the medieval Wealden woollen industry.

The church had a spire once but it burned down centuries ago and the present 'snuffer' that crowns the wooden top of the tower was added some time before 1700.

Marden has grown substantially in recent times and is still growing but its most strikingly 20th century feature, apart from the industrial estate on the north side of the station, is the stained glass in the windows of the church chancel. It was designed by Patrick Reyntiens in 1962 and represents with vivid modernity the vision of St John in Revelations.

In 1998, Kent Wildlife Trust extended by nine acres Marden Meadows Nature Reserve, one of the best remaining examples of unimproved hay meadows, with a huge variety of wildlife, some of it quite rare.

Marden Fruit Show is the biggest show of its kind in Britain and is now known as the National Fruit Show.

🍁 MATFIELD

Although 20th century building has made Matfield virtually an extension of Brenchley (or possibly Brenchley an extension of Matfield) the two villages could hardly be more different from each other. Brenchley wears its antiquity like a medal; Matfield looks as if it is equally proud of its modernity.

Like Brenchley, Matfield is surrounded by orchard farmland, as suggested by its relatively simple village sign, which stands on the village green. It is a wrought iron hoop with the name across the middle, two apples dangling above it and the date 1981 in a horizontal diamond at the bottom.

It is a pleasant place in which to wander, with its white painted boarded Wheelwrights Arms overlooking the cricket pitch and the pond and with some attractive Georgian houses for neighbours.

The First World War poet Siegfried Sassoon was born in Matfield and the village was the setting for one of Kent's more spectacular murders during the Second World War. In 1940, Dorothy, wife of Walter Fisher, and their daughter Freda were shot to death in an orchard immediately behind Crittenden Cottage, just outside the village. Their housemaid, Charlotte Saunders, was also found dead inside the house. The murders were investigated by no less a person than the head of Scotland Yard's famous Flying Squad. He suspected an attractive young widow named Florence Ransome, a frequent visitor to Crittenden Cottage where she sometimes spent the weekend with Walter Fisher. The (then) unconventional lifestyle of the people involved served to divert some public attention from the London Blitz, which was at its height during the Old Bailey trial. Florence Ransome, although she maintained her innocence throughout, was found guilty. She was not executed, however, but certified insane and sent to Broadmoor.

More recently, the parish was thrust into international headlines when, in 1997, Badzel Park farm and rural centre became the final refuge of the notorious Tamworth Two. The porcine pair were on their way to the slaughterhouse when they took to their trotters in a bid to save their bacon. After a short but well-publicised spell of freedom they were finally rounded up, reprieved by public demand and became two of Badzel Park's most famous residents.

 MEOPHAM

Cricket on the green, Meopham.

Meopham (pronounced Meppum, by the way) is chiefly notable for two things: for being the longest village in Kent and for having a windmill that is one of the best-preserved in Kent. It is a large village on the North Downs, south of Gravesend, and it is also well known for its cricket green, claiming that the game has been played there for at least 250 years.

The mill, which overlooks the green, is a six-sided black wooden smock mill with white sweeps standing on a two-storey brick base. It was probably built some time after 1801 by the Killick brothers and it worked by wind power until 1927, when a petrol engine took over. Later still it was worked by an electric motor, with the mill generating its own electricity until it was linked to the mains.

By 1958 the structure was in a bad state of repair and was given, with the land on which it stands, to Kent County Council, which leased it back to the owner for 999 years. Restoration was begun and a trust set up to take over the lease and bring the mill back to working condition. Very practically, the base of the mill was put to use as a parish council meeting room.

The mill is, in fact, unique in Kent for being six sided. Eight sides were more usual and it is supposed to have been built originally from the timbers of an old battleship dismantled at Chatham dockyard.

Probably the reason why the green and its presiding windmill have come to typify Meopham is because the village has very little else to commend it to the visitor's eye. It is a bit of a straggle along the A227 between Wrotham and Gravesend, having exchanged its former rural reason for being there for an almost wholly commuter-based community.

Most of the people who live in Meopham now have no recollection at all of the historic broadcast made by Harry Price, the famous psychic researcher, from Dean Manor in 1936. During the broadcast, one of his pieces of equipment, designed to record changes in temperature, created some excitement when it suddenly twitched, first upwards and then down well below normal, for no apparent reason.

Mr Price thought such behaviour could only have been provoked by some paranormality that he did not, however, identify. Later during the night that Price spent in the house with BBC technicians and others, mysterious footsteps were heard and could not be accounted for, and there were reports of other ghostly sights and sounds from Dean Manor, too.

It was in Meopham church that John Tradescant, Charles I's Dutch gardener, married in 1607 and his son, also John, was christened there a year later. They were both botanists and travellers and together they introduced many plants hitherto unknown in this country, including lilac, plane and acacia.

In the housing shortage aftermath of the Second World War, Meopham was scheduled to become one of London's proposed new satellite towns with 11,000 homes housing another 40,000 people, plus industries to employ them. The scheme was abandoned because it would have taken up too much good farming land, which was even more valuable at that time, but the village has grown nevertheless, although on a less dramatic scale.

🍁 MEREWORTH

The whim of an earl's son who wanted a better view from his new house put Mereworth (pronounced Merryworth) where it is now.

When the Hon John Fane, later Earl of Westmorland, inherited the manor of Mereworth early in the 18th century, he was a man who had everything – except a Palladian-style mansion which was the 'in' status symbol of his day. So in 1720, he had one built to a design by Colen Campbell. Today, Mereworth Castle can be glimpsed from the Maidstone-Tonbridge road: a domed and porticoed confection of a house, as unlike a castle as anything that can be imagined, with flues cunningly built between the inner and outer shells of the dome so that the perfect lines should not be marred by chimney stacks.

It is privately owned and out of bounds to everyday sightseers at the end of its parkland drive although the house was used as a setting for the James Bond film *Casino Royale.* But when it was built it overlooked the old village, which its owner decided spoiled the view. So he built new homes for the villagers where they would be hidden from his fine new house and had the old ones demolished.

He built the villagers a new church, too, and it is the steeple of Mereworth church that identifies the village to travellers today. It is the most incongruously ornate village church spire in Kent, looking for all the world as if it had been evacuated from the City of London. In a way, it was. The church was modelled on Inigo Jones' St Paul's church in Covent Garden, but with a steeple copied from that of St Martin in the Fields.

The memorials in the old church were conscientiously removed to the new one and have since been joined by others, including one to Rear Admiral Charles Lucas, who distinguished himself during the Crimean War. As a Royal Naval Lieutenant, he picked up a live enemy shell from the deck of his ship and tossed it overboard, an act of bravery that led to his becoming the first man to win the Victoria Cross.

One of the treasures of the church was a unique and very valuable 9ft 6in by 6ft 6in Persian rug of unknown age, depicting the Crucifixion, which hung 20 feet from the ground on one of the walls. It was given to the church in 1994 by the Arab owner of Mereworth Castle and stolen by person or persons unknown in 1997.

It was not the first theft from the church. In 1995, workmen stripping paint inside the church accidentally started a fire. They thought they could put it out themselves but when they went for the fire extinguisher they found it had been stolen and had to send for the fire brigade.

Milton

Like a number of other villages elsewhere in Kent, Milton has been virtually absorbed into the apparently endless inflation of an overwhelming neighbour, in this case Sittingbourne. So much so, that the two are spoken of in the same breath and there will be those who will wonder at Milton's inclusion among the county's villages.

But Milton (properly Milton Regis) was a royal manor long before Sittingbourne mattered at all and in Saxon times the Isle of Sheppey was just part of the manor of Milton, where stood the mother church for chapels in villages for several miles around.

Milton was Alfred the Great's town of Middleton and its creekside location would have made it a significant little port. Holy Trinity church claims to be the second oldest in Kent still in use. There was certainly a church on the site in AD 680, although most of the present flint and stone building is 14th century.

It was that same creekside location that brought the 19th century paper mill that completely overwhelmed the little 18th century fishing village. The mill's need for water drained the creek (although nowadays, its water comes from its own wells) and the creekside area became lost among industrial development.

The Dolphin Yard sailing barge museum is on one branch of the creek, into which the tide still flows, and Holy Trinity church, with its exceptionally massive tower, keeps watch over the Milton and Kemsley marshes and particularly the immediately neighbouring Church Marshes Country Park.

Despite all the expansion of Sittingbourne that has blurred its boundaries and the new building that has bloated its own appearance, vestiges of the old Milton are still to be found. The beamed and peg-tiled old court house still stands, defiantly incongruous today, in the main street.

Minster-in-Sheppey

In writing about some parts of the Isle of Sheppey there is an underlying sense of a need to get the words down quickly because tomorrow may be too late. The seaward coastline can change quite dramatically and very suddenly whenever another bit of the clay cliffs crumbles and fall into the sea.

The island is highest east of Sheerness and it slopes away to flat marshy grazing and mud levels on the southern, Swale, side. It was on the heights (though that is perhaps too grandiose a word for the reluctant eminence that serves as high land on the island) that the first settlers built their homes. There, too, a widowed Kentish queen, Sexburga, built a monastery in about AD 670, on the spot where an angel told her that before many more years had passed a heathen people would conquer the nation. The abbey was one of the first in Kent and was specially a place to which royal or noble widows or spinsters could retire from the stresses and strains of the man's world in which they lived. The ex-queen, fittingly enough, became its abbess.

This was the part of the island that became known as Minster and the angel was quite right: 200 years later the heathen Vikings did descend on the Saxon nation and, eventually, conquered much of it.

But at first they came not to conquer but to plunder and one of the more accessible places in which to do that was Sheppey. The minster there offered worthwhile prizes for any raider and in fact so hospitable did they find this 'island of sheep' that when they came in force, bent on conquest rather than mere plunder at last, it was on Sheppey that they made their first headquarters and where they established a beach-head for their advance towards the west. They remained masters of Sheppey until the Normans came and took it from them yet, oddly, they left no recognisable traces of their occupation – that have yet been discovered, at any rate.

The old abbey gatehouse has been restored and made into a local history museum and the surviving main tower of the abbey is undergoing restoration. One of its many exhibits is a headstone incribed beneath the exortation: 'O Earth cover not my Blood' with the explanation: 'To the memory of a man unknown who was found murdered on the morning of the 22nd April 1814 near Scrap Gate in this parish; but his head was severed from his body. A subscription was immediately entered into and 100 guineas reward offered on conviction of the perpetrators of the .....'. The bottom of the stone is broken off and the rest of the inscription illegible.

At least one miracle is credited to the minster. At some time (the date seems to have been lost in the telling and re-telling of the story) a year-old child called Ann Plott who lived in a cottage nearby was run over by a loaded dung-cart and crushed 'flat as a pancake'. A passing woman led prayers for the child, who miraculously returned to life and actually spoke her mother's name for the first time as she did so. Before night fell that same day, the child was dancing in the street again, evidently tempting fate to send another dung-cart to do the same thing all over again.

When an inventory of the abbey's possessions was taken for Henry VIII in 1536, when he was dissolving the monasteries, among the items listed was 'a chamber hanging of painted paper'. As far as is known, this was the earliest use of wallpaper in England.

In the early 20th century, Sheppey was seen by speculative developers as a kind of blank cheque on which to write their own fortunes. A man called

Frederick Ramus bought about a thousand acres of farmland on which he laid out roads and drains and then offered for sale small plots of land on which buyers could build their own homes. It probably sounded lovely and in fact he sold some 3,000 of these plots to about 1,000 Londoners. Many had no doubt read the *Daily Express* comment in August 1903 which wondered why no one had thought of converting 'this semi-circle of grassy cliffs, swept by the breezes of the German Ocean' into a health resort.

Well, after the Second World War the population of Minster had swollen from about 250 people in 100 homes to about 5,500 in 1,800 homes. Since then, it has continued to grow and is now very near that point when it can no longer be considered a village but has become a small town.

MINSTER-IN-THANET

The 'in Thanet' is necessary to distinguish this village from the quite different one of the same name 'in Sheppey'. Both took their names from very early religious houses (minsters), this one from the nunnery founded in the 7th century by King Egbert of Kent for Ermenburga, Queen of Mercia.

Ermenburga took the religious name of Eva and became known as Domna Eva or Domneva, to be succeeded as Abbess of the Minster by her daughter, Mildred, who is still regarded as the patron saint of Thanet.

Parts of the old minster that gave its name to the largest parish on the Isle of Thanet still stand, probably one of the oldest inhabited houses in England. At the Reformation, it became a private home, which it remained until 1937 when it was restored to a small community of Benedictine nuns from Bavaria, refugees from the Nazis. It can be visited at certain times.

Today, the village sign, which stands on the pavement outside shops in the village centre, shows a white deer with the date AD 670. The built-up centre of the village is, for the most part, no more than a century old although the present church of St Mary dates from 1150. It has been restored since then, particularly over a period between 1861 and 1863 and again, more thoroughly, in the 1970s.

Of a number of interesting old houses in the parish, Cleve Court deserves a special mention. The house was bought by Sir Edward Carson, lawyer and politician, in 1920. He is probably best-remembered for his cross-examination of Oscar Wilde in 1895. He was given a life peerage in 1921 and died at Cleve Court in 1935.

His widow lived on at the house until she died in 1966. While she lived, Lady Carson was convinced the house was haunted by a Grey Lady who appeared whenever there were children in the house. In his book *Ghosts of Kent*, Peter Underwood recounts a local story about a previous owner who kept his wife locked up until at last she died, childless, although her greatest wish was to have a son or daughter. Andrew MacKenzie of the Society of Psychical Research conducted an investigation into the Cleve Court hauntings, but the house has since been altered and divided up and the ghosts seem to have been laid now.

🍁 NETTLESTEAD

It is said that Nettlestead church owes its stained glass windows to a 15th century Agincourt veteran who came back from France very impressed with what had already been done with stained glass decoration for churches there.

The man was Reginald de Pympe and his son, John, added more stained glass later in the same century. The de Pympes made quite an impression upon Nettlestead in their day. Reginald moved into Nettlestead Place, which he rebuilt at about the same time as he had the church rebuilt and embellished with the new glass.

By that time, the family had already earned a certain notoriety as a result of one of its sons, Philip, having been committed to Canterbury prison for harbouring an outlaw in 1318. The same Philip was pardoned for homicide in 1337. Another member of the family fought with Edward IV in France and then afterwards sided with the Duke of Buckingham in his rebellion against Richard III's claim to the throne. That was a mistake, because the rebellion was crushed and the de Pympes had their estates confiscated, although they were restored to them later, after Henry VII became king in 1485.

After the de Pympes, Nettlestead Place was owned by a family called Scott whose men seem to have had a weakness for strong-willed wives. Sir John Scott once locked his wife in a room in the house during a quarrel, but she escaped by digging away the mortar round some of the stones with a bodkin.

Then a 17th century Scott, Edward, who backed Cromwell in the Civil War, found himself at variance with his wife, Catherine, who was so whole-heartedly Royalist that she reputedly bore the illegitimate son of Prince Rupert, the dashing Cavalier cavalry leader and, later, naval commander.

Edward might well have found that a bit too partisan for his liking even if he had shared her loyalty to the Crown. As it was, he took a particularly dim view of the affair and during a family row that went on for some days, Catherine waited until Edward left the house and then slammed the door in his face when he tried to come back in again.

Her husband laid siege to the house, resolved to starve her out and presumably carry on the row to a rather more satisfactory conclusion, but Catherine escaped and the domestic fracas ended with Edward deciding that all he could do was acknowledge the little bastard, who was called Thomas, as his own son.

Yet another Nettlestead Scott, Sir Thomas, was one of the leaders of some 10,000 men who formed a 16th century Home Guard and stood ready to repel invaders should the Spanish Armada force a way past the English ships and make a landing on Kentish soil.

Later, Nettlestead Place fell into less caring hands and might well have crumbled into total disrepair as a neglected farm store during the 19th century. But in 1920 enough of it remained intact to encourage a Mr R. Vinson to buy it, and restore it to a family home, still with its old stone gatehouse and a remarkable 13th century undercroft. Since then it has been converted into flats.

Nettlestead village is barely distinguishable from its larger neighbour, Wateringbury. Both suffer from traffic which diverts from the A26 Tonbridge road in order to take the more direct route through the riverside villages to the Paddock Wood industries.

The church of St Mary the Virgin has been in need of repair for some time and by 1998 the 13th century tower was recognised as being in a dangerous condition.

🍁 New Ash Green

We tend to think of villages as invariably old, but New Ash Green is a reminder that this is not so. It was developed as a 'green fields' site in the 1960s, borrowing its name from the nearest existing village of Ash, in unspoilt North Downs countryside between Gravesend and Wrotham. The plan was to house 6,000 people there, including some of London's 'overspill' population, in 2,200 homes built on 430 acres of farmland.

The houses would be built around The Minnis, an open green, in a pattern of neighbourhoods separated by woodland but linked by footpaths and vehicle-free roads. A compact shopping centre, with a large car park where shoppers could leave their cars and move about without having to worry about traffic, would provide for all the needs of the villagers. It would, its developers promised, be unique and 'one of the most unconventional private housing developments in Europe'.

When the idea was first put forward, Kent County Council turned it down.

So did a Government inspector at a public inquiry. But Richard Crossman, then Minister of Housing, over-ruled them both and building began in 1967.

All did not go smoothly. The Greater London Council, which had said it would rent 450 of the homes for 'overspill' Londoners, pulled out. The developers lost financial backing and quit the project, leaving it started but far from finished, and the village was labelled an experiment that failed. But in 1971 another developer took over the site of the half-completed village and realised the original concept. The finished result was, indeed, something new in housing development and today the village has about it the lived-in look of an established community with the highest proportion of young people in the UK, almost a quarter of the 7,000 population being aged 11 to 21.

All villages acquire legends and New Ash Green's concerns a mysterious nine foot tall wooden statue which appeared overnight in the village. It was a figure of a man, his chin resting on a staff, and because of the expression on his face he was dubbed the Weary Traveller. No one claimed him but he was adopted by the village and made to feel welcome. One night he disappeared again, as mysteriously as he had arrived, to be rediscovered later, lying in a ditch. He was recovered and resited in private ownership. He must have sent out word that this was a good place for carved wooden men because in 1986 another, smaller, wooden statue appeared in woodlands half a mile away. This one was given the name of the Wanderer but he, unfortunately, burned down, as mysteriously as he had arrived, a few years later.

🍁 NEWENDEN

When 16 year old Prince Edward was at Newenden in 1300, money was paid from the Royal exchequer for him to play at 'creag' with his friends. Cricket historians like to use this as evidence that cricket (creag?) was being played on Kentish soil by a future king of England almost 700 years ago, but there is no proof that creag was, in fact, cricket.

The village is the last – or, of course, the first, depending upon how you look at it – in Kent, literally teetering on the edge of the Kent Ditch county boundary with East Sussex. It is also one of the smallest Kent villages, comprising very little more than a tiny church, a single pub, and a handful of houses.

Yet for centuries after His Royal Highness played creag there (whatever it was), Newenden continued to be a town and River Rother-side port of some consequence. Castle Toll is the site of a prehistoric hill fort and the port was

sacked by Saxons when it was the Roman town of Andredscaster and by
Danes when Saxons knew it as Eopenburnen. Each time it was rebuilt.
Edward I owned estates here and it was the site of one of the first Carmelite
houses in England. As late as the 16th century it is said to have had no fewer
than 16 inns or taverns and Newenden shares with Faversham the distinction
of being one of only two market towns in Kent named in the Domesday
survey.

Then the Rother changed its course, Newenden lost its reason for being and
today, only the 500 year old White Hart remains to offer its hospitality to
travellers. The church is smaller than it once was and still looks too big for a
population of only a few hundred people.

🍁 NEWINGTON

There are two Newingtons in Kent: one near Folkestone, which has been
practically extinguished by the Channel Tunnel terminus, and this one, near
Sittingbourne, which is larger and stretches along the A2, almost linking up
with Rainham.

Neither has imprinted itself particularly deeply upon the county
consciousness, although the A2 Newington has at least won a place in county
lore.

In 1936 a great stone was moved from the corner of Church Lane to the
entrance to St Mary the Virgin's church. It is known as the Devil's Stone,
identified by a metal plaque which, however, does not tell the story that
belongs with it. According to legend, the Devil was once so disturbed by the
ringing of Newington church bells that he went to the belfry one night and
gathered the bells up in a sack. Then, with the sack over his shoulder, he
jumped down.

But as he landed, he tripped over the great stone and fell, leaving his
footprint stamped into the stone and spilling the bells out of the sack. They
rolled down the lane towards Halstow and into a stream which, the story
always ended, flowed clear as a bell ever afterwards. The footprint remains to
be seen – with a little imaginative perception – to confirm the truth of the story!

🍁 NEWNHAM

I couldn't be sure whether it was the village that lent its name to the valley or
the valley that gave rise to the village. It hardly matters now. Village and

valley have lived together too long and harmoniously to question the precedence of either.

The point is that Newnham is a surprisingly little-spoilt village with very little depth on either side of the street and with one particular gem, timbered Tudor Calico House. Once it was the vicarage and the house was altered in 1712 when the outside walls were plastered and painted with a design of flowing foliage in a terra cotta colour. Large pieces of the plaster remain, still with their painting on them.

🍁 OARE

From its eminence above Oare Creek, an arm of Faversham Creek, Oare looks down on mainly flat marshy countryside and thinks itself lucky to be, for the most part, well above flood level.

The old windmill, stripped of its sweeps, is a private home behind a pub of the same name and its former glory is better commemorated in the village where the local inn sign depicts it as it may have looked once.

The approach to Oare, through the sprawl of Faversham's industrial overflow, is discouraging but the village itself is rather appealing. Oare Creek marina is crammed with small craft right up to the road which passes both the Windmill and the Castle public houses and climbs steeply up to the Three Mariners in the village itself. One road leads to the neighbouring hamlet of Uplees and another meanders off towards the church, which stands back a little, gazing out across the creek.

🍁 OFFHAM

The quintain on Offham green is the only one still in use, albeit very occasionally, in England. Some say the sport of quintain tilting was known to the Romans. It was certainly practised by medieval knights and is capable of entertaining equestrians and spectators still.

It is, in fact, a wooden post with a freely revolving arm on the top, a bit like a weathervane. One end of the arm is flat and from the other end hangs a wooden truncheon or some other substituted unpleasantness. The object of this unique relic of medieval horseplay is to ride full tilt at it, strike the flat end with the point of a lance and gallop on in order to get out of range before the business end swings round and catches the rider a fourpenny one. Great fun!

The quintain, Offham.

Offham village lies just comfortably off the A20 west of West Malling, a pleasant place around its green but with ragstone quarries and landfill sites for uncomfortably near neighbours. In 1994 planning permission was given, in spite of local opposition, for further ragstone quarrying at Blaise Farm on condition that quarrying started within five years. In 1998, the company asked for the deadline to be extended, again arousing a chorus of opposition from villagers who foresaw more years of rubbish tipping into the resulting hole in the ground when quarrying ended. At the time of writing, the outcome of the application is still unknown.

🍁 OLD ROMNEY

When you remember that New Romney, which is a town and so has no place in this book, was built before 1100, you get some idea of the age of Old Romney. Before that date there was only one Romney, and this was it, the one named among the original Cinque Ports.

It became stranded well inland as a result of successive and successful attempts to win land from the sea. The first of the 'innings' were on the estuary into which the River Rother emptied, between Lydd and Romney. All the marshes hereabouts belonged to the church and it was the church that first began the business of enriching itself by turning unproductive marshland into good fertile grazing land.

As the sea was held ever further back, Romney had to reach out towards it and the old town retired into village status, well inland of the last and persisting site of the new one.

Old Romney church – St Clement's – used to overlook the town's wharf in those long gone days when it had a wharf. Now it presides over a few houses and a lot of open countryside. It was extensively restored in 1959 thanks to the help given as a result of a deal done with the Rank film organisation which wanted to film locally some scenes for a Dr Syn film. One of the more successful examples of collaboration between God and Mammon. There has been further restoration since then, too.

The church makes a pretty picture with its different roof lines and its heavily buttressed tower topped by a hipped steeple, surrounded by trees and grass and the warmly welcoming red-brick houses of the village. In 1967 when much of the restoration work was afoot, one of the workmen was wheeling a barrow through the porch into the church when he noticed that where the grass had been worn away a slab of stone was showing through. He thought it was probably a long-lost memorial stone but he was interested enough to get the rector's permission to dig it up and lo! it proved to be nothing less than an even longer-lost pre-Reformation stone altar table. It was an item of church furniture that was banned by Royal command of Edward VI in 1550, so it was reasonable to conclude that instead of being destroyed, as the king presumably intended, it was taken out and buried, perhaps in the hope that the edict would be lifted or the hazards of ignoring it lessened by the passage of time.

It was quite a find and it was later provided with a wooden frame and set up under the east window of the north chapel to serve the sort of purpose it would have served 400 years or more ago. It joined another treasured curio of the church, the font, which dates from about 1300 and is made with a square bowl of Purbeck marble standing on an octagonal stand with supporting pillars, all the capitals of which are different.

When William Cobbett rode through Old Romney in 1823, he was moved to remark on the height of the local corn, and its yield. 'I never saw corn like this before,' he enthused. He went on: 'At this Old Romney there is a church (two miles only from the last, mind!) fit to contain 1,500 people, and there are, for the people of the parish to live in, 22 or 23 houses! And yet the vagabonds have the impudence to tell us that the population of England has vastly increased.'

Since his day, the population of Old Romney, certainly, has increased, but whether or not Cobbett would still be impressed by the local corn I couldn't say.

🍁 Old Wives Lees

The temptation to include a village with a name like Old Wives Lees is irresistible, and I wish I could say how it got the name. But if anyone knows, I have not yet met them.

The village is spread around a minor crossroads on the Downs above Chilham, almost wholly residential and relatively modern, with a spacious village green, the Star Inn and some extensive views over a countryside fruitful with orchards and other farmland.

Formerly, it was distinguished for the annual race that was held, when two village youths and two maidens competed for a prize endowed by Sir Dudley Digges of Chilham Castle. But even that little peculiarity died out with the coming of the 20th century as village youths and maidens no doubt found other prizes to compete for and now there really is little more than the name – but what a name! – to attract any attention to it at all.

🍁 Ospringe

Time was when Ospringe drew much of whatever prosperity it had from the London-Dover road on which it sat. Pilgrims travelling to Canterbury, messengers hot-hoofing it between London and the coast, occasional royal entourages following the same route and, later, stage-coach travellers – all had occasion to be grateful for the hospitality of this little wayside oasis a mile from Faversham.

As the 20th century aged, Ospringe joined in the chorus of A2 villages demanding a bypass to rid it of the increasingly troublesome traffic. The opening of the M2 in the 1960s did not altogether meet those demands and now another road carries traffic from the industrial north of Faversham to the A2 without the need to go through Ospringe.

The village is administratively part of Faversham, having been brought within the borough boundaries in 1935. A great deal of building on the north side of the A2 long ago erased any physical separateness there once was.

The flint and timber buildings on the corners of Water Lane, which leads off the A2 towards the church and the elevated M2, are part of the 13th century Maison Dieu, which was once a travellers' rest with buildings on both sides of Watling Street (A2). Now, the building on the right looking into Water Lane is a museum, and that on the opposite corner is a private house. The Ship Inn occupies the corner site on the other side of the A2.

Until the 1960s, Water Lane lived up to its name. A stream ran through ancient Queen Court Farm further along the lane and in times of flood – which happened every year and often several times a year – flowed into the lane. Water Lane became, for a day or two at a time, the bed of the stream before it went under the A2 and emerged again to water the watercress beds and power the 17th century Faversham Chart Gunpowder Mill on its way to Faversham Creek.

Then, when the M2 was built, the lane was dug up, hollowed out with a huge double-barrelled culvert occupying the complete width of the carriageway, and relaid again. Since then, no more water has flowed on the surface of Water Lane; it all flows under it. Much more tidy, more comfortable for everyone, especially the occupants of the cottages with front doors opening onto the footpath, whose front rooms were once flooded every time a car drove along the flooded lane – but undeniably less picturesque.

🍁 OTFORD

One of the attractions of the Bull at Otford is a high-backed oak settle that once – it is claimed – belonged to Thomas a Becket himself. If it is true, no doubt the archbishop's saintly person once sat in it and modern customers at the inn are invited to do likewise and to make a wish. I can only report that I found it too uncomfortable to sit in for long enough to finish my lunch and my wish was not fulfilled. It was still raining when I went outside again.

The Bull was once the refectory at Otford monastery and was granted a licence by papal bull (hence the name, despite the beast on the inn sign) in 1538.

The Archbishops of Canterbury had a palace at Otford for 500 years or so.

Of course, there were archbishops' palaces all over the place, never more than a day's riding apart, so that travelling prelates could be sure of a comfortable night's rest when they were pursuing their necessarily peripatetic profession. The one at Otford was improved and enlarged after Thomas Becket used it.

According to legend it was Becket who provided the place with water when he struck the ground with his staff and a spring gushed forth. He is also said to have banished nightingales from the palace precincts after one disturbed his prayers with the splendour of its song, and to have laid a curse on all blacksmiths at Otford, condemning them never to prosper there after one accidentally lamed his horse while shoeing it.

In fact, I am told nightingales do sing in Otford and blacksmiths did prosper there long after Becket had gone to gory glory. Perhaps canonisation gave the prelate a change of heart so that he lifted his ban and his curse post mortally.

After Becket, successive archbishops stayed at Otford. One, Archbishop Winchelsea in 1313, died there. Cranmer wrote his *Thirty-Nine Articles* there and it was he who gave the palace to Henry VIII, after the king, queen and 5,000 retainers stayed there on the way to Dover and the Field of the Cloth of Gold.

The king was characteristically ungrateful, grumbling that it was a 'rheumatick' place and deciding that he would use Knole at Sevenoaks whenever he travelled this way in future, and the rest of his household could stay at Otford. In fact, he quickly tired of both places. Otford was sold to pay Army wages and its roof stripped of lead to make ammunition. After that, inevitably, it soon declined into ruin and today almost nothing is left, apart from a bit of a tower and a few cottages. The village declined with it.

Then came the railway in 1862. It brought some growth, although the village remained mainly agricultural until the 1930s, when the railway was electrified. Since the Second World War Otford has become almost entirely another Kent commuter village.

But at least it is a thriving village, with a school, shops, a car park and the only 'listed' duck pond in the country, where the ducks actually get a food allowance from the parish council.

🍁 OTHAM

So far, Otham has remained almost desperately aloof from neighbouring Maidstone, although apparently always on the verge of being swamped by the encroaching spread of modern homes to which it seems it must inevitably succumb before very long.

Otham is a village that is rightly celebrated for some very fine 14th and 15th century timber-framed houses: Synyards, Gore Court, Wardes and Stoneacre. Stoneacre was the home of a gentleman in 1467 although the present house dates from about 1480. It was beautifully restored and extended between 1920 and 1926 by the then owner, Aylmer Vallance, who having completed his work capped it generously by giving it to the National Trust. It is open to the public, although it is still occupied as a private home.

Wardes, in Otham Street, was thrust into the limelight in July 1985 when raiders murdered gardener Bill Austin, who lived there, and wounded the owner, 74 year old widow Ellen Ditcher, with rifle bullets and a crossbow bolt.

Otham church is still very much a village church, a little away from the centre of population. Its well buttressed tower is topped by a weatherboard belfry and, on top of that, a broached, shingle-clad spire that looks like some kind of hat that has been pulled down rather too firmly against the weather.

In the churchyard is buried the author William Stevens (who used the pen-name 'Nobody'), who died in February 1807 aged 74. A stone was erected to his memory by the Society of Nobody's Friends, which was founded in 1800 as a charitable organisation.

The village sign split villagers in 1997 as a result of a referendum organised by Otham parish council. The sign, which stood in front of the village war memorial, had become rusted and was removed for restoration. Some of the villagers felt it should be re-erected somewhere else. Some even wanted it demolished. But in the end it went back to its original site where it is, indeed, one of Kent's most unusual village signs: an open box framing a collection of ancient tools. A plaque on the ragstone plinth on which the all-metal sign is mounted says simply: 'OTHAM Parish council 1894-1994. The tools that shaped our village.'

Whatever you think of the sign, it is difficult not to envy its position on the large grassy village green overlooking a spectacular view of the surrounding countryside.

🍁 PATRIXBOURNE

It is generally accepted, I think, that it was at Patrixbourne that Julius Caesar's expeditionary force met and defeated the British during his second invasion of Kent. He couldn't have chosen a nicer spot for it.

Patrixbourne is just north of the A2, south of Canterbury: a pretty collection of half-timbered and thatched houses. The 12th century church has a rare circular east window and a main doorway rich with Norman stone carving rivalled only by the much better-known one at Barfreston, away to the south-east.

The Big House here used to be Bifrons, former seat of the Marquess of Conyngham, the great favourite of George IV. The house is no longer there, but Highland Court still stands. This was the stone mansion built about 1904 for Count Louis Zborowski, the racing motorist who, with Captain John Howey, was responsible for the famous Romney, Hythe and Dymchurch (The Little) Railway. Count Zborowski, a naturalised Briton, built and raced the famous Chitty-Chitty-Bang-Bang cars. He already had his own 15-inch gauge railway at Highland Court when he met and became friends with Howey.

With locomotive designer Henry Greenly, they dreamed up the idea of creating a real, but miniature, railway. Zborowski died when his car skidded on an oil patch into a tree while he was competing in the 1924 Italian Grand Prix at Monza and he never saw the work begun on the Romney Marsh railway which has since become one of Kent's major tourist attractions.

🍁 PEMBURY

Road traffic has loomed large in Pembury village life since before the road from Sevenoaks to Woods Gate at Pembury became the first in Kent to be turnpiked in 1710.

In fact, it was the traffic on that road that put the village where it is. When stage coaches began using the old packhorse road and passengers in them clamoured for refreshment along their way, the good people of Pembury forsook their centuries-old church of St Peter in the centre of what was then Pepenbury and rushed a mile or so south to set up shop alongside the suddenly lucrative coach route.

The village can even claim to have played a part in founding the Automobile Association. After an early motorist, a German called Schlemtyne, told friends at the Fanum Club in London how he missed the corner outside Woodsgate House at Pembury one night and crashed into a wall, it was decided there and then to form the AA and to provide the Pembury corner with a gas lamp as one of its first acts.

The old village church, now isolated, has in its churchyard the tomb of Anne West of nearby Bayhall. She once dreamed she was buried in a trance and ordered that when she was, in fact, buried the lid was to be left off her coffin and one end of the tomb left open. She also left instructions for her butler to bring food and drink to the opening every day for a year – just in case.

When she died in 1803, aged 34, her wishes were respected and until 1947 one could still look down into the vault through an opening at one end. Poor Anne West. Her Bayhall, once the home of the great Kentish Colepeper (or Culpeper) family and also of a Duke of Buckingham, became a ruin, said to be haunted by her ghost.

Hers is not the only ghost hereabouts, either. The tale is told that when the owner of Hawkwell Mansion, west of Colt's Hill, died he left the house to his widow and two daughters. One of the daughters married and went to live with her husband in London, but he ill-treated her so cruelly that she left him and walked home to mother in Pembury, carrying her baby in her arms.

When she arrived, however, she found the house had been burned down and her mother and sister gone to stay with friends. Too tired to walk any further that night, the young mother laid down with her child in the grounds of the ruins of her home. Next morning, they were both found, frozen to death, and it is the young woman's ghost that is said to haunt the site still.

One ghost that does not seem to haunt the village is that of Margery Polley, a widow who was burned at the stake at Tonbridge in 1555, possibly the first woman victim of the Marian persecutions. But she is not forgotten. A horse trough on the green, alongside the A21, is her memorial, placed there by voluntary subscription in 1909 and now used as a flower-bed.

There was considerable development between the wars, and since, but the village centre, around the school, post office and Royal Oak public house, has kept its 'villagey' character and is all the better for having been bypassed at the end of the 1980s. Pembury has a vineyard now, and in 1998 it became a pioneer among Kent villages when the parish council opened its doors to the world with its own Internet page.

🍁 PENSHURST

Thousands of people arrive by car, coach and bicycle every year to visit Penshurst Place, one of Kent's most stately of stately homes and ancestral home of the Sidneys. They follow a well-trod trail: accounts of visits to Penshurst Place are to be found in the diaries of 17th century diarist John Evelyn and others.

The house was already old when its most famous owner, that Sir Philip Sidney who was such a favourite of Elizabeth I, was born there. Sir Philip it was who was expressly forbidden by Her Majesty to go with Sir Francis Drake on his second expedition to the West Indies, lest – as she put it – 'we should lose the jewel of our dominions.'

Instead, she appointed him Governor of Flushing in the Low Countries at a time when Holland was at war with Spain and so was at least in some measure responsible for his being fatally wounded at the Battle of Zutphen in September 1586. However, he contrived to earn immortality with the words, 'Thy necessity is yet greater than mine', with which he refused a drink of water on the battlefield and instead quenched the thirst of another dying soldier. Sir Philip himself died 25 days later, aged 32, and was brought home to England for a State funeral at Old St Paul's, where his memory outlived his memorial which was destroyed in the Great Fire in 1666.

Penshurst Place fell into ruin and had to be rescued during the 19th century by succeeding generations of the family. Today, one of the great glories of the ancient house is the splendidly restored Great Hall with its unrivalled 60 foot high chestnut-beamed roof.

The village of Penshurst, which grew up around the house, has become used to taking second place to it, though it deserves better. It lies between two rivers, the Medway and the Eden, each crossed by a bridge by visitors coming or going in either direction, and the last century has been rather kind to it, largely by leaving it pretty much alone. Some of the Tudor-style buildings are actually Victorian, although some are genuine.

Penshurst claims one of the most modern vineyards in England, which is open daily to the public throughout the year.

🍁 Plaxtol

Many of Kent's villages are resisting change of almost any kind; some are absorbing change, so that it requires a certain amount of diligence to discover where it has taken place. Some, though, bear the scars of changes that have not been kind and Plaxtol, I think, is one of those.

It is still a pretty village but the timelessness that clung to it even a decade ago seems to be deserting it now and it has about it an air of trying not to lose the will to live. In 1994 the local metal works closed after 20 years in the village; the old bakery, which once employed nearly a hundred people and served thousands of customers every week, is also closed and abandoned, as is the former garage; and the distinctively-named Rorty Crankle inn has been decommissioned and is now a private house.

An effort to keep the village alive was made in 1998 when the village stores in The Street became one of the first village shops to benefit from a new Rural Development Commission scheme to help small businesses survive. It received a grant to help pay for, among other things, the setting up of a sub-post office in the store, a major life support aid in itself.

The village still has its school and the church and its neighbouring white weatherboard cottages still make an eye-catching group. The church has no dedication, having been built in 1649 during the Cromwellian Commonwealth as the inscription over the door testifies.

Until the Victorians had their wicked – well, sometimes misguided, anyway – way with so many old churches, this one was the only complete 17th century church in Kent. The particularly fine hammer-beam roof remains, as does the Cromwellian oak altar in the Lady Chapel, and the churchyard contains some particularly interesting gravestones, including some examples of the kind unique to West Kent and East Sussex, made of ragstone shaped like human figures with carving on the 'heads'. The transepts and chancel, however, were added during the alterations in 1885 and 1894.

Excavations in 1857 uncovered evidence of an extensive Roman villa on the banks of the River Bourne, where a Minerva statuette was found, and there was a Roman cemetery at nearby Ducks Farm.

There are a number of 14th, 15th and 16th century houses in the vicinity, the best-known of which is Old Soar Manor, a mile east of the village, which is the remains of a medieval knight's hall house with a 13th century solar (family quarters). It is owned by the National Trust. A red-brick Georgian house now covers the site of the old manor hall. The manor was once owned by the Culpeper family, which looms large in Kentish history and whose menfolk were rumoured to have founded their fortunes as the biggest landowners in Kent and Sussex by marrying all the available heiresses of the day.

The house is said to be haunted by the ghost of a 17 year old servant girl called Jenny who, in 1775, was called in to help prepare food for a great Christmas feast. While she was busy in the dairy, the family priest, who had been getting himself into the Christmas spirit, took it upon himself to initiate a nativity of his own. When Jenny's personal advent made itself known as a result, she asked the parson what she should do about it and he told her she should marry her boyfriend – a solution that left poor Jenny so unreassured that she fainted, hit her head on the font and drowned in it. When she was found, it was assumed she had committed suicide and she was buried in unconsecrated ground, from which she returns from time to time to haunt the old house.

Another notable local property is Fairlawne House, once owned by Sir Henry Vane senior, Secretary of State to Charles I. His son, also Henry, became Governor of Massachusetts in America but was later executed by Royalists for his Puritanical support in 1662. The house has been suggested as the likely model for Shipley Hall, home of Lord Uffenham, one of the characters created by P. G. Wodehouse. His daughter, Leonora, lived there after 1932 when she married Major Peter Cazalet, who trained race horses for both the Queen and the Queen Mother.

 PLUCKLEY

All villages lay some claim to fame, or at least distinction. But little Pluckley, near Ashford, got a bit carried away when it claimed to be the most haunted village in England. Nobody seems to know quite how many ghosts do haunt Pluckley. There is always someone who knows of one the others hadn't heard about.

Jack Hallam, in his *Ghost Tour* (1967), put Pluckley 'very near the top of the league table for the most haunted village in England.' In 1975, Andrew Green wrote in his *Shire Album of Haunted Houses* that it was 'the most haunted village in Britain'. Peter Underwood, in *Ghosts of Kent* in 1985, decided there were 'about a dozen' ghosts that haunted or had haunted the immediate area. And there have been other accounts that have come to similar conclusions.

However many there are, they include a schoolmaster who hanged himself; a highwayman who was run through by a sword at (appropriately enough) Fright Corner; a mysterious Red Lady, a member of the formerly prominent Dering family, who searches for her child among the churchyard gravestones; another Dering lady whose spectre wears the red rose her adoring husband dropped into her coffin; a former miller; a monk; and an old gipsy watercress seller who burned to death when she fell asleep and dropped her clay pipe onto her straw bedding.

There has even been a report of a complete fife and drum band marching through one house, and in the 700 year old Black Horse inn furniture has been said to rearrange itself.

It all seems a bit excessive, especially as Pluckley could just as easily have settled for its distinctiveness upon those intriguingly domed Dering windows that are a feature of so many of the local houses, including the Black Horse.

There is, of course, a legend attached to them. It claims that one member of the Dering family discovered that a forebear of his during the Civil War once escaped the consequences of his equivocal politics by leaping through a window of that shape. Deeming such windows to have been lucky for his ancestor, 19th century Sir Edward Cholmeley Dering had all the windows on the estate replaced with ones of the favoured pattern.

The family home, Surrenden Dering, was burned down and only the stable block now remains, parts of which have been converted into private homes around the old cobbled courtyard. The family is remembered today, as well as by the Dering windows, by the black horse family emblem that still remains on the vanes of several of the cowls on top of local oast houses.

 ROLVENDEN

Once, long ago, Rolvenden was by the sea. Now it stands above Romney Marsh, between Tenterden and the county boundary at Newenden, on the A28. It is not unlike Tenterden, in fact, though on a smaller scale, with its wide village street, the grass verge and its houses of weatherboard and brick.

Originally two hamlets, one – Rolvenden Streyte – was virtually burned down during the 17th century Great Plague and the remaining villagers moved a mile away to Rolvenden Layne. Later, however, the Streyte was rebuilt and became the main village centre, attracting several antiques shops and a motor museum and generally wearing an air of self-confidence that is by no means usual among villages today. Rolvenden Layne is almost wholly residential, centred upon a large recreation area and the Hooden Horse pub.

Although a relatively small village, Rolvenden has several claims to fame. Lady Jane Grey, who was Queen of England for nine days in 1554 until Queen Mary ended her reign by chopping off her head before the crown could be placed upon it, lived at nearby Halden Place. She may have known the Rev John Frankish of Rolvenden, who became one of the Kentish Marian martyrs when he was burned at the stake at Canterbury in 1555.

Hole Park was where Edward Gibbon lived. He became famous as the author of the monumental *Decline and Fall of the Roman Empire*, which was published between 1776 and 1788.

The Georgian style mansion, Great Maytham Hall, was designed by Sir Edward Landseer Lutyens. Part of it is now apartments but some, together with 18 acres of surrounding parkland, is open to the public at specified times. Once it was let to Frances Hodgson Burnett, author of *Little Lord Fauntleroy*, and was noted for its 'secret garden' which is generally reckoned to have been the inspiration for the book of that name.

Rolvenden's restored postmill, rare in Kent, is probably the best surviving example in the county. There has been a mill on the site since 1596 at least. Its restoration was carried out in 1956 as a memorial to John Nicholas Barham who 'lived his short life within sight of it' and died in August 1955, just before his 18th birthday. The mill, which is privately owned, featured in the Tommy Steele film *Half a Sixpence*.

Rolvenden Station is an embarkation point for travellers on the privately-owned Kent and East Sussex Railway, a nostalgic regeneration of the good old days of steam trains.

🍁 Royal British Legion Village

Although part of Aylesford parish, the village deserves a mention of its own. Founded on Preston Hall Hospital, it grew out of the efforts of the British Legion (before it was distinguished with the Royal prefix) to provide for ex-servicemen needing continuing support during and after convalescence.

The present house, despite its Jacobean style, was built in the 1850s and was part of an extensive manor that dated back to the 12th century when the Colepeper family held it during the reign of King John. Much later, the estate came into the ownership of Edward Ladd Betts, a railway engineer who built the present Preston Hall before he was ruined by financial speculation. As a result, the property passed to the Brassey family.

Later still, another owner, Madame Sauber, let the Hall for use as a Red Cross Convalescent Home during the First World War and when the war was over it became a hospital for ex-servicemen.

The village was built around it, providing homes and workshops for the families of patients at the hospital until the men could return to work themselves. The author George Orwell was one of those who received treatment for tuberculosis at Preston Hall. It was taken over by the National Health Service in 1948 as a chest hospital and later became a general hospital until the new Maidstone General Hospital in Hermitage Lane opened in 1984. Today, Preston Hall houses the headquarters of the West Kent Health Authority and is also the site of the Heart of Kent Hospice, which was opened in 1992 by Diana, Princess of Wales.

British Legion Industries still provide work for ex-servicemen in the village. Most of the original houses have now been replaced, although the distinctive Preston Hall Colony bungalows are still in use on the opposite side of the A20, alongside Hermitage Lane.

🍁 Ruckinge

Ruckinge is one of a series of villages that overlook the Royal Military Canal from the lower slopes of the old Romney Marsh shoreline, strung out along the B2067 from Lympne westwards to Ham Street, where the two features part company.

It isn't a big village, and it might well have avoided notice altogether but for a few notable residents. Some of them were more notorious than notable, including several members of the Ransley family. The family name was linked, during the 18th and 19th centuries, with the infamous Hawkhurst Gang and, later, the Aldington Gang of smugglers, both of which featured in nefarious exploits throughout Kent.

Two Ransley brothers who were hanged in 1800 on Penenden Heath at Maidstone for highway robbery lie buried in Ruckinge churchyard and George Ransley became a leader of the notorious Aldington Gang, known as The Blues, in the 1820s. George was born in 1782 and was a ploughman and a carter before his big break came when he found a smugglers' cache of spirits which he sold for enough money to enable him to build his own house, the Bourne Tap, at Aldington. When the Gang was broken up finally in 1827, he escaped the death sentence and was instead transported to Tasmania, where he seems to have lived out his life as a law-abiding farmer.

More recently, Ruckinge was home to Thomas Aveling, pioneer of the steam traction engine in the 1860s. It is Aveling – or, more accurately, his engine – that is featured on the village sign, outside Ruckinge village hall.

St Mary Magdalene's church is of Norman – perhaps even Saxon – origins, with a startlingly massive low tower capped with an odd-looking spire that looks like an inverted funnel. Only devoted locals could call it an attractive building and inside it is almost entirely devoid of any kind of architectural or even memorial features. It is much bigger than the size of the present village, even with its modern additions, warrants and must once have catered for the spiritual needs of a much larger community.

🍁 RYARSH

Ryarsh is not a particularly distinguished little village, a mile or two north of West Malling, but it deserves a mention if only because its Victorian vicar for 38 years, the Reverend Lambert Blackerell Larking, became the first secretary of the Kent Archaeological Society and launched the record of its activities, *Archaeologia Cantiana*, which is still going strong.

He wrote more than 200 pages of the first volume. He was an authority on Saxon and other ancient manuscripts and made a translation of the Domesday Book which was published after his death.

Today, Ryarsh is the workplace of Birling parish, and bricks from Ryarsh

Brick Co have protected Middle Easterners from the heat of the sun and scientists at King Edward Point from the freezing temperatures of the Antarctic, not to mention lions in the lion house at London Zoo from the vagaries of the English climate.

In 1998 plans were put forward to turn the local sewage works, for long an eyesore, into public gardens which, if the scheme goes ahead, could make a significant improvement to the village generally.

❧ ST MARGARET'S BAY

In 1910 J. Harris Stone published a guide to St Margaret's Bay which he called *The Piccadilly of the Sea*. When John Jewell, archivist to St Margaret's Bay Local History Society, updated that book in 1980, he gave his own book the same title, which was originally intended to apply to the Straits of Dover, then as now the busiest seaway in the world.

At the western end of St Margaret's Bay is the coastguard station at Langdon Battery which monitors that seaway, and much of the land behind the Bay is owned by the National Trust. The Saxon Shore Way long distance coastal walk crosses some of that land.

Local tradition claims that the first of the Huguenot refugees to arrive in England landed here. Could be. It is far more certain that smugglers used the Bay and the cliff-top village behind it, though we are back to tradition when we recount the old story of a certain parish clerk who is said to have stored in the church tower ropes and tackle for hauling smuggled goods up the cliffs from the beach. The illicit but very popular trade must have been seriously inconvenienced, though probably nothing more, when Capt Philemon Phillips, RN, persuaded the Government of his day to set up a coastguard station, with six men and a boat, there in 1737.

St Margaret's Bay joined the modern world in 1865 when Lord Granville, then the new Warden of the Cinque Ports, decided the little fishing village should blossom into a popular seaside resort. At different times it has hosted such famous visitors and temporary residents as Lord Arthur Cecil, Lord Byron, Max Beerbohm, Noel Coward, Ian Fleming and Peter Ustinov. The Bay is also a popular starting point for cross-Channel swimmers.

In 1918 the last bomb to be dropped on England in the First World War fell on St Margaret's and when the Second World War began the area, like many others along the south coast, was evacuated of all unnecessary civilians and occupied by troops in readiness for the expected invasion. It was near here that the big naval guns, nicknamed Winnie (the popular abbreviation of

Winston Churchill's name) and Pooh (after Winnie, of course!) were sighted on France. When they were fired they did more damage to local property than they did to their target area, but there is a story that after Winnie fired her first salvo of the war, her commander telephoned the Prime Minister to report a direct hit. Back came the query: 'Direct hit on what?' 'On France, sir,' was the reply.

Today, a bronze statue of the man himself, Winston Churchill, is a prominent feature of the six-acre garden of The Pines, at the top of the steep road down to the little bay itself. The garden is open to the public, as is the local museum opposite. The statue was unveiled by the wartime Prime Minister's grandson, also Winston Churchill, in November 1972. The Dover Patrol Memorial was there first, however, unveiled by Edward, Prince of Wales, in 1921.

🍁 St Mary's Bay

Author Edith Nesbit, who found fame late in life as the author of such children's classics as *The Railway Children, The Wonderful Garden* and *The Treasure Seekers*, came to St Mary's between the wars, with her second husband Captain Tucker. They lived in two former air force huts which were connected by a covered way; one they called the Long Boat and the other the Jolly Boat. When she died in 1924, she was buried in the churchyard in the old village of St Mary in the Marsh, just inland of the Bay, where there is a memorial to her inside the church.

Another writer who knew the whole Romney Marsh area well was Anne Roper (1903-1988). She is remembered both by a memorial tablet inside the church and also by the little leaflet guide to the church which is on sale to visitors and which she wrote in 1983.

St Mary's Bay is a popular holiday resort, with its own Romney, Hythe and Dymchurch Railway station serving local holiday camps.

It was after the First World War, during which there was an emergency landing strip there, that the Bay became part of that Arcadia on the South Coast described by Dennis Hardy and Colin Ward in their book *Arcadia for All*. Seaside bungalows were built and soon it became a popular little residential area, growing quickly into a new village with all its own amenities almost literally 'a stone's throw' from the sea. Until just before the Second World War there was no church and weekly services were held in a local garage. But then a modern church was built and St Mary's Bay was created a parish with a resident vicar.

The inland village of St Mary in the Marsh hardly warrants the name. It is a very small cluster of mainly modern homes beside the church of St Mary the Virgin and the Star Inn. The church was there long before the Bay became built up and assumed the dominant role. There was a wooden Saxon church before the Norman one was built and the present building dates from about 1133, with later additions and alterations. The little mound on which it stands would once have offered a refuge from regular flooding of the surrounding countryside and, like all the Marsh churches, it has its own (always unsubstantiated) tales of being used by smugglers down the centuries.

🍁 ST NICHOLAS-AT-WADE

The village earned its name and, no doubt, its existence, by being at a point where it was possible to wade across the Wantsum. The old channel once made a true island of Thanet but has since become little more than a drainage ditch at its northern end as a result of centuries of land reclamation on either side.

It is a pleasant little village, with a main street that is actually in two parts: High Street and The Length, both with a pleasant mix of old and newer houses. There are some typically Dutch gabled houses and a really rather fine church which dates from the 12th century, with a 14th century tower that is still a landmark for shipping in the Channel.

Among the memorials inside the church are several brasses, including one of charming simplicity to William Henaker who died in 1609. It says only that he lived to the age of 39 'or thereabouts' and then died and was buried. The church also boasts one of the county's best 17th century pulpits, with a little cartouche dated 1615.

In 1983 a workman inside the church put his foot through a hole in the tiled floor while he was replacing a light bulb. Investigations led to the discovery of hundreds of human bones, equivalent to 15 or 20 bodies, in an hitherto unsuspected burial area inside the church.

The bones were reinterred and the pit made safe but before that happened the vicar had the foresight to put a time capsule (well, a biscuit tin wrapped in a plastic bag, if we are being prosaically exact) into the cavity. It contained a 20p coin, a picture postcard of the village, a parish guide and a copy of the parish magazine. It will make an interesting find in a few centuries time, if it does, in fact, survive that long.

SARRE

Unusually, this little village in which the main Canterbury-Thanet road forks to Margate and Ramsgate, has no church of its own. Since the 16th century, it has been part of the parish of neighbouring St Nicholas-at-Wade.

What it does have, however, is the 15th century Crown Inn, an early posting inn that for 300 years has been famous for its cherry brandy. The front of the inn is embellished with painted panels containing the names of some of its celebrated patrons, who have included people like Charles Dickens, Rudyard Kipling, Ellen Terry and Sir George Robey. So celebrated has it become for its cherry brandy, that it is now better known as the Cherry Brandy House.

The King's Head hotel, which first welcomes the visitor into Sarre from the Canterbury direction, declares itself to have been an alehouse since 1630, so between the two, the inns have a long record of dispensing hospitality to wayfarers through the village.

More of a landmark, though, is Sarre windmill, which occupies a high spot between the Ramsgate and Birchington roads. The smock mill of tarred brick and weatherboard, with a boat-shaped top, was built in 1820 and later heightened, in 1856, when the base was converted from one to two storeys. Although it ceased to work in 1920 as a windmill it then became the first Kent mill to be worked by steam. The sweeps were dismantled but have since been restored and the mill now offers yet another haven for travellers as Sarre Mill tea rooms.

 SEAL

The A25 saunters through Seal before it nudges the northern fringes of Sevenoaks, passing what is probably the village's most eye-catching building, Grumbles. The timbering is not original but part of a 16th century 'restoration'. The house was a 14th century pilgrims' rest and has been many things since then. At the moment it is an Italian restaurant.

It stands on the corner of the A25 and the road that descends from Kemsing, passing the 600 year old church of St Peter and St Paul, with its avenue of clipped yews. Above, the particularly tall 15th century ragstone tower watches benevolently over the little village and offers a fine view over the Darent valley.

Once, Seal was part of Kemsing parish, and did not become an independent ecclesiastical parish until 1874. In the 13th century, the lord of the manor was granted the right to hold a Monday market at Seal and a fair on the festival of St Peter and St Paul, so it is likely the church – or, at any rate, a church – was already there then although the actual date of its foundation is not known. Indeed, there is some evidence that there was a Saxon church on the site some long time before the present one was built.

From a niche over the porch doorway, St Peter, with his crossed keys in one hand and a book in the other, is as much a memorial to the Miss Hensman of Sevenoaks who carved him as a reminder of his shared patronage of the church.

Every village has its particular story to tell and Seal's is of the church rood screen which was taken down during the Civil War and stored for safe-keeping in the manor house. But after the Restoration of the Monarchy, instead of being restored to the church, the screen was made into furniture, including a sideboard which was finally given to the church in 1947 and is now to be found near the lectern.

The church also boasts a particularly fine brass of Sir William de Bryene, Lord of Kemsing and of Seal, and the last of his line, who died in 1395. The 54 inch tall knight in armour is in the chancel and it is in very good condition for its age.

Seal used to be a rather pretty little village, but it is in danger of succumbing to the sprawl of 'greater Sevenoaks' and being sucked into the town's expanding suburbia. Even so, aside from the main road, it is still a pleasant enough place, where the preponderance of relatively new building nestles in harmoniously enough with what little remains of the village the church alone remembers.

🍁 SEASALTER

The name hints at the origins of Seasalter because this was one of the parts along the North Kent coastline, between Faversham and Whitstable, where seawater was once allowed to flood, at high tide, into troughs. At low tide, the water was boiled off, leaving highly prized salt to be harvested.

Today, the sea wall prevents any such activity and the former low-lying salt-pan areas are sites for holiday camps and chalets. There are shops and a yacht station and during the summer the whole sea-front bustles with holidaymakers.

If there is a village centre, it is on the corner that takes its name from the Blue Anchor public house, although it was at one time known as Granny Hart's Corner from the name of a proprietor of the inn. Although the present building is Victorian, there has been a house of the same name since 1756 and before that it was the Crown.

Most of the old village, which consisted of a church, the inn, a few farm buildings and a parsonage, had gone by the 1960s. The Saxon church was destroyed by the sea in about 1100 and in 1472 a chapel dedicated to St Alphege served a very small settlement known as Seasalter Street. The dedication commemorated the fact that the body of the Saxon Archbishop Alphege rested at Seasalter on its way to Canterbury for burial.

The building of the sea wall made it possible to farm the hinterland, although the sea demonstrated its disdain for such barriers during the disastrous east coast floods in January 1953. In the 1960s and 1970s speculators bought up plots of the former marshland and split them up into so-called 'leisure plots' of about one-tenth of an acre each which were sold, often with no legal access to them and certainly no planning permission for any kind of development. Some of the plots were used as allotments but many were simply abandoned.

For more than a hundred years the Seasalter Company operated as a cover for local smugglers, for whom the deep littoral of sand and mud and the even deeper area of flatland between the shoreline and Blean Woods might have been purpose-made.

Much of this whole coastline, which is actually watered by the Swale, the channel that separates the Isle of Sheppey from the mainland, is a nature reserve, for some of which Kent has to thank Red China. Henry Newlyn was a retired civil engineer who had spent much of his life in the Far East before he retired to Tunbridge Wells, and in 1973 he bequeathed £50,000 to the Society for the Preservation of Nature Reserves and another £50,000 to the Chinese People's Republic. But the Republic felt unable to accept the money from a Western Capitalist and so it, too, went to the SPNR. Part was used to buy land for a nature reserve at Sandwich Bay and the rest bought 15,000 acres between Faversham and Seasalter, to add to the reserve already leased by the Kent Trust for Nature Conservation.

In 1998, Seasalter was again in the news when evidence of a potentially very exciting Iron Age settlement was discovered under housing development on a derelict caravan park.

🍁 SEVENOAKS WEALD

Which areas of land were in the Weald in Kent and which were not once mattered a great deal more than it does today. Woodland in the Weald, for instance, was exempt from tithes, payable by landowners for the support of the church, and juries were called upon to decide whether land was or was not part of the Weald. Today the matter is more of academic interest but the little village of Sevenoaks Weald permits of no doubt about where it stands.

It is a village of some 1,500 people, below the ridge on which the town of Sevenoaks stands, just west of the A21, with a large green surrounded by trees and overlooked by the school and memorial hall. The post office, which wears its Kent Best Kept Village Shop first prize award (1995) and other awards like medals, looks across the green at the Windmill pub and the whole effect is pleasantly attractive rather than picturesque.

This is one of several Kent villages that claim to have been the birthplace of William Caxton, father of English printing. The man himself said he was born in the Weald, but he left very few clues about exactly where. When the writer Vita Sackville-West married Harold Nicolson, they went to live at Long Barn in Sevenoaks Weald and they believed this was the house in which Caxton was born.

The house is old enough. When the Nicolsons were renovating it, in 1915, a coin dated 1360 was found behind some plaster on one of the walls. But in Tenterden, which likes to think it is the most likely birthplace of Caxton, the Sevenoaks Weald claim tends to be dismissed as a fairly clumsy attempt by the Kentish Men to usurp the claim of the Men of Kent.

Probably the most imposing local house is Wickhurst Manor which, although mostly 19th century or modern now, has a medieval stone hall at its core and 16th century panelling.

🍁 SHEPHERDSWELL

Or is it Sibertswold? The village itself seems to be in some doubt about which it should properly be and map makers tend to make up their own minds, which can be a bit confusing.

By whichever name you find it, the village stands at a crossroads just east of the A2, and on the Canterbury-Dover railway line, some ten miles south-east of Canterbury. As well as the main line railway, Shepherdswell (as I shall continue to call it because, I find, most of its residents seem to use that name) is the starting place for the East Kent Railway line, which once wound its way through Eythorne and Tilmanstone to Eastry. The line was built in 1911-17 to serve the East Kent coal mines and link up with a proposed new port at Richborough. The project petered out however, and the line was closed in 1987. It has since been reopened to Eythorne by volunteers and is one of several such 'nostalgia' lines operated by steam train enthusiasts.

It is a village that seems to keep itself very much to itself and is reticent about whatever contributions it has made to Kentish history. Even its church, St Andrew's, has an almost apologetic look about it, as though it knows it is a modest newcomer, having been built in the 1860s for an economical (even then) £1,500. But it is the fourth church to be built on the same site, the first having earned a mention in the Domesday survey so its ancestry is nothing to be ashamed of.

There was a Methodist chapel in the village, where services were held from 1870 until 1995 but since then Methodists and Anglicans have both shared St Andrew's church, which is something else in which the little church might take some pride.

🍁 SHIPBOURNE

It was in Shipbourne (pronounced Shibbun) that Christopher Smart, poet and friend of Dr Johnson, was born in 1722. In 1752 he published a blank verse poem of no less than 700 lines, which was a sort of 'teach yourself' treatise for would-be hop growers, detailing at painstaking (almost tedious) length all that anyone could possibly need to know about the subject.

He called it simply *The Hop Garden*, and having unburdened his creative ambitions of such a weighty masterpiece he went mad, apparently the victim of a surfeit of two equally dangerous opiates, alcohol and religion. Smart was one of the sons of a steward of the Vane family and while he was in an asylum he wrote with charcoal on the walls the first lines of his much less famous poem, *Song to David*.

Milton's friend Sir Henry Vane owned Fairlawne between 1615 and 1640 and was Charles I's Secretary of State. His son, also Sir Henry, became Governor of Massachusetts in America in 1635 and despite his Parliamentary sympathies, provoked Oliver Cromwell into exclaiming: 'The Lord deliver me from Sir Harry Vane!' and then engineering his own deliverance by having Sir Harry imprisoned. After the Restoration, Charles II found a more permanent solution to any problems Sir Harry gave rise to and had him beheaded in 1662.

The Vanes were followed, as owners of the extensive Fairlawne estate, partly in Shipbourne and partly in neighbouring Plaxtol, by the Cazalet family. In about 1880 Edward Cazalet gave the village its heart: the present church, with its huge gargoyles, a pub called the Chaser, and some cottages, most of which surround the very large village green.

The church of St Giles is virtually a memorial to the Cazalet family. They, too, have gone now, the last one commemorated by a marble tablet with his portrait and those of his pet dog and horses. But it was a Cazalet who made Fairlawne famous as a racing stable and Major Peter Cazalet became the trainer of horses owned by HM The Queen Mother.

In the 1970s, as a by-product of his research for his book *In Search of Blandings*, Norman Murphy concluded that Fairlawne was in fact the model upon which the author P. G. Wodehouse based Shipley Hall, 'the ancestral seat of George, sixth Viscount Uffenham'. Wodehouse's daughter Leonora married Peter Cazalet in 1932 and she and her husband were living at Fairlawne during the time her father was writing stories about Lord Uffenham.

# SHOREHAM

> When I went down to Shoreham
> Some time another year,
> I found a cross for sorrow
> And pain for men to bear.
> For lads I knew aforetime
> Were sleeping otherwhere.

Those words, from a poem entitled *A Kentish Lad* by George H. Vallins included in his *Kent Ways* in 1923, refer to the great white memorial cross on the hillside across the River Darent opposite Shoreham church. It was dug in 1920 as a memorial to local men killed in the First World War and is still a prominent landmark today.

Dorothy Gardiner described her own visit to Shoreham in her *Companion into Kent* in 1934, in which she recounted a story she was told about some smugglers who arrived at the Old Crown Inn there early in the 19th century, with a wounded Spaniard. The foreigner was nursed back to health by the daughter of the owner of the inn, a man known as Squib the Maltster. When he was fit and well again, the Spaniard married Squib's daughter and for a while they lived together in the village.

But then one day the Spaniard was taken by the press-gang and his wife died giving birth to their child. Many years later (so the tale concluded) the Spaniard returned to Shoreham but when he learned his wife was dead, without another word he turned round and walked away again, never to be seen thereafter.

Methodist John Wesley used to visit Shoreham to see his great friend and supporter the Rev Vincent Perronet, who was vicar there for 57 years. Wesley is said to have had to be rescued by the Perronet family from an unsympathetic audience when he preached from a stone near the bridge over the Darent, but the experience did not stop his preaching in the vicarage kitchen.

Artist Samuel Palmer lived in The Water House with his father and nurse from 1827 until 1833. His work was considered eccentric in his day but is regarded more highly today. He used to entertain a group of artist friends known as The Ancients, who used the village as a sort of artists' colony until the 1830s. Another of Palmer's friends was William Blake, who visited Shoreham at least once.

A more recent distinguished resident was the writer Lord Dunsany, who was president of the Shoreham Players in the 1950s and wrote a one-act play about the village called *The Road.*

Shoreham church preserves a large painting depicting the return from Africa of Lieutenant Verney Lovett Cameron, RN, son of a former vicar. He headed an expedition to Africa to find Dr David Livingstone but met bearers bringing the explorer's body to the coast. Cameron went on, however, and became the first white man to cross Africa from the Indian Ocean to the Atlantic. After his triumphant homecoming, Cameron settled down and became a writer of boys' books. When he died at the age of 50, as a result of being thrown from a bolting horse in Bedfordshire in 1894, his body was brought to Shoreham for burial.

Papermaking was once a local industry but the mill closed during the First World War and although it was reopened in 1920 it finally closed in 1925. Today Shoreham's one shop is well outnumbered by the five public houses and its railway station houses a Countryside Centre.

🍁 SHORNE

An elongated village on the northern slopes of the North Downs, about equidistant from Gravesend and Rochester, Shorne is, in the words of the ubiquitous estate agent, wholly 'res' and most definitely 'des'. The church tower looks out across the estuary towards Essex and London although St Paul's Cathedral in London which, in 1771, Richard Hayes of Cobham told his diary he could see with the naked eye from Shorne windmill is no longer one of the local sights.

Just outside Shorne is the lost village of Merston, apparently a stockaded

Saxon settlement which got a mention in the Domesday Book, unlike Shorne. An archaeological dig in 1957 revealed foundations of a small Norman church, but the village seems to have been deserted by 1445, possibly as a result of a visitation of plague.

The village was the medieval home of Sir John Shorne who had a reputation for being something of a healer. He was credited with having blessed a well in Buckinghamshire which became a certain cure for the ague and he was said to have captured the Devil in his boot, too, although subsequent history suggests that it was not a very secure incarceration.

The church of St Peter and St Paul was built during the 13th and 14th centuries, with a tower added in the 15th century, and has been in continuous use ever since. When students at Canterbury College of Art were commissioned to design stained glass for the church the result was the abstract representation of the four seasons to be seen in the church porch.

Dickens knew this part of Kent very well and he once remarked that he thought Shorne church had one of the most peaceful and secluded churchyards in Kent, forming 'the fairest spot in the garden of England'.

Today, that particular accolade might be applied to the 174 acres of Shorne Country Park, which was once a clay pit on part of Cobham Hall estate and is now claimed to have become, since it was opened in 1987, the most popular public open space in Kent.

🍁 SISSINGHURST

This is another of those Wealden villages that suffers – or, perhaps, benefits; it is difficult to be sure which – from being almost wholly outshone by one local feature, in this case nearby Sissinghurst Castle. The Castle, which is nothing of the sort and never was, is world famous especially for its gardens. The village is virtually unknown outside its immediate neighbourhood.

The Castle is, in fact, all that remains of the splendid Elizabethan mansion built by Sir Richard Baker some time before 1573, when it was visited by Elizabeth I, and whose family owned it until 1730. History, with its love of all larger-than-life characters and legends, and with its special fascination with the bizarre, has pretty well dismissed most of the Bakers, but it remembers very well indeed that 16th century Sir John, sometimes known as Bloody Baker or even the Kentish Bluebeard.

History claims Sir John as a lawyer and a politician, a Kent Member of Parliament, Under-Sheriff of London, Recorder of London, Attorney-General, Chancellor of the Exchequer and Speaker of the House of

Commons. Legend would like to label him a seducer of local girls, rapist and murderer – when he wasn't satisfying his blood lust with his enthusiastic support of the religious persecutions of Catholic Queen Mary, who he once entertained at Sissinghurst.

But history casts a good deal of doubt upon whether or not that reputation was justified, at least by anything more than general ill-will towards a man who undoubtedly feathered his own nest very cosily at the expense of others in a period when there was plenty of scope for such perfectly conventional behaviour. Sir John was lucky enough to die naturally, aged 70, just as Elizabeth I succeeded Bloody Mary on the throne. If he had not, he might very well have died judicially very soon afterwards, or at best ended his days in prison. Elizabeth did not hesitate to clear the decks of Mary's supporters when she came to power.

After his death the great house at Sissinghurst became a prisoner of war camp during the French Seven Years' War, when it first became known as Sissinghurst Castle. The prisoners almost demolished it between their efforts to burn everything combustible to keep warm and to remove everything else in efforts to escape. By the time the war ended, the house was estimated to be worth only about £300.

It was Cranbrook's parish workhouse for more than 50 years, after which it provided homes for farm labourers for another 50 years. Then, in 1930, Sir Harold Nicolson and his wife, the writer Vita Sackville-West, found it. Vita told her diary: 'Fell flat in love with it', and her love affair with the house and its gardens lasted the rest of her life.

She dubbed it there and then Sleeping Beauty's Castle and she wrote a poem about it, which she called simply *Sissinghurst*. She and Sir Harold spent a great part of their lives creating the world-famous gardens that are still a place of pilgrimage today, long after both of them died, she in 1962 and he in 1968. It is her personality that has over-ridden any impressions earlier owners left on the house, or what now remains of it, and the gardens which are now owned by the National Trust and visited by garden enthusiasts from all over the world. The tower study where she worked is lined with her books, including her gardening books, and is preserved just as it was when she was writing in it. Visitors can look, but cannot go inside.

The house is not to be confused with Georgian Sissinghurst Place which was destroyed in 1948 by fire caused by an electrical fault. Vita Sackville-West wrote about that fire in her novel *Easter Party*.

 SMARDEN

Smarden has laid claim, with some justification, to the title of the prettiest little village in Kent. The 12th century church of St Michael the Archangel sits behind the Flying Horse pub with almost matriarchal pride at the centre of its clustered family of white painted weatherboard and beamed cottages with some of the most colourful gardens to be seen anywhere, a gleaming 15th century pub and a general air of just slightly self-appreciative reserve.

Its very arrangement is different from that of most villages of its size: a place of nooks and sudden corners where the visitor is confronted by unexpected oddities. Like the archway formed by the upper storeys of houses that invites entry into the churchyard and boasts no fewer than ten plaques recording Kent's Best Kept Village Competition wins; and the glimpse of the River Beult in Water Lane, at the back of the Chequers Inn.

Parsonage House is at one side of that entrance to the churchyard and the nearby 15th century Thatched House once fulfilled the role of the home of Agatha Christie's detective, Miss Marple, played by Angela Lansbury in the film *The Mirror Crack'd*. The village is one of those that owes much to an injection of commuters who continue a long tradition in the Weald of Kent of adopting some of its best bits as havens from the stresses of successful careers in the City and elsewhere.

All of which makes it particularly unfortunate that Smarden has been tainted with the reputation for being the place where BSE (so-called mad cow disease) began. A local insecticide manufacturing plant was blamed for a spillage of toxic chemicals which began the worst case of pesticide poisoning in the UK in 1963. Two thousand tons of polluted soil was mixed with concrete and dumped into the sea, where it was assumed to be safely disposed of. Although experts differ about the consequences, the chemical, which was later found to be a mutation agent, may have polluted a local pond from which cows drank and, as a result (it is claimed), died. The dead animals were rendered down into feed for other cattle which contracted BSE which emerged in the 1980s.

Part of the enormous tragedy of what followed is that a beautiful little village like Smarden should have been blamed, rightly or wrongly, for it.

🍁 SNARGATE

The Romney Marsh villages are rather like members of a family, each one different but all sharing a common likeness. They are almost all small; some little more than a church, a pub and a few cottages. Perhaps it is that which makes the visitor feel that he is under scrutiny all the time.

Snargate exemplifies this very well. It is a tiny village on the B2080 between Brenzett and Appledore amid open farmland where a handful of houses keep just a respectful distance from 13th century St Dunstan's church and the Old Rectory next door.

The 17th century Red Lion pub is the most reliable village marker. Miss that and you've missed the village. When Cobbett rode through in 1823, he found only five houses and 'a church capable of holding two thousand people'. He seemed puzzled by it but, of course, it was in Snargate that the Lords of the Level (the earliest practitioners of real local government in unified England) held meetings during the 13th century – and perhaps before that – and it would have been an important gathering-place for centuries. It is the size of the churches on Romney Marsh that hint at the extent of the decline of the population of the Marsh generally.

This was one of the churches served by *Ingoldsby Legends* author, the Rev Richard Barham. He was born in Canterbury but he came to live at Warehorne, another Marsh village, and was rector of Snargate from 1817. Later, in 1821, he became a minor canon of St Paul's Cathedral and achieved some fame with his *Legends*, which related embellished stories of several Marsh churches, villages and characters, including Snargate's St Dunstan's church.

Like most of the Romney Marsh churches, St Dunstan's has tales to tell of being pressed into service by smugglers and in 1743 Revenue men siezed a quantity of tobacco hidden in the belfry and a cache of gin under the vestry table. It is said that the north aisle was sealed off from the rest of the church and was used as a regular hide for smuggled wares.

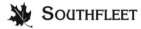 SOUTHFLEET

Southfleet is upstream of Northfleet on that tidal creek or fleet which, having baptised both of them, has since dried up completely.

Considering the extent to which industry, and particularly the cement industry with its associated excavations, has hedged it about for centuries, Southfleet has a surprisingly rural look about it. The new development blends well with older properties like the thatched Black Lion, the Ship Inn and the timber-framed houses opposite. Church Cottages are over 400 years old, the Old Rectory was built in the 14th century, or perhaps even earlier than that, and Chapter Farm House dates from 1470.

The Rectory had a number of ghost stories told about it, including one about a monk said to have been bricked up in one of the rooms, and a Brown Lady who was supposed to have been locked away to die in the cellar. Whether the two were associated in life and whether that association, whatever form it took, had anything to do with the manner of their deaths seems to have become lost among the lumber of local lore.

The church of St Nicholas, although mainly 14th century with relatively recent repairs to the damage caused by fire in 1944, stands on the site of a very much older Roman temple, and rather a lot of Roman remains have been found in and around the village. Southfleet school was founded in 1637 and claims to be the oldest school of its kind in the country.

SPELDHURST

Although part of the parish of Groombridge, Speldhurst is an attractive little village in its own right. It is recognisably another of those villages where the population is very substantially boosted by commuters, but that is no bad thing. 'In-comers' as they are sometimes called tend to come in because they like what they see and many of them have the resources to defend it against unwelcome change. Many of our Kent villages have owed much to in-comers through the centuries.

The George and Dragon at Speldhurst claims to trace its origins back to about 1212 and there has been a village church for at least 700 years, probably since Saxon times. After the Battle of Agincourt in 1415, Sir Richard Waller of Groombridge Place brought back as his captive Charles, Duke of Orleans, who was held prisoner at Groombridge while his family scraped together the ransom that was demanded for him. The local story claims he could have been ransomed earlier than he was, if he had not indulged his enthusiasm for architecture by spending some of the money on restoring the church of St Mary the Virgin at Speldhurst, allegedly as a show of appreciation for his treatment here. It seems rather a pity to have to say, however, that there are variations of this story and the benefactor may have been someone else altogether.

Sadly, the church was destroyed by fire in 1791 when the wooden spire was struck by lightning. A new church was built but it did not satisfy its congregation and was pulled down in 1870 when the present church was built on the same site. The spire was not added until 1923, though.

The church is particularly notable for its windows, most of which were designed by Edward Burne-Jones and made by William Morris.

🍁 STAPLEHURST

The oldest architectural treasure in Staplehurst is without doubt the south door of the church. It may be the oldest church door in England; the remnants of wrought iron that illustrated aspects of Norse mythology suggest that. Once, no doubt, the whole door was decorated with similar ironwork, probably made at one or other of the nearby Wealden foundries, though by whom and quite how such unashamedly pagan symbols came to embellish a Christian church we shall almost certainly never know.

All Saints' church has a memorial window to Henry Hoare and his wife. He was a London banker who, in the 1840s, settled at Iden, then outside the village but now part of its southern end. He restored the church and transformed Little Iden farmhouse into an Italian style villa in which he lived with his wife and their twelve children and a large staff. They called it Staplehurst Place but what remains now is known as Staplehurst Manor nursing home. Iden Manor, built by Henry's son, William, in his father's Iden Park, is now part of the estate belonging to the Convent of the Good Shepherd.

Industrial modernity clusters around the railway station at the very northern edge of the village. Inasmuch as it forms a sort of all-of-a-piece annexe, it does not intrude unduly upon the rest, although that may be less true if a proposed new supermarket is built in the railway station car park.

A memorial obelisk at the side of the village main street commemorates three Staplehurst women and a couple from nearby Frittenden who were executed for their Protestant convictions during the 16th century persecutions that stained the reign of Queen Mary.

A century later, though, Staplehurst had one of the first Baptist churches, in 1644, and in 1647 the rector, the Rev Daniel Poyntel, found himself unable to comply with the requirements of the 1662 Act of Uniformity and was deprived of his living. He became the first Nonconformist pastor there, preaching from his own home on the site where the present Congregational chapel was built.

In 1763 John Wesley preached in Staplehurst, at a house whose owner and 14 other people were summoned before local magistrates for breaking the law. They were charged under an Act of 1664, the magistrates apparently unaware that the law had been changed more than 70 years earlier. The Methodists appealed for a retrial to Maidstone Quarter Sessions and then, when that was rejected, to the King's Bench which granted the appeal and the sentences were quashed.

It was just outside Staplehurst that a train in which Charles Dickens was a passenger crashed in 1865. The accident happened after a ganger in charge of line maintenance works failed to stop the Folkestone-London express, which was derailed on a bridge over the river between Staplehurst and Headcorn. Dickens was in the first of the derailed coaches, returning home from holiday in Paris with his young mistress, Ellen Ternan, and her mother. Dickens was

53 by then, but he climbed out of a window and rescued the two ladies before returning to help the wounded and the dying. He suffered severely from shock and never really recovered from the experience. When he died on 9th June 1870, friends were quick to find significance in the fact that it was five years to the day after the Staplehurst train crash.

The village is the largest of the Maidstone satellites with a population of about 6,000 and both the village and the parish contain some picturesque old houses, including Tudor Loddenden Manor, Great Pagehurst farmhouse and Iden Manor from which the local herb farm takes its name. Another local attraction is the Brattle Farm museum, started in 1976 on a working farm with a fine collection of vintage cars, tractors and agricultural machinery and equipment and a farm trail.

🍁 STOCKBURY

The Stockbury Viaduct, which carries the M2 over the dry valley through which passes the A249 that links Maidstone with the Isle of Sheppey, is as much a local landmark now as Stockbury's old St Mary Magdalene's church.

But the church is higher, seeming to crane its neck to see past the viaduct to the Swale and the Medway estuary beyond. Near the church are the remains of a Norman motte and bailey castle which must once have frowned down upon the surrounding countryside. Pevsner thought Stockbury's church was one of the most interesting in Kent. It is actually a little way out of the village centre, its only near neighbour the adjoining farm. But the grassed churchyard is well-tended and surrounded by old trees and the view from its two-tier burial ground, over surrounding farm land and orchards, has a gentle peacefulness about it that subdues the ceaseless activity of the main roads on two sides.

The entire village is a memorial to St Simon Stock, from whom it takes its name. He lived in a hollow tree hereabouts before he became the head of the Carmelite Order in England at their Aylesford Priory.

It is a small Downland village with a post office and store, and ancient and modern houses clustered around a modest triangle of village green, where the village sign features the church, three squirrels and a harrow. The Three Squirrels is the name of an inn below the village alongside the A249 and the Harrow Inn overlooks the green. It has pictures painted on one wall showing Stockbury in Spring, Summer, Autumn and Winter.

🍁 STURRY

The curving village street at Sturry was quite picturesque a century ago. It might have remained so but for the interference of a couple of high explosive bombs which dropped on the village in 1941. The village claimed to be one of the most severely bombed places in England, size for size, during the Second World War and the centre of the village was practically wiped out. It has since been redeveloped, giving the place a new look, although in fact it is very old.

It stands at the junction where the roads from Thanet and Reculver meet to go on together into Canterbury and the Romans thought it necessary to build a fort to protect the nearby River Stour crossing.

The Manor House, which was built in 1583 and rather prides itself on its medieval tithe barn, was once owned by St Augustine's Abbey at Canterbury. Now it is the junior boys' school of King's School at Canterbury.

Inevitably, at such a junction of roads up from the coast leading into Canterbury city, Sturry saw a good deal of smuggling activity during the 18th and 19th centuries. Several incidents were reported in the local press at the time and one of those reports refers to an occasion when Excise officers and a soldier set out from Canterbury to intercept a band of smugglers known to be heading for Sturry.

The smugglers were warned of their coming and hid their contraband in a wood before they went on into the village where they sought out the officers. They pulled the soldier from his horse and beat him up pretty severely and threatened the rest with instant death if they touched the hidden cache. Nevertheless, the officers, reinforced with a party of dragoons, searched the wood and found 18 tubs of gin and brandy and about 250 pounds of tea.

It was not always the smugglers who won, by any means.

🍁 SUNDRIDGE

Sundridge lies alongside the A25, whose travellers can easily go through the village before they have properly appreciated they are in it.

To find the best of Sundridge, it is necessary to turn aside and seek out some of the picturesque old houses on, say, the Ide Hill road, or to visit Coombe Bank, now a girls' school but once the home of Dr William Spottiswood, Queen's Printer and President of the Royal Society. He entertained all the great scientists of his time there: people like Darwin, Huxley and Herbert Spencer. When the house became the first locally to be wired for electricity, the work was supervised by Michael Faraday himself.

The house was bought in 1720 by Col John Campbell when he married Mary Bellenden, maid of honour to Queen Anne. He was Groom of the Royal Bedchamber. His wife died young but he lived on at the house with their children until 1761 when he became the Duke of Argyll. It was inherited by the Duke's third son, Frederick, and was restored and added to after a disastrous fire in 1807. In 1924 it became a convent and in 1972 a school.

Sundridge is specially favoured by its surroundings and the tourist-trap gardens of Emmetts are National Trust owned.

🍁 SUTTON VALENCE

The main one of the Three Suttons – the other two being East Sutton and Chart Sutton, which are close neighbours – Sutton Valence was earlier known as Town Sutton.

But for the fortunes of war, East Sutton and Sutton Valence might well have evolved as one after they were united under the ownership of Reginald Lord Gray in the 14th century. Unhappily for his lordship, he also owned land in the Welsh border country where he was kept pretty constantly occupied in beating off the raids of Welsh war lord Owen Glendower, who later declared himself Prince of Wales. It was in one of these clashes that Reginald was taken prisoner and he had to sell some of his Sutton lands to raise the ransom to secure his release. That sale led to part of the Kent estate becoming the property of the St Ledger family.

A very large part of Sutton Valence today is occupied by the public school which spreads over a hundred acres of hillside overlooking the Weald. The school was founded more than 400 years ago by William Lambe, who was baptised in St Mary's church in about 1495 and grew up to become a Freeman of the City of London Company of Clothworkers in 1568 and its Worshipful Master in 1569.

It was he who built the almshouses at Sutton Valence and in 1576 he founded Sutton Valence Free Grammar School for about 20 boys, making the Clothworkers Company its trustee. Today the school educates about 360 boys and, since 1983, a smaller number of girls as well.

The school playing field is known as Bloody Mountain, which has nothing to do with how some of the less enthusiastically sporting of the boys feel about it but bears out the tradition that a Saxon battle was fought there about a thousand years ago. A more recent tradition is perpetuated every Midsummer Day in a ceremony in which the chairman of the parish council hands one red and one white rose to the headmaster of the school in payment of the rent due for the use by the parish of the village green, which is actually part of the school grounds.

The ruins of Sutton Valence castle stand on the southern slopes of the hill; a small building by the standards of some castle ruins, with an internal floor space of only about 20 feet square. But in its days of now departed glory, whatever its defensive qualities, it must have been the envy of many a larger castle's owner for the superb view over the great sweep of the Weald from its site on the Greensand ridge. What remains is no more than part of the keep, now protected by English Heritage, but this would have been the castle to which William de Valence gave his name when Sutton was granted to him by Henry III, his half-brother, and from which the village, too, got its name.

The Greensand Way long distance walk passes through the village, which is very picturesque, especially around the green. In the churchyard there is a memorial to John Willes (1777-1852) who was born in Headcorn and died in Gloucester. He is remembered as the man who introduced round arm bowling into cricket. It is said that he copied the style from his wife who, when they played cricket together, found she could not bowl conventional under-arm because her hooped skirts got in the way.

It did not make him popular. In a match between 13 Men of England and 23 Men of Kent on Penenden Heath outside Maidstone in 1807, he earned catcalls from the spectators who became so incensed against him that they invaded the pitch and uprooted the stumps rather than let him carry on with his unconventional style of bowling. Violence at sporting encounters is not as new as all that!

In 1820 the Marylebone Cricket Club ruled that the ball must be bowled under-arm and when Willes bowled an over-arm delivery in a game at Lords in 1822 and was given 'No Ball', he stormed off the pitch vowing he would never play another game. The Sutton Valence memorial describes him as a 'patron of all manly sports and the first to introduce round arm bowling to cricket.' He lived at Bellingham House in Sutton Valence and was cricket coach to the famous Alfred Mynn, so-called Lion of Kent.

🍁 SWALECLIFFE

When I first knew Swalecliffe, there was a path which led one between the houses in St John's Road to St John's church, which stood among the fields of Swalecliffe Court Farm. The path went on, through the churchyard and past the farm buildings, over a precarious wooden plank bridge across a stream and then ended abruptly on the edge of a four or five foot high jump down onto the beach.

It was a perfect combination of countryside and seaside, with miles of low-water shingle and mud upon which to enjoy that special kind of solitude that is only to be found on unpeopled beaches. Even the nearby caravan camp was acceptably remote and as anxious to keep itself to itself as the village was. It is very different today. The little church is still there, but now it is jostled by houses and estate roads busy with the new villagers' cars and its churchyard overlooks a necessarily much enlarged sewage treatment works.

The village main street turns a hairpin bend where the railway station is, extending from the Wheatsheaf inn at the Tankerton end to Eddery's (formerly the Plough) at the Herne Bay end. Most of the shops are on that bend, where the railway bridge gives access on to the Thanet Way roundabout.

The rest is all housing, almost all of it built during the last 60 years and much of it more recently than that. So much is new that it seems unlikely that history has had much to do with Swalecliffe. Yet the place was found by those diligent bureaucrats the Domesday survey clerks, who recorded finding eight cottagers there. There has been a Swalecliffe church since about 1200 and the first rector was appointed in 1296. Kent historian Edward Hasted noted that there were eleven houses there in his own 18th century, and that it seemed there were the same number when a return was submitted to Queen Elizabeth I in 1565. The parish seems to have been always too poor to maintain the church and after it was several times rescued from terminal decay, in 1875 the present church was built for the village population of 167 people. It cost just £1,410.

Early in the 20th century there was a brickfield at Swalecliffe. The chimney of the brick works was a landmark on this bit of the North Kent coast, but after 1914 the industry began to decline and in 1935 it was decided that the time had come to demolish the chimney. Quite a crowd gathered to see the familiar landmark toppled, but 75 minutes before it was due to be brought down by explosives, it was blown down by a wind that couldn't wait, and spectators and workmen alike had to scatter for their lives.

🍁 SWANLEY VILLAGE

Swanley village stands apart from the much bigger town of Swanley, brooding over a past that was virtually obliterated by the arrival of the railway at what became known as Swanley Junction.

The village was, and to some extent still is, an agricultural community where even the local jam factory relied heavily on local fruit. This, in fact, was one of the chief market gardening areas of Kent and its glasshouses once supplied a major part of London's demand for vegetables. It had been settled since Anglo-Saxon times at least and was almost certainly occupied long before that.

The arrival of the Rochester-St Mary Cray railway line in 1861 began a change. The hamlet where the station was built had only three houses in the 1850s but it quickly became known as Swanley Junction and a new church was built there for the new ecclesiastical parish that was created to cater for the rapidly expanding population.

When a separate civil parish was created in 1901, for some reason it was decided it should be called Swanley, laying the foundations for confusion that still arises, since town and village, a mile or so apart, continue to exist side by side. The situation became even more confused when, during the 1974/75 reorganisation of local government, the village was formally absorbed into the town, even though it still identifies itself as a separate community.

🍁 TANKERTON

Virtually continuous development has made Tankerton almost one with Whitstable; a cobweb of mainly 20th century residential streets behind and beyond the single shopping street which runs parallel with the sea front and The Slopes.

Tankerton Slopes spread a wide green apron alongside the sea-front road before rolling steeply down to the beach huts that parade in review order above the shingle beach. It is a popular playground for children and a splendid place from which to view the maritime traffic and sailing regattas that take place from time to time in the bay.

At the Whitstable end of The Slopes, Tankerton Castle was built in the late 18th century by Londoner Charles Pearson as a summer home. Unlike some mansion houses dignified with the title of castle, this one does actually look like a small castle. It was later owned by the Member of Parliament Wynn Ellis, who added to it in the 1830s. He built the nearby almshouses as a memorial to his wife before he died in 1875.

The gatehouse, which is what catches the eye on the hill up from Whitstable, was built by a later owner at the turn of the century and after 1935 it became the offices of Whitstable urban council. The grounds were opened to the public as part of the local Royal Silver Jubilee celebrations. Now, it is used as a Canterbury City Council community centre.

Tankerton always seems to me to be unable to make up its mind if it is a seaside resort or a slightly haughty residential area. The sea-front area has none of the bucket-and-spade shops that tend to distinguish most promenades and several of the shops in the wide main shopping street, too, have an almost reserved air about them, as though they would much rather be somewhere else.

In the early decades of the 20th century, Tankerton beach was much more welcoming than it is now, with children's swing boats and tearooms. Perhaps the children were hardier then for although it is pleasant enough on one of those relatively rare warm English summer days, it can be very bracing indeed and nowadays it is more common to see people sitting in their parked cars, perhaps devouring ice cream from the ice cream parlour, and wondering what to do next.

One of the intriguing features of Tankerton's beach is the shingle bank known as The Street. It used to be assumed it was the remains of a Roman road built on land that has since surrendered to the sea. But a more credible suggestion is that it is all that remains of a medieval town called Graystone. Certainly, the shingle all the way along the beach contains fragments of tile and other bits of building debris.

The popularity of Whitstable as a place to visit at the beginning of the 20th century led to the building of Tankerton Hospital. It served as a naval and military hospital for wounded servicemen during and after the First World War before becoming a National Health Service general hospital.

🍁 TESTON

We can imagine William Cobbett climbing thankfully off his horse and easing the aches out of his saddle-filling end after one of his Rural Rides brought him to Teston. Then, as he waited for the numbness to wear off, he no doubt reached for his notebook to record his opinion that the view from the riverside below the village was one of the most attractive in Kent.

That was more than 150 years ago, but his spiritual successors who stop off at the Teston Bridge country park, for example, and take time to enjoy the view across the valley or downstream from the 14th century five-arch ragstone bridge will, surely, echo his sentiments almost exactly.

The village of Teston (pronounced 'Teeson', by the way) has grown a good deal since Cobbett's day. The church of St Peter and St Paul was there then, but the houses that line the little approach lane were not. The church is unusual among others in Kent for being in the classical style, reminiscent of some of the City churches of Christopher Wren, and yet somehow more at home in its rural setting than many of them would be.

On one wall of the church, under a window, is a memorial tablet to a former vicar, the Rev James Ramsay. He was Rector of Teston and Nettlestead from 1781 until he died in July 1789 and he was a friend of Pitt and Wilberforce and worked with them for the abolition of slavery. That was in no way inconsistent with his relationship with his black servant/companion of 22 years, Nestor, who died before the rector and is also commemorated at the church as well as in the name of nearby Nestor Court, a little cul-de-sac of modern houses a few yards from the church.

Barham – originally Berham – Court is a fine old house made even more interesting by association as the home of Randal FitzUrse, one of the knights who murdered Archbishop Thomas Becket in his cathedral at Canterbury in 1170. As a result of that deed, FitzUrse fled to his lands in Ireland and the manor passed into the ownership of his kinsman, Robert de Berham. The de Berhams prospered in Kent and became one of the great families of the county. Richard Barham, author of the *Ingoldsby Legends*, was one of their descendants.

But at the end of Elizabeth I's reign, the property passed to Sir Oliver Boteler and his wife, Anne. The Botelers (later they changed the name to Butler) were Royalists and Barham Court was sacked by Cromwell's New Army during the Civil War. Their son, Sir William Butler, was imprisoned in London for his support of the Kentish Royalists' petition of 1642. The last of the Butlers, Sir Philip, was responsible for changing the course of the old Tonbridge-Maidstone road, which used to run north of the church and then south of the house on its way to Barming and Maidstone. He had the road moved 'some hundred rods' (say 550 yards) to the south.

In the 18th century, Edward Hasted described Barham Court, then owned by the Bouverie family, as the greatest ornament of this part of the county. William Wilberforce was a frequent house guest of the first Lady Barham, who is said to have inspired and supported him in his fight against slavery. He loved the place and once wrote that 'for the charm and softness and elegance I never beheld a superior to Barham Court.' Today, part of the house has been converted into apartments and the rest into Barham Court business centre. Currently, there are plans to build houses in the parkland around the house.

Teston is soon to lose the cricket and hockey ball factory which was established there in 1808. Thomas Mann founded the enterprise in the mid-

19th century as a part-time business conducted in a single-storey workshop at the back of the village shop and post office, and after he retired it was taken over by Alfred Reader. The present factory was built after Alfred's death in 1927 and after the workers formed their own trade union, the Teston Independent Society of Cricket Ball Makers, the smallest in the country. Now, though, the owners have decided the factory has outgrown the village and they plan to move, leaving the site to be sold for housing development.

 ## TEYNHAM

> He that will not live for long
> Let him dwell at Murston, Teynham or Tonge.

Thus the old rhyme, which probably had some relevance in days gone by when these low-lying Swale creekside villages tended to be pretty unhealthy spots. Today Murston is lost among a mass of post-war homes and is wholly a suburb of Sittingbourne. Tonge (pronounced as though it had no 'e' on the end) has withered down to an isolated church and an old watermill. Teynham, however, continues as a somewhat sprawling village between the A2 and the railway line linking Sittingbourne and Faversham, the result of infilling between the once separated centres of population.

When William Lambarde wrote his *Perambulation of Kent* in the 16th century, Teynham was still a garden within the Garden of England. It was here that, during the reign of Henry VIII, Richard Harris planted his orchards of sweet cherries and apples that made the village 'the most dainty piece of all our shire', as Lambarde put it in his first of the English county guide books.

Harris was born locally; a house called New Gardens at nearby Conyer is sometimes claimed to have been his home. The story goes that when he heard of Henry VIII's passion for cherries and some of the apples he had found growing in France on one of his visits there, the Kent businessman went to the Continent himself and bought some trees which he brought back with him and planted on his own land at Teynham.

Teynham church is another that looks as though it had crept quietly away from the imperfections of the village it was built to serve and now broods peacefully among the orchards which protect it from the bitterly cold winds that sweep across the marshy flatlands bordering the Swale. But there was no protection from the Civil War skirmish that left the scars of the combatants' bullets on its massive old door.

The A2 forms the main street through the village, with the Fox inn at one end, the Swan and the George next door to each other half-way along and the Dover Castle inn at the other end. The older village centre was at Teynham Street, near the church and the site of a former archbishops' palace, where the now separate village of Conyer was its creek-side wharf.

🍁 THURNHAM

Thurnham had its great days 800 years ago, when people like the de Thurnham brothers, Stephen and Robert, sallied forth from their castle in Kent to go crusading with Richard the Lionheart and the rest of the nobility of Europe.

Robert de Thurnham was given command of the English fleet, while his brother Stephen was entrusted with escorting the Queen Mother, Eleanor, on a mission to collect His Majesty's betrothed, the beautiful Berengaria of Navarre. Stephen saw the king and his bride safely married in Cyprus, where Robert was made Governor, and later on Stephen was sent back to England, again as escort to the Queen and her mother-in-law.

It was Robert who acted as chief fund-raiser when the crusade-impoverished flower of the English peerage was dunned into subscribing to the ransom demanded by the Emperor of Austria if they wanted their king-napped monarch back again. King's men through and through were the de Thurnhams, and yet they survived all the hazards of their day to die peacefully in their beds at Thurnham.

Where all the villagers who ploughed and sowed and harvested the lands that supported their castle lived and died we really do not know. Probably not far from the overgrown heap of rubble that is all that remains of that castle today, on the highest part of the parish on the Downs above Bearsted and Detling, in an area that is protected for its outstanding natural beauty.

Even before the castle was built there was a big Roman house at Thurnham. The foundations were unearthed in 1833 but the excavators omitted to say where. Exactly a hundred years later, in 1933, a Roman building was found about a mile from the castle ruins. It may have been the same building, or another one. Either way, part of it is now under the M20 that bypasses Maidstone. In 1913 Anglo-Saxon graves were found but the most splendid of all local archaeological finds was the 7th century gold cross set with garnets which was ploughed up in a field in 1967.

Now, there is no recognisable cluster of homes that could be called a village and there are no shops at all. St Mary's church has existed since before 1066 and earned a mention in the Domesday Book in 1086. It is just beside the old

Pilgrims' Way, behind Thurnham Court, and it serves almost as a memorial to the village that was but which is now so scattered that there is no place to which one can go and say: 'Here, then, is Thurnham.' Even the Black Horse public house stands alone, looking as though it were waiting patiently for thirsty wayfaring pilgrims to drop in.

Yet the names of its villagers have sounded through history. One, Richard Thurnham, was clerk of Canterbury; another Richard was Town Clerk of Sandwich in 1490-93. In 1977 a stained glass window was installed in the church to the memory of Col Alexander Thurnham who was directly descended from the first Sir Robert de Thurnham in the 12th century.

One of the people remembered here is Alfred Mynn, that Lion of Kent who distinguished himself in the game of cricket. He was born at Goudhurst and lived for some years at nearby Bearsted, but when he died in 1861 it was to Thurnham churchyard that they brought his body, and there he lies still.

In 1882 Sir Herbert Beerbohm Tree, the actor-manager, was married here, with the young Max Beerbohm, although only ten years old, acting as best man. The occasion was celebrated with two triumphal arches of flowers and branches, one at the gate of the church and the other at the garden gate.

Thurnham today shares its parish council with Bearsted, yet obstinately refuses to lose its identity completely. When, in 1980, British Rail changed the name of the railway station, which is wholly within the old Thurnham parish, from Bearsted & Thurnham to just Bearsted – without, which is what so upset the villagers, so much as a 'Do you mind?' – there were bitter protests. They didn't make any difference and Thurnham had to get used to the loss of one more shred of separate identity.

🍁 TOVIL

Pronounced Tovvul, despite the 19th century *Kentish Dialect* by Parish and Shaw, which lists 'Tovil (pron. Toavil): a measure of capacity and possibly a corruption of two (or twice) fill.' In other words, two fillings of a particular measure.

Once a bustling mill village, its riverside busy with barges, Tovil is now one of the more sadly frayed edges of Maidstone. St Stephen's church, which has left its name to Church Street, was declared redundant and closed in 1982 and now only a few headstones remain to mark the spot where it once stood.

The paper mills that gave the old village its life are gone, too, and little more than the public house, the Royal Paper Mill, remains as a memorial to mills that were making paper at Tovil as early as the first half of the 16th century.

Upper Tovil Mill changed hands many times before it was bought in 1896 by Albert Reed, who also bought nearby Bridge Mill in 1907. Mr Reed had already laid the foundations for the giant Reed International papermaking group before he abandoned Tovil and spread himself over several acres of new ground at downstream New Hythe and Aylesford. New homes have been built on the sites of the demolished Tovil mills and papermaking has given way to a whole range of industrial and commercial enterprises.

Leading away from what, for want of a better description, must be regarded as the centre of the village, where the village sign stands, Straw Mill Hill takes its travellers into Stockett Lane and past the County Fire Headquarters, or by way of a swoop down Cave Hill, to the little hamlet of Bockingford. Here is the building that is still called Hayle Mill, which probably had its beginnings beside the stream before 1550.

The mill was still making paper in the 1980s, when it was the only commercial mill in Britain producing its very special hand-made paper but now it, too, is given over to other purposes. However, the tiny community of mill-workers' cottages in Hayle Mill Road, alongside the mill stream and ponds, retains a character all its own and evokes memories of an industry that flourished here for centuries. In character, it is a thousand miles from Tovil and the county town yet, geographically, it is little more than a literal stone's throw away.

🍁 TROTTISCLIFFE

The countryman with kindly face
When strangers ask: 'What is this place?'
Gives them a shock when he says crottiscliffe:
'This 'ere durned place is just called Trottiscliffe!'

Of course, the joke is lost if you try to say that to anyone. It needs to be written; then it is a useful reminder that, for some reason, the village name is always pronounced 'Trosley'.

It is a pleasant little place, squatting in the southern lee of the North Downs and, in recent years, rambling up the lower slopes in a rather untidy straggle of new-ish homes.

The church, which stands well clear of the village, in a farmyard, was mentioned in the Domesday Book in 1086. The land on which it stands was given to the See of Rochester by Offa, King of Mercia, in AD 788. Over the years, the church has acquired a great many second-hand treasures. In a

Coldrum Stones.

glass case on one of the walls inside the church are exhibits of finds at the nearby Coldrum Stones, a prehistoric burial site forming a large mound ringed with great sarsen stones and trees. They include some of the remains of 22 people, an ox, cat, deer, rabbit and fox, all discovered when the site was excavated by the archaeologist Benjamin Harrison, of Ightham, to whom there is a memorial plaque fixed to one of the stones.

Then, during the 18th century, the church acquired the pulpit from Westminster Abbey. It was, shall we say, an irregular acquisition and the Dean and Chapter had to be persuaded, after it was really too late for them to do anything else, to agree to make a gift of it to the village. There is a seat below the west window that came from St Paul's Cathedral. In 1865 the little orchestra that used to play in the minstrel's gallery was replaced by an organ which came from Meopham and remained in use until it was replaced in 1937 by the present organ, which came from the church at Leybourne.

Trottiscliffe is well off the beaten track and has had no shop since the former post office in Taylor's Lane closed in 1984. It still has two public houses, though: the George and the Plough, both about 500 years old. The chimney at the George collapsed into the inglenook one lunchtime in November 1980 and among the debris were found some shoes, a leather purse and a clay pipe, all of which had apparently been bricked in at least a hundred years before.

Nearby Trosley Park country park takes its name from the former Trosley Towers mansion. The estate was taken over as an army training camp in the Second World War and in 1952 permission was given for 350 acres to be developed. That was later reduced to 165 acres which were to provide 600 homes for about 2,500 people.

But then the planners changed their minds again and a Law Lords majority ruled that the permission had expired and the development could not proceed. In 1976 the estate was opened as one of Kent's first country parks, with 69 acres of North Downs woodland and 51 acres of hillside grass and scrub affording some of the finest views south across Kent to be found anywhere in the county.

🍁 TUDELEY

In 1749, the Kent historian Edward Hasted said Tudeley was 'obscure and unfrequented'. Today, it is internationally known for the stained glass windows in its little All Saints' church.

When Sarah d'Avigdor-Goldsmid was drowned in a sailing accident in 1963, her parents, Sir Henry and Lady d'Avigdor-Goldsmid of Somerhill at Tonbridge, commissioned memorial stained glass windows from one of the great artists of the century, Marc Chagall. The glass was installed when the church was restored in 1966 and the 'paintings in light', as they have been called, are now the principal treasures of this little country church.

The church itself is 18th century although it is built on Saxon foundations and was one of only four churches in the Weald of Kent at the time of the Domesday survey in 1086. Tudeley was one of the possessions of Bishop Odo of Bayeux and one of the early iron smelting centres which provided iron for the Roman Empire. It is known that metal forging continued there into the 16th century. The church was completely rebuilt during the first half of the 16th century and was again restored and rebuilt 250 years later, when the brick tower was built. There were further alterations and repairs to the church in the late 19th century and again in 1966.

The Jacobean house, Somerhill, on the hill above Tonbridge, was bought in 1849 by Sir Isaac Lyon Goldsmid who extended the park and surrounding estate to include Tudeley and the neighbouring hamlet of Capel. The family were major employers of local labour, with a great many indoor and outdoor servants.

230 @ ⬛ ULCOMBE

The even smaller church of St Thomas a Becket (now redundant) at Capel made its own claim to fame in 1927 when a series of 13th century wall paintings were uncovered in the nave. The parish today combines the two names: Tudeley-cum-Capel.

🍁 ULCOMBE

In 1985 volunteers working on a £100,000 restoration scheme at Ulcombe church dug out hundreds of human bones, boars' teeth and other assorted relics from around the bottom of All Saints' church ragstone walls.

At the moment the first shovel hit the first bone, a flash of lightning ripped across the sky and there was an exceptionally loud crash of thunder followed by heavy rain. In that moment, 2,000 years of Christian teaching fell away and betrayed lurking pagan apprehension among the diggers! However, the work went on and as more and more of the funerary bits and pieces were uncovered, weekly reburial services had to be held by the parish priest to re-inter them with appropriate 20th century ritual. Nobody really knows how old the bones were, but it has been suggested that the church was possibly built on a pre-Christian burial site and that the remains recalled those long-ago interments.

Ulcombe's All Saints' church is one of a line of churches along the Greensand ridge that separates the North Downs from the Weald and perhaps waymarks an old forgotten highway, presumably to Canterbury. Local tradition claims that William the Conqueror himself once stood on the site and ordered a church to be built there. It is certainly a Norman building, altered and enlarged in the 13th and 15th centuries, with two enormous old yew trees in the churchyard, one of which makes some claim to being as much as 3,000 years old.

Inside the church, on the left of the door, is a table on which is displayed the handwritten *Memories of Albert Chapman (1876-1975)* about the village. One paragraph records that he dug the first grave in the cemetery in 1896 and had interred nearly 400 people and exhumed one, 'a German soldier which was cremated at Charing and his ashes sent to his mother in Germany. After 17 years in the grave he fell a victim of the RAF and fell from his plane in the meadow opposite Street Farm his plane landed in the orchard back of oast in front of school during the 1939 war Battle of Britain.'

The sequence of events becomes less unlikely if the author's somewhat individualistic punctuation is corrected by the transfer of the full stop from where it is, after 'Germany', to where it should be, after 'grave'.

The village was home to the most famous of Kent bellfounders, Joseph Hatch, who lived at Roses Farm on the Broomfield-Ulcombe boundary. He died in 1639 and was succeeded in the business by his nephew William who, however, never achieved the same degree of recognition. Many of Joseph's bells still hang in Kent churches.

In 1850, Ulcombe had one of the first village schools in Kent, at a time when only about a dozen of the county's villages could boast such a thing. In 1998 the village became another victim of its time when the village shop and post office closed amid lamentations and predictions of resulting decline.

🍁 UPCHURCH

The eye of the visitor to Upchurch is drawn quite irresistibly to the almost grotesque two-piece spire on top of the squat little church tower. The first tier of the spire is normally pyramidical, but then, half-way up, it disappears into an octagonal second storey that seems to have been plonked down on top of it.

A plaque in the porch recalls that the clock and chimes were installed by the people of Upchurch as a thanksgiving for Victory and Peace at Christmas 1918.

Upchurch village is a quiet jumble of pleasant enough houses on the inland edge of the Medway estuary marshland between Sittingbourne and Rainham. In 1560 its vicar was a man called Edmund Drake, father of Sir Francis Drake as well as of eleven other sons. Before the family arrived in Upchurch from Devon, Edmund had been prayer-reader to the fleet in the Medway and had lived on one of the hulks. It may well have been during this time that young Francis, the eldest of the vicar's twelve children, learned his love of the sea that made him one of the great Elizabethan seadogs.

🍁 UPNOR

Old photographs of Upnor show it as a riverside resort of some popularity in the 1920s, with a pier and tea gardens and a miniature train. The old *Medway Queen* paddle steamer used to pick up and set down passengers at Upnor pier and the arrivals went up into the neighbourhood woods, on Upnor Hill, for picnics. The riverside is still busy, but now its visitors are more likely to head for the marina which harbours hundreds of small craft of all types.

In 1998 the village High Street underwent improvements costing £144,000. The street leads down to 16th century Upnor Castle which stands like a

monument to its own shame. For the castle was built in 1567 to a design by Sir Richard Lee, a notable Elizabethan military engineer, who employed Humphrey Lock to oversee the building work. The castle's specific job was to add to the defences of Chatham dockyard on the other side of the River Medway. The only time it was called upon to do that was in 1667 when the Dutch fleet under de Ruyter sailed contemptuously past it up the Medway and attacked the British fleet, burning several of the ships and actually carrying off the pride of the fleet, the *Royal Charles*, back to Holland in triumph.

On 30th June, Samuel Pepys travelled to Chatham and from there, in heavy rain, went by boat to Upnor to see for himself where the boom chain was broken. Diarist John Evelyn called it 'a dreadful spectacle as ever any Englishman saw and a dishonour never to be wiped off.' He was somewhat prophetic in that. Whenever Dutchmen and Kentishmen meet, the Dutch can seldom resist the obvious temptation of recalling the event, good-naturedly now, to be sure, but it still smarts.

During the Civil War some prominent Kent Royalists were held prisoner in Upnor Castle and in the risings that began on 23rd May 1648, Upnor was one of several Kent castles that were taken by the insurgents.

A hundred and fifty years ago the river off Upnor was full of the infamous hulks; pensioned-off ships of the fleet, stripped of their masts and guns and anything else that could be sold, and used as floating compounds for prisoners of war and, later, for ordinary criminals. The City of London claimed legal authority over the Medway as far as Upnor, where the upper limit of that authority is still marked by the London Stone, down on the river front.

Today, the river at Upnor is as full of small craft as the streets of Rochester or Chatham are of motor vehicles, for this is the water sport resort of the Lower Medway.

🍁 VIGO VILLAGE

Vigo began as a squatters' camp in the aftermath of the Second World War when abandoned Army camps were simply taken over by families who, made homeless by the war, moved into huts and created 'villages' for themselves.

In the case of Vigo, the area had been used as a wartime training camp – one of the largest in Kent, covering about six and a half square miles – for D-Day infantry commanders. The 800-plus huts had electricity and water connected, there were concrete roads and walkways. When the squatters moved in, in August 1946, rather than enforce evictions, the local authorities accepted responsibility for them and acknowledged the new community, which became known as Squatterbury. Gravesend borough, together with Strood, Malling and Northfleet urban councils, used the 'new town' to house their own overspill populations.

Since then, the area has been developed in a series of woodland enclaves comprising some 780 homes. The 165 acre estate was originally advertised as 'a new concept for living', being designed to discourage a lot of traffic movement, and it has become a North Downs commuter village whose residents seem to be generally agreed that it is a great place to live, especially for young families. The first residents moved in in October 1965 and now there is a purpose-built village centre, with shops and the Villager pub and a primary school with about 230 pupils.

The whole village is on the edge of one of the county's most spectacular country parks, Trosley Park, which tumbles down the southern slopes of the North Downs towards the village of Trottiscliffe below.

At present, Vigo is part of neighbouring Meopham parish, but is pressing for independent status. It takes its name from the Vigo Inn, which has stood since 1471 but was renamed by a man who bought it after service at Vigo Bay in 1702, when the British navy won a great victory over a combined French and Spanish fleet.

 WALTHAM

A small village among the wooded downlands south of Canterbury, Waltham has a history that certainly began before the Saxons arrived. Evidence of Roman residence has been found, perhaps more likely a military camp than a civil settlement. But a Saxon college of priests here became an abbey in 1177 and Henry II was present at the foundation ceremony. It was owned first by the Knights Templars and then by the Knights Hospitallers of St John of Jerusalem until the Dissolution.

The village was the subject of a Victorian three-volume novel by G. R. Gleig, published in 1835 and entitled *The Chronicles of Waltham*. The story opens with a description of the village: 'There are not many villages in England of which the general appearance is more attractive, without in the most remote degree bordering on the romantic, than Waltham, in Kent.'

It goes on: '... if ever village bore about it an air of perfect innocence and contentment, Waltham may fairly lay claim to the honourable distinction. It consists of a single street, broad, unpaved and shaded on either hand by rows of stately trees. This, about the centre, makes a curve so as to place the fine old church at the base, as it were, of a triangle.'

And there, save that the single street is now paved, and I would describe St Bartholomew's church, a little way out of the village centre, as the point rather than the base of a triangle, you have it.

❧ WATERINGBURY

This is one of a chain of Upper Medway valley villages where the river is very much a part of everyday life. From Allington Lock, below Maidstone, to Tonbridge the river is well trafficked all summer by holiday cruisers and the riverside at Wateringbury is always lined with craft of all kinds.

For centuries, though, the village played a very muted second fiddle to the other settlements in the parish, one of which was Chart, a community that has now vanished virtually without trace.

It has been suggested that the houses at Chart may have been burned down at one time, possibly deliberately because of an epidemic that raged. However, the most we can say today of Chart is that it was probably somewhere near the Pizen Well end – which is itself probably older than the present Wateringbury village – that it held a charter for a weekly market and an annual three-day fair ... and that the rarest of Wateringbury's historic relics originally belonged there: the Dumb Borsholder of Chart.

Today, the Dumb Borsholder, a three foot five inches long wooden staff fitted with metal rings and a wicked looking iron spike in one end, is lodged in Wateringbury's church of St John the Baptist. Its history reaches back to Saxon times, when it was customary for small communities to appoint an elder to be the borsholder and represent them at meetings of the Hundred Court. As time went by, the staff that originally symbolised the office became known as the Dumb Borsholder and was carried by a deputy to the court meetings. One man held the Dumb Borsholder for a year at a time and was paid a penny by each of the other householders in his community to do so.

The practice continued through the centuries until one Thomas Clampard, blacksmith, became the last holder of the office in about 1740. He died in 1748 and was buried in Wateringbury churchyard, remembered with an epitaph shared with blacksmiths all over the country (see Blean). It was about that time, too, that Wateringbury emerged as the chief village of the parish and took charge of the ancient relic, which is thought to be the only one of its kind left in England.

Pizen Well is a road at the west end of the parish. The name is not as ominous as it sounds, probably deriving from a family name, although another possible derivation might be that water from the well was used for the piscina in the church. The water was locally thought to have remarkable properties and until quite recently it was the custom for local newly-weds to drink it in order to ensure that they had healthy children. For all I know the custom is carried on still. I doubt if a modern bride would admit it if she did nip out under cover of darkness and take a sip.

For much of the history of Wateringbury, researchers are indebted to former Clerk of the Parish Edward Greensted, who died in 1797 – or, as his memorial stone preferred to put it, 'dropped like ripe fruit into its Mother's lap.'

It was he who left a very graphic account of a disastrous summer storm that swept across this part of Kent in August 1763. It only lasted about half an hour but in that time the wind rose to hurricane force, the thunder and lightning were almost continuous and hailstones up to ten inches round battered trees, crops, houses and wildlife. According to Greensted, some of the hailstones lay in heaps for more than a month and still measured four or five inches round at the end of that time. They provided a tourist attraction while they lasted and some were sent as curios to be exhibited in London.

Wateringbury Place is a lovely Georgian house built by Thomas Style in 1707 to replace an older building. The property remained in the Style family until 1851 and then returned to it after a break, although it is now in other hands again.

The Style family became linked with the Winches in the Maidstone brewery of Style and Winch. The old Phoenix brewery at Wateringbury was closed in 1982 and given permission for redevelopment for housing in 1984. Its distinctive gold-coloured weathervane lived on for some time on a neighbouring public house, but has now been replaced by a smaller version, more in scale with the building, above The Wateringbury Hotel that has replaced the pub.

As well as the Dumb Borsholder, Wateringbury used to boast about a particularly fine and unusual sundial which stood on a plinth near the church porch. It was about 200 years old, the work of a local man, Thomas Crow, who was born in 1772. It told the time all over the world, accurately to within a couple of minutes and was valued at about £600 at the time it was unscrewed from the plinth and stolen in 1981. It has never been recovered.

🍁 WESTBERE

This very pleasant little village lies on rising ground off the main A28 road that links Canterbury with the Isle of Thanet. It has been claimed that beer took its name from the village where the first hops to be cultivated commercially in Britain were grown during the 15th century at Hopland Manor. It is one of those claims that villages make but which do not bear too close examination. Another explanation of the name is that it derives from an Old English word for a swine pasture, 'boer', lying to the west of the original settlement.

The village sign is an unusually shaped one that imitates the outline of the church, All Saints, with three bells in a little open bell-cote. Below the bells, the sign depicts a swan and local fauna on and around the nearby Westbere lakes.

In 1990 the owners of Westbere House transferred ownership of a small plot of land in order to give the village a little green, which was opened in June 1990 and the village sign was erected on it in July 1991. The enclosed green is opposite a very attractive old thatched cottage and the church, which is of mainly flint construction, has the date 1673 over its door although it is mainly 13th and 14th century. There are a number of picturesque old timbered houses, too.

Opposite the church is a graveyard which has been designated a wildlife conservation area and a survey in 1994 identified more than 60 different species of trees, flowers and grasses, and very many insects and other forms of wildlife flourishing there.

🍁 WEST MALLING

West Malling used to be known as Town Malling and the approach road to its centre from the A20 is still called Town Hill. Residents are divided about whether they want to be villagers or townsfolk, and there will be those who will question my judgment in including it among Kent villages.

But it has a villagey feel about it: a very distinctive little community, most of the centre of which is a designated conservation area. It was first mentioned, as Town Malling, in AD 945 but the nunnery was founded by Bishop Gundulph of Rochester in the 11th century. It was destroyed, together with most of the houses, in 1190 and rebuilt for a community of Benedictine nuns. Legend has it that Becket's assassins hid in the Abbey during their flight from Canterbury after they had launched the Archbishop upon his gory way to early canonisation.

The Abbey in Swan Street is still occupied by Anglican Benedictine nuns, who have as close neighbours the Anglican Cistercian monks of Ewell Monastery in nearby Water Lane.

The High Street is lined on both sides with some fine Tudor, Jacobean and Georgian houses. Just outside the village, the 18th century manor house built by Thomas Augustus Douce is now a commercial training centre, separated from the parkland it overlooks (now a local authority country park) by the road that goes through the hamlet of St Leonard's on its way to join the Maidstone-Tonbridge road at Mereworth.

The mansion was a rest base for airmen operating from the Second World War West Malling airfield. Its cellar was the war-time Twitch Inn, on the ceiling of which airmen, including some of the famous air aces of their day, wrote their names in candle flame soot. The airfield is some way out of the village: 530 acres bought from the Ministry of Defence by Kent County Council in 1973 and 1974 and now developing into a high quality, low density business park and Kings Hill village.

St Leonard's is chiefly notable for its tower, perhaps the finest early Norman keep in the country and all that remains of the house that Bishop Gundulph built there. The Startled Saint public house, which used to amuse customers and passers-by with its inn sign showing the saint looking appropriately startled by Battle of Britain Spitfires flying overhead, is now a private house.

West Malling was rather more obviously deserving town status in the days when local industry included tanning, brewing, glass blowing, clock-making and the manufacture of straw hats. Today, it is almost wholly residential, but it still contends with several other Kent villages for the honour of being the one where cricket was first played in the county, claiming that the game was first played on the local ground in 1705.

The 1974 local government reorganisation combined the former Malling rural council with Tonbridge urban council to form Tonbridge and Malling district (later borough) council and in 1998 it was decided to sever yet another link with the past by closing the West Malling magistrates' court, opened in 1866, from January 1999.

🍁 WEST PECKHAM

Some distance and very different in character from East Peckham, West Peckham is quite small and rather remote. It lies just west of the A26 between Mereworth and Hadlow and the approach road comes to a dead end at the very fine village green. Its unpretentious little village church of St Dunstan presides over the occasional game of cricket or village fete with an air of studied impartiality.

The entrance to the village is guarded by a big timber-framed house now known as Dukes Place, once the Commandery of the Knights Hospitallers of St John of Jerusalem. They were given the manor by Sir John Colepeper in 1408. Sir John also built a mansion house which he called Oxenhoath some distance from the village and he founded a chantry, with a chaplain to pray for himself, his wife Katherine, and for King Henry IV and his second wife,

Joan of Navarre, and others. Sir John and Katherine were buried in the chantry vault and so were later owners of Oxenhoath and also of Hamptons, another of the local big houses.

One of the descendants of the Colepepers married into the family of Lord Edmund Howard, whose daughter Catherine became Henry VIII's fifth wife. She is said to have stayed at Oxenhoath and to have met there a distant relative, Thomas Colepeper of Bedgebury, who was accused of misconduct with her and executed for it in 1541. She followed him to the scaffold in 1542.

Oxenhoath descended to the Geary family, the last of which, Sir William Geary, bart, died in 1944 but the last interment in the family vault was in 1871. When the old Colepeper chantry inside the church was being restored in 1887, a Mrs Maximilian Dalison offered £1,000 towards the cost of removing the 200 year old steps leading from a square pew for ten people down into the chancel. The vicar and churchwardens – who may well have had an eye on the £1,000 that would help to pay for other renovations as well – agreed that the steps should be removed, but Sir Francis Geary, who owned the pew at the time, did not. The church authorities wanted access to the pew to be from outside the church only. Sir Francis claimed his right of access from inside the church. The issue became one of some moment and in the end the vicar and churchwardens took the matter to the Consistory Court, where Sir Francis won the day. The Geary family continued to use the pew until the last one, Sir William, died in 1944.

Behind the elevated pew is a monument, enclosed within iron railings, with effigies of Leonard Bartholomew in a full wig and 18th century finery, and his wife, who both died in 1720 and are buried in the vault below.

In 1594, John Comper of West Peckham earned a sort of reflected immortality from the names with which he baptised his three children. His son was called Remember Death and his two daughters rejoiced (if the family allowed any such emotion) in the names of Lament and Sorrow. Whether or not they all lived happily ever after we do not know.

Actress Fay Compton used to live in West Peckham. She claimed her house was plagued by a poltergeist and had it exorcised. The vicarage has also been said to have been haunted in the past and about 20 years ago a local man claimed he saw a ghost near the Hurst which was thought to have had something to do with a notorious highwayman called Jack Diamond.

In 1997 an intemperate outburst by the vicar of East Peckham caused a row when he said thieves who stole twelve wooden statues, worth about £2,000, from his church should have their hands chopped off. The publicity attracted by the outburst resulted in the return of the statues by a North London antiques dealer who had bought them.

WHITFIELD

Whitfield village lies aloof from the A256 Sandwich-Dover road and the roadside development would deceive the traveller into thinking Whitfield was almost entirely modern. In fact, the village is part of one of the oldest of all Kent parishes. Excavations have unearthed evidence of Roman and Saxon settlements although the name is derived from 'white field' and is explained by the chalkiness of the land here on top of the White Cliffs above Dover.

The village was still being called Beauxfield (Beuesfield or Bewesfeld) until the time of the Commonwealth and that was the name of an early owner of the manor. The Domesday survey in 1086 recorded two separate manors of Bevesfel and Pineham. Early in the 14th century, the manor was held 'by service of holding the king's head between Dover and Wissant whenever he travelled between the two' – not all English kings were good sailors by any means.

In AD 772, King Offa of Mercia (who held sway over Kent at that time) gave part of the area to St Augustine's at Canterbury and there was a church here, St Peter's, in about 1070. The present building still has two of the original Saxon windows. The church has never had a tower and the single bell has been housed in successive wooden bellcotes. The present bell is said to be the oldest in Kent, dating from the early 13th century and possibly a little earlier.

During the 19th and early 20th centuries, Whitfield became a favoured home for some of Dover's most prosperous residents and it was they who built homes along the then new main road which bypassed the village.

A curiosity of Whitfield is its village sign, alongside the main road. The sign itself is a painting of the church, with the name of the village under it, but it is mounted on a stout wooden upright which is studded with dolls' masks. The faces recall the five sons and six daughters of William and Jane Cross, who all died in infancy between November 1821 and August 1835. Only one of their daughters, Marian, survived to maturity and even she died before her parents did.

🍁 WICKHAMBREAUX

There is something almost toy-like about Wickhambreaux (pronounced 'Wickhambroo') which is beside the Little Stour and between the A28 Canterbury-Thanet road and the A257 Canterbury-Sandwich road. Together they make it fairly certain that no unnecessary traffic finds its way into the village.

The local pub is the Hooden Horse, a reminder that this is 'hoodening' country, where farm labourers used to go from door to door collecting money or gifts from neighbours for a Christmas feast (see Lower Hardres).

Originally the village was simply Wickham and the suffix was added after it came into the possession of William de Breuse in 1285. Wickhambreaux was once one of the Kentish estates of the original Fair Maid of Kent, Princess Joan Plantagenet, who was born in 1328, daughter of Edmund, Earl of Kent and grand-daughter of Edward I. The French chronicler Froissart called her 'the most beautiful woman in all the realm of England, and the most loving.' Before her, the manor was owned in the 12th century by the Clifford family, whose daughter Rosamund captivated the heart of the young Henry II and became known as the Fair Rosamund. The earliest rector was the fourth son of William de Longspee, a son of Henry II by the Fair Rosamund.

The village green is surrounded by attractive buildings, including the weatherboarded watermill which, although 19th century as it stands, is on the site of earlier ones, perhaps including one of the two mentioned in Domesday. The oldest house is the chequered stone and flint Stone House which may be, in part, Norman. This is where Joan, the Fair Maid of Kent and by then the widow of Sir Thomas Holland, Earl of Kent, was courted by Edward, the Black Prince, who she eventually married and by whom she became the mother of Richard II.

At one end of Wickhambreaux's village green is the Rose Inn, with neighbouring 16th century Bell House which was once the schoolroom. The church has an unusual weatherboarded porch and its several treasures include an ancient tapestry showing Christ as Charles V of Germany (1550) and his son Philip II of Spain who, in 1554, married England's Queen Mary, daughter of Henry VIII. Other figures are also authentically historical.

A late 19th century memorial window to Countess de Gallatin, who is buried in the churchyard, has a uniquely American stained glass depiction of the Annunciation and there are wall paintings in the nave and elsewhere.

 WINGHAM

The very attractive East Kent village of Wingham is built around the T-junction formed where the B2046 north-south road meets the A257 Canterbury-Sandwich road. It is a relatively large village, with a handsome, tree-lined High Street. Several of the trees commemorate Trees in the Village competition awards.

It has a prosperous look about it and, indeed, it has enjoyed a measure of prosperity since Saxon times when it was one of the richest manors in Kent. In the 13th century a College for six secular canons was founded here and Canon Row, opposite the 13th century church of St Mary the Virgin, remains as a reminder that the college was, in fact, one of the most notable medieval colleges in Kent. It was dissolved in 1547 by Edward VI and the buildings were sold.

The village has had a front seat in much of the history of this part of Kent. Archbishop Thomas Becket passed through Wingham on his way back to Canterbury from exile on the Continent, unaware that he would be slain in his own Cathedral less than four weeks later. Richard I (the Lionheart) stopped here on his way to London when he returned from captivity in Austria in 1194, and King John stayed here in 1213. In 1255, the King of France gave an elephant to Henry II as a gift and the animal must have caused quite a stir as it walked through Wingham on its way to Canterbury. Edwards I, II and III all visited Wingham during the 13th and 14th centuries and Elizabeth I followed in their footsteps in 1573.

After about 1540, when the church had been allowed to get into such a state that one day it just fell down, a Canterbury brewer called George Foggard sought and was given permission to collect money for rebuilding it. He was evidently a persuasive collector for it seems he raised £224, quite a considerable sum for that time – so considerable, indeed, that Master

Foggard could not bring himself to part with it when the time came and the money never did find its way into the fabric of the rebuilt church. One consequence of that was that the church was rebuilt with a nave arcade of octagonal chestnut pillars instead of stone ones, to keep down the cost.

The church boasts a number of impressive monuments, none of which eclipses the 17th century Oxenden monument in the south transept. In black and white marble, it is an ornately carved obelisk on a square base with ox-head corner supporters for the four putti at the corners.

A 14th century widow of the Earl of Kent, who retired to a convent, broke her vows and secretly married at Wingham a French Wars veteran called Sir Eustace de Aubrichecourt. The marriage caused quite a scandal at court and outraged the Church which imposed penances upon the pair, requiring them to eat nothing but bread and drink nothing but water for a whole day once a week, and recite the psalms every day. In addition, the bride had to walk barefoot to Becket's shrine at Canterbury. The couple seem to have accepted the penances stoically and to have fulfilled them for more than 50 years, during which time they had one son.

In 1795, William Miller was born in Wingham, grew up to join the Army and travelled to South America where he fought with Simon Bolivar, the Spaniard who freed part of Peru from Spanish dominance and gave his name to the new state of Bolivia. Miller so impressed the Spaniard that he was given command of his whole army in South America, but the call of Kent proved too strong after a year or two and he returned to be made a freeman of Canterbury. He did not stay long, though. He was a rover at heart and died at sea in 1861.

Between 1925 and 1947 Wingham was unique in Kent for having three railway stations. That was because it hovered on the verge of becoming one of the county's mining villages and a railway station was built to serve the intended colliery. But Wingham colliery was never developed and the project was abandoned in 1914. The three stations remained open until the railways were nationalised in the late 1940s, when Wingham went off the rails, in the nicest possible way, for good.

🍁 WITTERSHAM

Although normally included among the Romney Marsh villages, Wittersham is really the largest village on the Isle of Oxney, an area of slightly higher land which was once a true island in the delta that became the Marsh. The village sign is a reminder of this, featuring a cut-out metal Roman galley under sail.

The Kent historian Hasted, in 1799, described it as a lonely, unfrequented place made grossly unhealthy by the air of the adjoining marshes. Today it is less lonely, not particularly unfrequented and the marsh air is probably generally regarded as healthy rather than the reverse. Part of the village is a conservation area, including the 13th century church of St John the Baptist and several nearby listed buildings. Among them, 19th century Wittersham House is one of Sir Edward Landseer Lutyens' designs, encasing an earlier building.

Palstre Court is 16th century, altered during the 18th century – a rambling old farmhouse on a hilltop overlooking the Rother Levels. It is most notable for being one of the few South Kent place names of Latin origin, deriving from *vivi palustres*, which translates pretty freely as 'men of the marsh'.

The church clock was donated in 1960 by the parents of Flying Officer Michael Fitt, RCAF. He died at the controls of his crashed Sabre jet because he chose not to bale out in order to make sure the plane did not fall on a French village.

Stocks windmill, a mile or so outside the village, was probably built in 1781 and was restored with Kent County Council help.

🍁 WOODCHURCH

Although it has grown a great deal in recent times, Woodchurch is still an attractive village, with its big triangular green, its unusually tall spired All Saints' church and, of course, its windmill.

The windmill is as much a landmark as the church's broach spire which, as a result of subsidence of the tower, leans some two feet from the perpendicular. The mill was in working order until 1926 and at one time it was the only windmill in Kent to be listed as an ancient monument.

Windmills are particularly vulnerable to the ravages of time and weather because of the necessarily exposed hilltops on which they were usually built and the one at Woodchurch was no exception. It was presented to the parish in 1947 by Sir Sydney H. Nicholson but was doomed to collapse after the Second World War until Ashford borough council began a rescue mission. Now it has been restored and is open on Sundays during the summer.

The mill is the survivor of a pair that once stood close together and were known, as many such pairs of mills were, as Jack and Jill. The present one was probably built in 1820 and one of the millers, John Parton, met his death in 1831, at the age of 49, when he was beheaded by one of the mill sweeps. The last of the Woodchurch millers, though, was a man called Albert Tanton.

The windmill is reached by way of a short public footpath which starts between the Bonny Cravat and the Six Bells public houses. How, you will naturally ask at this point, does a public house in possibly the most independently minded and self-concerned corner of England come by a name as obviously Scottish as the Bonny Cravat?

The explanation is that the name has nothing at all to do with Scotland or cravats. It is probably a local version of the Bonne Crevette (which can be interpreted as the Good Prawn and which no doubt sounds less ridiculous to a French fisherman than it does to a Kentish landsman). It is usually thought to be the name of a French fishing boat once active in the smuggling industry in these parts.

Currently, the windmill is a rather less popular tourist attraction than the nearby South of England Rare Breeds Centre.

🍁 WOODNESBOROUGH

It is a rather grand-sounding name for a very small village built around a minor crossroads between Ash and Eastry or Sandwich and Chillenden, depending upon which of the roads you travel, amid open East Kent countryside, but it invites speculation about its origins.

The little church of St Mary the Virgin stands on a slight knoll which is generally supposed to be the site of a Saxon grove sacred to Woden worshippers. The area may well have been a gathering place for the out of doors worship practised by pagan Saxons, from which the name derived. It is largely conjecture that the site had religious or mystical significance for the Britons even before the Saxons arrived here. There is a local tradition that the last British king of south-east England, Vortigern, expressed a wish to be buried here, so that his remains would deter the Saxon raiders who were ravaging this coastal area.

In fact, the Saxons finally drove Vortigern and his people out of Kent altogether and although we do not know where the British king was buried, we can be fairly sure it was not at Woodnesborough which, of course, must have had a different name, if tradition is to be trusted, before the Saxons introduced Woden to Britain.

Certainly, nearby Eastry was the centre of the Saxon royal manor to which it gave its name and Sandwich was the chief port of this part of the south coast – in fact, it was the most important port in the country for centuries – so the tradition has plenty of circumstantial evidence to support it.

But apart from that, it is very easy to imagine that there is something about the place, and particularly about the church, with its odd little cupola-capped wooden addition to the almost elegantly balustraded tower, as though it were aware that it is, in some slightly eerie way, special.

The present church is probably restored 12th century and there are those who believe the local traditions justify their conviction that it is somewhere beneath its foundations, inside that knoll on which it stands, that lies buried the fabulous golden Woden that remains a persistent feature of East Kent legend.

🍁 WORTH

Considering how many quite large villages in Kent have no village sign at all, it is slightly surprising to find that a village as small as Worth, just south of Sandwich, has one. A very distinctive one it is, too, because both the illustration and the lettering are reminiscent of a particular kind of seaside postcard or, perhaps, a slightly dated advertisement poster.

The result is cheerful and warmly welcoming at the top of the road that plunges seawards from the A258 Sandwich-Deal road and comes to a slightly bemused end in the village, just past the St Crispin inn. It shows a veteran local yokel leaning on his walking stick in front of a typical five-bar field gate and pointing down the road towards the village, as though some wayfarer had stopped to ask him the way. The legend under the picture promises, 'There's Good Worth in Word', which is about as enigmatic as it could be until you learn that the name of the village derives from the Old English 'word', meaning an enclosure. Even then, it remains a bit enigmatic!

Edward Hasted, the 18th century Kentish topographer, said the parish of Worth had three boroughs, one of which was Worth Street, the present village. Early in its history, Worth was a creekside community and Roman finds have encouraged speculation that some of Caesar's legions may have anchored their ships in the creek. It was certainly a Bronze Age settlement and much later one of the local streams was used to drown Sandwich criminals whose bodies were then borne out to sea by the tide. Now, much of the land on the seaward side of the village is part of the famous Prince's and Royal St George's golf courses.

Some say that Archbishop Becket, when he fled from the consequences of his dispute with Henry II, left England from Worth Creek rather than attempt to take ship from Sandwich, which would have been teeming with loyal subjects of the king.

Local legend also claims that Henry V, returning from his St Crispin's Day

(25th October) victory at Agincourt, disembarked at Worth and there met and fell in love with a village ale-wife. The story goes that the two lived together for a time at the local inn which has ever since been known as the St Crispin. Another rather more believable version of the same story names one of Henry's courtiers, rather than Henry himself, as the ale-wife's beau.

🍁 WOULDHAM

Travelling downstream on the River Medway, along the tidal reach from Allington Lock to the impressive concrete span of the M2 bridge at Rochester, the only village actually to reach down to the water on the Men of Kent's eastern bank is Wouldham.

It is worthwhile for any river traveller to disembark to see the village, if only to visit the church or, at any rate, the churchyard where the grave of local man Walter Burke is marked by a headstone. The original inscription is now almost wholly illegible but it has been repeated on the back of the stone. The new inscription, carved in 1955, tells how Burke was purser on HMS *Victory* at Trafalgar and that it was in his arms that 'the immortal Nelson' died. Walter Burke left the Navy and came home to Wouldham where he owned both Purser Place and Burke House. Both were removed to Maresfield in East Sussex in 1937 and materials from both were used to build one new house, also called Purser Place. Burke died on 12th September 1815, aged 70, and every year since local schoolchildren have laid flowers on his grave each Trafalgar Day.

For centuries there was a ferry crossing the river whenever hired to do so from Wouldham to Halling and it may be that there was, before that, a ford across the river at this point, possibly where Romans and Britons fought for the way to London. In 1843 workmen found what, at the time, was thought to be a Mithraic temple at Wouldham, although later experts decided it was more likely to have been part of an old farmhouse cellar. No one can be sure because no details of its location have survived, so no one now knows where it was found.

The ferry service ended in 1963, when the Stevens family, who had operated it for many years, gave it up. Nowadays, it is assumed that anyone who wants to cross the river will have the means to travel the few miles north or south to the nearest bridges at Aylesford or Rochester.

Out on Wouldham marshes, north of the village, the 14th century remains of the house called Starkey Castle were brought back to life in the 1980s by retired barrister Gerald Davies. The house was originally built for Sir

Humphrey Starkey, Recorder of the City of London in 1471 and later Chief Baron of the Exchequer in 1483. The Royal Commission on Historical Monuments described Starkey Castle as a monument of national importance and one of the few medieval manor houses to have survived more or less in its original condition.

Today, Wouldham is mostly a village of terraced cottages originally built for 19th and early 20th century cement workers. The church is at one end of the village street, its wall prettily overhung by flowering trees. Inside, a list of rectors begins in 1283 and the font is hewn from a solid slab of stone which is capped by a carved wooden pyramid cover with brasswork decoration.

🍁 WROTHAM

King Henry VIII was staying at Wrotham when he received news of the death of Anne Boleyn in 1536. Eighteen years later, Henry was dead and his daughter Mary was on the throne and planning marriage with Philip of Spain. Sir Thomas Wyatt of Allington Castle, just downstream from Maidstone, opposed the marriage, and some of his supporters were intercepted on Blacksole Field at Wrotham and defeated in a pitched battle with soldiers led by Lord Bergavenny. There is a road called Battlefields in Wrotham today.

The protest achieved nothing but the execution of Wyatt in London and the continuation of 'Bloody Mary's' reign of religious persecution, during which more than 70 people in Kent were burned at the stake, the last of them being John Corneford of Wrotham, who died at Canterbury in November 1558. It was probably a potential Protestant victim of that persecution who hid a parchment-wrapped bible behind the wall plaster in a house in Wrotham High Street, where it was not found until 1966.

Wrotham used to have an archbishop's palace, just behind St George's church, but it was pulled down by Archbishop Simon Islip in 1349 and the materials were carted away to be used for his new riverside palace at Maidstone.

The church, incidentally, is thought to have been one of the first in England to be dedicated to St George. It is a particularly fine, spacious building, with a number of memorial brasses, an ornate pulpit and some rather beautiful stained glass. Several of the memorials are to members of the Betenson family, including that Sir Richard Betenson who was described as 'an ancient Baronet' and who died in 1786, and Helen Betenson, the last survivor of the family, who died in 1788 aged 68 leaving £10,000 to various charities. In a niche over the entrance to the porch is a little statue of St George which was sculpted by Willi Soukip, RA and exhibited at the Royal Academy before it was installed in its present position in 1973. It replaced an earlier one which was stolen in 1971.

Where the High Street dog-legs and Bull Lane offers its invitation to visit the old Bull Hotel, opposite the ornate iron gates of Wrotham Place, there is a stone set into a wall commemorating the day in June 1799 when 'Near this place fell Lieut Colonel Shadwell, who was shot to the heart by a deserter.' The stone relates that the assassin, with another deserter, was immediately secured and brought to justice.

Wrotham (pronounced 'Rootham', by the way) has put on a lot of weight in the last 50 years, because of all the new building behind the still very picturesque old village centre. Thanks to the lie of the land, though, the new does not intrude upon the old, which survives very well an altogether disproportionate amount of major road building nearby.

Wrotham was always a travellers' staging point and well-known to the smuggler community, who necessarily travelled rather more than most of their contemporaries. One local man, known as Old Sobers, left a detailed account of his father's involvement in the trade during the 19th century. The family had a legitimate transport business, carrying goods between London and Sandwich, that served as a splendid cover for an equally successful and probably even more lucrative smuggling enterprise.

One of Old Sobers' stories told how, at the age of 17, he took a cart load of brooms to sell in London and returned next day with £1,000. Most of the money, of course, came from the sale of silks, lace, tobacco or spirits that had travelled with him, hidden among the brooms.

🍁 WYE

New building has given Wye something of the character of a small town, although the heart of the place, around the church and the neighbouring Wye College, is still unmistakably villagey, mainly Georgian or later.

Wye is – if a little licence can be allowed – between the Devil and the deep (well, not all that deep, actually) River Stour. The Great Stour chuckles across one side of the village while, on the other side, the road climbs abruptly to a stretch of the Downs where motorists are encouraged by provided lay-bys to pause and contemplate the south-westerly distance across that remarkable feature, the Devil's Kneading Trough. The walk down, skirting the incredible scoop of dry valley to the Brook road at the bottom offers breathtaking views, though if you've left your car at the top the walk back up again is very much more breathtaking and the view loses some of its charm.

Due west of the village, the Downs display perfectly the turfed chalk crown shaped on the hillside by Wye College students in 1902 to commemorate Edward VII's coronation. The College was founded by John Kempe, a native of Wye, who was Cardinal Kempe and later Archbishop of Canterbury in 1447. It has expanded a great deal since then and is now, since 1892, the Agricultural School of London University. It is a famous centre for research into various aspects of farming, horticulture and the countryside generally, and is perhaps especially well-known for its work on hop cultivation.

An old Kentish rhyme says:

> Naughty Ashford, surly Wye,
> Poor Kennington hard by.

But why this rather cheerful village should ever have been thought surly is one of those mysteries history keeps to itself. History is less reticent about other features of the village. From being a Saxon royal manor, it grew into an important medieval market town and resting place for pilgrims bound for Canterbury.

In 1941, Olantigh House, a little way outside the village, was the Second World War divisional headquarters of the Army's Southern Command, under the command of Lieut-Gen Sir Bernard Montgomery, later, of course, the Field Marshal affectionately known to the nation as 'Monty'.

🍁 YALDING

Yalding is one of those 'dumb-bell' villages with the two parts joined by the U-shaped High Street. It grew up where the rivers Beult and Tiese join together before they flow into the River Medway, and it may have derived its name from an old expression meaning 'twin ford'.

There is no need to ford the rivers now, nor has there been for centuries. They are crossed by bridges: Yalding Town Bridge, which has been there since the 15th century, crosses the Beult and Twyford Bridge, which is generally regarded as one of Kent's – indeed, one of the south-east's – finest medieval stone bridges, spans the confluence of the Tiese and the Medway.

Despite the traffic lights which now control the Twyford Bridge crossing, it is still basically the same bridge that has borne wheeled vehicles and pack horses from one side to the other for at least 500 years. No one knows just how old it is, but it was certainly there in 1325 although it has changed a bit

since then. In 1939 part of it collapsed into the river but it was repaired and there have been further repairs since then.

The rivers which helped to locate Yalding where it is have done their best, over the centuries, to sweep it away again. As you walk along the street, you cannot help noticing the raised footways which have, over and over again, made it possible for pedestrians to go about their business when vehicular traffic has been forced to negotiate carefully the seasonal floods. Hopefully, upstream flood defence works above Tonbridge have now ended at least the worst of that particular hazard for Yalding.

Today's Yalding is based on four Saxon manors of which the manor of Twyford was once the most important. In the 14th century, Edward II gave permission for a weekly market and two annual fairs to be held in the village, and they were probably held on The Lees at Twyford, where the thatched Old Anchor Inn deceives its visitors. It is actually fairly new.

The old core of the village is south of the River Beult, but there are fine old buildings throughout the village and its immediate neighbourhood, including the church, Court Lodge and Cleaves, the 17th century school house, where the Kent poet Edward Blundell was brought up and where his father was schoolmaster. Town Bridge has for its neighbour the George Inn and some attractive beamed and white weatherboarded cottages which include the post office. On the Maidstone side of the bridge is Bridge House, the church, Church House, The Elms, Church Cottage and picturesque weatherboarded and thatched Randall Cottages. Alongside the war memorial in Vicarage Road, the old village lock-up, with its iron studded door and grilled window, backs on to Cleaves House, opposite the Walnut Tree Inn.

Yalding's village sign overhangs the entrance to Court Lodge, Old Barn and Hop Barn, a modern development of an old site. The sign has been there since March 1948 and depicts an oast house, a bridge, and two pairs of crossed keys and swords, symbols of the church's patron saints, on a green ground.

Still developing at Yalding are the organic gardens of the Henry Doubleday Research Association. A series of themed gardens, all cultivated organically, are open to the public just off the B2162 where it turns south (to the left) across Town Bridge.

The vaguely exotic onion dome on the top of the tower of the church of St Peter and St Paul makes it a very distinctive local landmark in a landscape that was once in the heart of the orchards-and-hops countryside. Although hops are still grown locally, they are much less a feature now than they once were.

Index